CDBRX-384

Wissenschaftliche Untersuchungen
zum Neuen Testament

Herausgegeben von
Martin Hengel und Otfried Hofius

80

Fathers of the World

Essays in Rabbinic and Patristic Literatures

by

Burton L. Visotzky

J. C. B. Mohr (Paul Siebeck) Tübingen

BR
67
.V57
1995

Die Deutsche Bibliothek − CIP-Einheitsaufnahme

Visotzky, Burton L.:
Fathers of the world: essays in rabbinic and patristic literatures / by Burton L.
Visotzky. − Tübingen: Mohr, 1995
   (Wissenschaftliche Untersuchungen zum Neuen Testament; 80)
   ISBN 3-16-146338-2
NE: GT

© 1995 by J.C.B. Mohr (Paul Siebeck), P.O. Box 2040, D-72010 Tübingen.

This book may not be reproduced in whole or in part, in any form (beyond that permitted
by copyright law) without the publisher's written permission. This applies particularly to
reproductions, translations, microfilms and storage and processing in electronic systems.

The book was typeset by ScreenArt in Wannweil using Times typeface, printed by Gulde-
Druck in Tübingen on non-aging paper from Papierfabrik Buhl in Ettlingen and bound by
Heinr. Koch in Tübingen. Printed in Germany.

ISSN 0512-1604

Acknowledgements

It is my pleasure to acknowledge the many scholars and institutions that have assisted me in writing this book. The essays in this volume were written during the last decade. For all those years and more I have had the privilege of being on the faculty of the Jewish Theological Seminary of America. It is truly the residence of a host of disciples of the sages who love the Torah. Daily I give thanks to God that I am among those who dwell at the Seminary. One could not ask for better teachers, colleagues or students. Among those whom I explicitly wish to thank are the late former chancellors Louis Finkelstein and Gershon Cohen. The current chancellor, Ismar Schorsch, has been extremely supportive, as have been his successive provosts, David Kogen, Raymond P. Scheindlin, Ivan Marcus and Menahem Schmelzer. I must also acknowledge my debt to the Abbell Research Fund of the Seminary for the generous financial support I have received and without which this book could not have been written.

In addition to JTS, two other institutions have hosted me during my writing and research. The Oxford Centre for Post-Graduate Hebrew Study invited me to be a visiting scholar in 1985–86. I particularly wish to thank Geza Vermes and Sebastian Brock for their warm hospitality during that stay. In the same year I was a visiting fellow of Clare Hall, University of Cambridge, where I was subsequently honored with life membership. I feel Clare Hall is a true home. I would like to thank N. R. M. de Lange and Profs. Henry Chadwick and Christopher Stead for their cordial welcome that year. My old friend Marc Hirshman not only shared the Cambridge experience with me, but was a student and colleague with me at JTS. He has sharpened my mind in both Rabbinic and Patristic literature.

My friends and colleagues of the Upper West Side Collegium Syriacum, particularly Shaye J. D. Cohen and the late Prof. Morton Smith should also be acknowledged, as should my now retired neighbors, Raymond E. Brown and J. Louis Martyn. It will be clear to the reader that the blessings I have received are in abundance. But, my thanksgiving would be incomplete if I did not acknowledge my perennial debt to my late teacher, Prof. Rabbi Saul Lieberman.

The many other colleagues and research assistants who have aided me in my work are thanked in the notes to the individual chapters. This volume has also benefited by the bibliography prepared by Kelly Washburn, the careful proof-reading of Jennifer Kraft and the meticulous typing of the indices by Efrat Halevi. To all of the above my thanks, yet the burden for errors remains my own.

Most of the chapters originally appeared in various journals, which are duly noted in the List of First Publications. "Mary Maudlin Among the Rabbis," was to have appeared in a volume edited by Phyllis Trible and Deirdre Good. Alas that volume has been unduly delayed and I pray that it will come out soon with my contribution appearing there as a reprint instead of an original.

This book is dedicated to the memory of Eleanor and Meyer Visotzky, mother and father of my world.

New York City   BLV

Contents

Fathers of the World: An Introduction

They were the fathers of the world. In their successive generations they begat rabbinic Judaism and Christianity. They fathered the transition from Temple and sacrifice to synagogue and study. They fathered the New Testament, churches, ecclesiastical order and ultimately, empire. Separately and together they fathered the transition from a pagan western world to a monotheistic (if not monolithic) Judeo-Christian culture. From the late first through the fifth centuries, these two groups of men reshaped the hellenistic culture bequeathed to them by Alexander the Great, his tutor Artistotle and their political and philosophical successors. A new world was begat by these fathers, a unique hybrid of biblical religion and Hellenism, Temple cult and academy. Two great religions were birthed by these fathers of our world.

Among the Jews the title, father, was used as an honorific, it denoted respect and authority. So the second century Rabbi Shimon ben Yohai can ask of the schools of the Hillel the Elder and his colleague Shammai, "How could the fathers of the world (*avot ha'olam*) disagree about the order of creation of heaven and earth; when in my opinion ..."[1] Or the title can denote philanthropy, as in the case of a certain father-of-the-Jews (*abbah yudan*) and his wife in Antioch who gave charity even when their fortunes took a turn for the worse. There was another giver called father-of- chicanery (*abba ramoi*) who used a bit of deception to get the Jews of Botsra to increase their charitable pledges (by witholding his own pledge) and then offered a matching grant.[2] It seems to have been a title, perhaps like Rabbi, for the late first century Abba Sha'ul and certain of his likenamed colleagues.[3] And, in a variety of forms, it served as a proper name for many of the sages of the Jews.[4]

Christians, too, used the term father. Jesus warns his disciples, "But you are not to be called rabbi, for you have one teacher and you are all

---

[1] Lev. Rabbah 36:1, ed. Margulies, 835, and parallels cited by Margulies, ad loc.

[2] Lev. R. 5:4, ed. Margulies, 110–114. The former is associated with early second century rabbis, the latter with an early third century rabbi.

[3] Pirqe Avot 2:8 and many other places in the Mishnah. Six other Rabbis of the Mishnah bear this title, see C. H. Kasovsky, *Thesaurus Mishnae* I, 5, s. v. Abba.

[4] See the onomastica and concordances to rabbinic literature, s. v.

brothers. And call no man your father on earth, for you have one Father,
who is in heaven" (Matthew 23: 8–9). Nevertheless the term persisted. In
New Testament Greek (and Latin), father means teacher (see the warning
about usage in I Cor. 4: 15) and in the late second century Irenaeus explains,
"When anyone has been taught from the mouth of another he is termed
the son of him who instructs him, and the latter is called his father" (*Adv.
Haer.* 4, 41, 2). First bishops, then all ecclesiastical writers were given the
title.[5] In the Syriac Church, the Hebrew/Aramaic *abba* referred to clergy,
whether monk, bishop or abbot (the term does persist, even in English).[6]

Of course, in both the Church and Synagogue God was granted the
title Father. In Hebrew, Latin, Greek, Syriac and Aramaic the fathers of
the world prayed to the Father of the World, Our Father in Heaven, the
Father of Mercy. But our concern in this volume is not for the Master
and Creator of all, but for God's creatures, those lesser, mortal fathers.
Despite their mortality, they live on. It was they who translated biblical
intolerence into ecclesiastical and then, temporal power. It was they who
shaped our Western worldview. It was they who molded pagan philosophy into a monotheistic mode. The process, however, was exceedingly
complex. Just as the fathers were changing Hellenism to fit the demands
first of Jewish law and lore, and then of Christian theology and doctrine;
so Hellenism had its pervasive effect on the fathers of the world. To lose
sight, even for a moment, of the influence of Hellenism on both religions,
is to misunderstand completely their relationships to one another and to
the *oecumene* in which they flourished.[7]

In the West and to a large extent of the East (up to the limes with the
Persian/Sassanian Empire, which includes all of Palestine and some parts
east) Judaism and later, Christianity, were Greco-Roman phenomena –
however unusual or suspect they may have been in pagan eyes. To say it
bluntly, the rabbis were Hellenists, much as were the Church fathers. Many

---

[5] On the term in the New Testament, see, now, *ABD* 1, s. v. abba. It is appropriate to
add here the concerns of feminist scholars, most recently ably represented by Mary Rose
D'Angelo, "Theology in Mark and Q: Abba and 'Father' in Context," *HTR* 85 (1992)
149–74. It is good early on in this book to apologize for the patriarchalism of the title
– it makes no claims to the role of men and women in the modern, or even ancient
era. It does, however, represent the ways the fathers of church and synagogue referred
to themselves in their own literature. For the later Church use I follow J. Quasten,
Patrology I 9–12.

[6] For Syriac usage, see the entries in R. Payne Smith, *Thesaurus Syriacus*, s. v.

[7] For the Church this proviso has been taken for granted as long as there has been a
distinction between Judaism and Hellenism. Now, however, it must be restated, particularly vis-a-vis Judaism. The classic statement of the issue is Martin Hengel, *Judentum
und Hellenismus, Studien zu ihrer Begegnung unter besonderer Berücksichtigung Palästinas
bis zur Mitte des 2. Jh. vor Chr.* (Tübingen, 2nd ed., 1973). The annotated bibliography
and collection of articles edited by Henry Fischel, *Essays in Greco-Roman and Related
Talmudic Literature* (New York, 1977) is also indispensible.

of the rabbis, if not most, were schooled in the same elementary educational system, learning letters and grammar in the same ways as their pagan counterparts. As Rabban Shimeʿon ben Gamaliel recalls, "There were one thousand students in my father's household. Five hundred learned Torah and five hundred learned the wisdom of the Greeks (viz. grammar and rhetoric)." This, for Jews associated with rabbinic Judaism and the patriarchate. One presumes other, less observant Jews to have been "properly educated" as well.[8] For the Church fathers, at least up to the reforms of Julian (361–363 CE), all education in letters was hellenistic education.[9] It is essential when comparing rabbinic and patristic literatures to view them both as products of this hellenistic milieu.

We will return below to the problems greco-roman rhetoric presents in the comparative study of rabbinic and patristic literatures. For the moment, some consideration must be given to the broader issues such comparisons raise. First and foremost among them is the simple question: What is to be compared? Since the literatures preserved are radically different genres this is a pertinent question. Church literature includes gospels, acts, epistles and apocalyptic among New Testament and patristic writings. Other patristic genres include homilies, commentaries and later, catanae. For the rabbis there is commentary, homily and Talmud.[10] For the most

---

[8] B. Sota 49b. For the Rabbis this is a complex claim not yet fully established in the secondary literature. See Hengel and Fischel, ibid, and see the materials collected in H. Z. Dimitrovsky, ed., *Exploring the Talmud* I (New York, 1976). Add to this the evidence amassed in S. Lieberman, *Greek in Jewish Palestine* (New York, 1965), esp. 1–67 (he comments on the quote on pp. 1 and 20f.) and see also his *Hellenism in Jewish Palestine* (New York, 1962), passim. A late fourth century Palestinian patriarch sent his son to Antioch to study with the famous rhetor, Libanius. See M. Schwabe, "Letters of Libanius to the Patriarch of Palestine," [Hebrew] *Tarbiz* 1/2 (1930) 85– 100. A monograph on hellenistic rhetorical practices in rabbinic education, especially the role of grammar and elementary rhetoric, remains a desideratum.

[9] The classic remains H. Marrou, *Histoire de l'Education dans l'Antiquite* (Paris, 1977: 7th ed). More recently, S. F. Bonner, *Education in Ancient Rome* (Berkeley, 1977), who does not, however, treat Christian (or Jewish) education explicitly. For the latter part of the period under study the influence of rhetors such as Libanius in Antioch (where church fathers, imperial officers and at least one of the Palestinian Jewish patriarch's sons [see previous note] studied together) has long been acknowledged. George Kennedy's works on the subject should be noted, e. g.: *The Art of Rhetoric in the Roman World* (Princeton, 1972), *Classical Rhetoric and its Christian and Secular Tradition from Ancient to Modern Times* (Chapel Hill, 1980), *Greek Rhetoric Under Christian Emperors* (Princeton, 1983) and *New Testament Interpretation through Rhetorical Criticism* (Chapel Hill, 1984).

[10] This list is representative and surely not meant to be exhaustive. On some aspects of comparison of seemingly similar rabbinic and patristic genres see M. Hirschman, "The Greek Fathers and the Aggada on Ecclesiastes: Formats of Exegesis in Late Antiquity," *HUCA* 59 (1988) 137–65 and, idem., *Mikra and Midrash: A Comparison of Rabbinics and Patristics* [Hebrew] (Hakibbutz Hameuchad, 1992). It is not the place here to determine the varieties of genres each literature encompasses.

part there is little point in comparing such disparate genres, so the issue
of "documentary integrity" cannot apply at this level. Rather, individual
traditions within documents will be compared.[11]

This still allows questions about the extent of knowledge that the rabbis
may have had about the New Testament – either as a document or through
its traditions. I have little doubt that the rabbis knew that something called
the New Testament existed, but I am dubious that they read it as such.
Rather, they cited sections and traditions that they had seen or heard in
other contexts. If the rabbis mention a text it is possible that they heard
it preached or more likely heard about it being preached. This means that
the rabbis will always be quoting New Testament out of context. Further,
the rabbis are most likely to hear the current local reading of a New
Testament verse. Using rabbinic parlance, they are more likely to know
the *drash* on a verse of the New Testament than to have any clue as to its
pshat.[12]

This is less so the case regarding more contemporary Church literature.
I think the rabbis may well have had a better grasp on patristics. Again,
I am dubious that they actually studied or even read such works. But,
the rabbis lived in a Holy Land regularly frequented by and significantly
populated by Christians.[13] The period they lived in was contentious – hot
issues of canon, trinity, mariology, heresiology and hamartology were regularly, publicly, vociferously debated. Theological, doctrinal and creedal
orthodoxies were being defined and Palestine was a battleground of ideas.
The rabbis could not avoid some fair knowledge of Church issues. Nor
could they resist probing those issues for weaknesses and opportunities
for polemic.[14] So, the student of rabbinic literature would do better to
expect the rabbis to know patristics than that they would know New Testament. It follows that more profitable comparisons may be made between
rabbinics and patristics than other Church literatures.

Does this hold equally true from the Christian side? This question
provides a good control for the hypothesis above. At first blush, the abun-

---

[11] Within individual Jewish or Christian religious traditions the concept of "documentary integrity" makes some sense and Jacob Neusner's cautions, first raised in his review
of Ed P. Sanders, *Paul and Palestinian Judaism* (Philadelphia, 1977) are given passing
attention – that is to say traditions are considered within the redactive critical framework of the document in which they are found. Once a redactive date and/or bias is
established for a given unit of tradition it is then compared to a parallel in the literature
of the sister religion.

[12] A case in point is argued below in "Trinitarian Testimonies."

[13] On Palestine as a Christian Holy Land, see, now, Robert Wilken, *The Land Called
Holy: Palestine in Christian History and Thought* (New Haven, 1992).

[14] This is a motif in the articles which follow. See "Trinitarian Testimonies," "Overturning the Lamp," "Mary Maudlin," and "Anti-Christian Polemic" for examples of
rabbinic knowledge of debated issues in the Church and rabbinic willingness to exploit
those very points in their encounters with Christians.

dance of studies which use rabbinics as "New Testament background" would seem to belie this contention. Jewish and Christian scholars eagerly plunder rabbinic literature to show the Jewish background of Jesus or Paul or even of gentile New Testament characters or books.[15] While this is methodologically dubious at best and possibly even pernicious,[16] it is nevertheless welcome. For far too long scholars have ignored the "Jewish problem" when studying New Testament. Although rabbinic literature may not be entirely apposite for its study, it is a breath of fresh air, possible only since World War II and Vatican II, that Christian scholars grapple with the problem of Jewish background. The bias of those who considered it a question of *Spätjudentum* is no longer welcome in the academy. We will have to endure inappropriate methodology for yet another generation until a surer means of using rabbinics or some other literature is discovered.[17] In the meanwhile all the usual caveats for the use of rabbinic literature in the study of New Testament must be recited ad nauseum (but not here).

Use of rabbinic literature for the study of patristics is as rare as use of patristics for the study of rabbinics. Since each is an arcane literature studied most often by those with a deep religious commitment, a certain narrowness of scholarly vision still holds sway. This is, of course, exacerbated by the methodological necessity for a scholar in Greek, Latin or Syriac texts to master Hebrew and Aramaic (and vice versa). Needless to say, those who move with assurance over such broad ground are few – their bibliographies will be discussed at the end of this chapter. This condition persists despite the testimony of Church Fathers like Origen and Jerome to their reliance on Jewish sources. It is enough for now to note that works like Louis Ginzberg's *Die Haggada bei den Kirchenvätern* come but once in a century.[18]

In both Rabbinic and Patristic literatures, methodological considerations loom large. Two discussions are called for here: first, a brief mention of methods and issues common to both disciplines separately (that is to say, rabbinics and patristics each require recognition of these matters whether or not they are being compared). Second, a lengthier discussion on prob-

---

[15] See, for example, the review of Lachs' *Rabbinic Commentary to the New Testament* or "Trinitarian Testimonies," below.

[16] As in the case of Paul Billerbeck's *Kommentar zum Neuen Testament aus Talmud und Midrasch.*

[17] A recent example of careful, well intentioned scholarship of this ilk is *The New Testament and Christian-Jewish Dialogue: Studies in Honor of David Flusser* ed. M. Lowe, *Immanuel* 24/25 (1990), with Flusser's bibliography published there, too.

[18] 1899–1935. Full bibliographic detail and some discussion may be found in Baskin, "Rabbinic-Patristic Exegetical Contacts in Late Antiquity: A Bibliographical Reappraisal," in W. S. Green, ed., *Approaches to Ancient Judaism* V (Atlanta, 1985) 53–80.

lems in comparing the two literatures follows, with special attention to the singular disturbances Hellenistic rhetoric provides to interfere with the comparison. Other methodological issues between rabbinic and patristic literatures are considered in the individual studies in this volume.

Both rabbinic and patristic literatures have suffered from a lack of critical editions of primary texts. Happily, this lacuna is being addressed in a variety of publications, doctoral dissertations and electronic databases. It is becoming easier to search for manuscript readings, phrases, bibliography and the like in both fields. Common research tools, such as a scriptural index to the literatures are either completed or now in publication. The ongoing task of updating dictionaries and concordances to account for these findings is also underway. By the end of the twentieth century anyone with sufficient computer memory will be able to access and search basic texts in both rabbinics and patristics.

Research tools are not, however, research; nor is memory interpretation. Historiography and exegesis are also in methodological flux. Techniques and schools of criticism, long common or now developing in Bible study are slowly being introduced in the fields of rabbinics and patristics. Redaction criticism, form criticism, rhetorical criticism, post-modern literary criticism in general and feminist interpretation in particular, combine with a more general interest in a history of religions approach, use of sociological techniques and social history methods in both fields.[19]

In the comparison of rabbinic and patristic literatures, a number of areas have garnered interest. Some recent studies have focussed on biblical verses and their subsequent interpretation in Church and synagogue.[20] This is a useful, if narrow, avenue of research. Key verses, particularly those that betray an overall attitude or *Weltanschauung*, are mined for material. Often, regrettably, little more than listings of the traditions are presented. Still, it is an important first step in the history of traditions and exegetical

---

[19] See most recently: in rabbinics, Judith Hauptman, "Contemporary Talmud Research," *Association for Jewish Studies Newsletter* 43 (Spring, 1993) – a brief general overview of trends – and my "Six Studies in Midrash and Methods," *Shofar* 10 (1992) 86–96. In patristics, see the first two numbers of the *Journal of Early Christian Studies* (Spring and Summer, 1993), where many of these methods are featured in the articles and noted in the book reviews.

[20] e. g. Sebastian Brock's studies of Syriac traditions on Hebrew scriptural themes in *Le Muséon* 87 (1974) and onward (e. g. vol. 99, 102) consistently compare the Syriac Father's interpretations with Greek and Latin Fathers and with rabbinic traditions. Jay Braverman, *Jerome's Commentary on Daniel: A study of Comparative Jewish and Christian Interpretations of the Hebrew Bible* (CBQ Monograph 7, 1978), Judith Baskin, *Pharoah's Counsellors: Job, Jethro, and Balaam in Rabbinic and Patristic Tradition* (Brown Judaic Studies 47, 1983), Steven Fraade, *Enosh and His Generation: Pre-Israelite Hero and History in Postbiblical Interpretation* (SBL monograph 30, 1984) and Jeremy Cohen, *"Be Fertile and Increase, Fill the Earth and Master It": The Ancient and Medieval Career of a Biblical Text* (Ithaca, 1989); to name a few. See Baskin, "Rabbinic-Patristic Exegetical Contacts" for more on this specific area.

study. Even more needs to be done in the exploration of whether these particular exegetical traditions are influenced by or in dialogue with one another.[21]

Other studies have traced parallel stories or *chriae* and their use in patristic and rabbinic literature.[22] Still others, small and large, have taken up a common theme.[23] Here, too, methodological limitations impose themselves. The larger works tend to cover such vast ground that it is impossible to do justice to more than one religious tradition. While the citation of rabbinic works in a study of patristic attitudes is welcome (or a study of patristic works in a scholarly tome on rabbinics), there is a need for such attention to become a regular part of scholarship. Translations of the primary materials are in sufficient abundance that linguistic barriers are no longer an excuse for overlooking the "other side's" point of view. Nevertheless, the only work that readily comes to mind which gives equal weight to both rabbinic and patristic tradition, and its theme demands such, is Marcel Simon's groundbreaking *Verus Israel*.[24]

When rabbinic and patristic literature on a given topic is patently polemical, hearing both sides of the argument is an absolute requirement. To list but one side is to indulge in the biases that characterized Church and Synagogue during centuries past. Rehearsing only one side confirms prejudice, study of both sides advances scholarship. In other instances, materials when simply juxtaposed can be seen to be polemical. In rarer instances, rabbinic and patristic writings will be in dialogue. The distinc-

---

[21] The small literature available now on Song of Songs comes to mind. All of the works cited below presume some sort of dialogue, apologetic or polemic. Careful reading of the primary sources does not demand these conclusions, however. Each of the sources may have been composed in isolation from the other traditions. See, Y. Baer, "Israel, The Christian Church and The Roman Empire ...," *Scripta Hierosolymitana* 7 (1961), 79–149; E. E. Urbach, "Homiletical Interpretations of the Sages and the Expositions of Origen on Canticles, and the Jewish-Christian Disputation," *Scripta Hierosolymitana* 22, 248–275 (a translation of the Hebrew, first published in *Tarbiz* 30 [1961]); R. Lowe, "Apologetic Motifs in the Targum to the Song of Songs," in A. Altmann, ed., *Biblical Motifs* (1966), 159–96; R. Kimelman, "Rabbi Yohanan and Origen on Song of Songs," *HTR* 78 (1980) 567–95. Mention of these works, each of which deals with Origen's writings on the Song of Songs, requires note of N. R. M. deLange, *Origen and the Jews* (Cambridge, 1976).

[22] E. g., see below, "Hillel, Hieronymus and Praetextatus".

[23] Small: e. g. my "Mortal Sins," below. Large, e. g. Peter Brown, *The Body and Society: Men, Women and Sexual Renunciation in Early Christianity* (New York, 1988) and Robert Wilken, *The Land Called Holy: Palestine in Christian History and Thought* (New Haven, 1992). As each of the latter two titles indicate, the primary interest is on patristic thought, the references to rabbinic are cursory.

[24] *Versus Israel: Etude sur les relations entre Chretiens et Juifs dans l'empire Romain* (Paris, 1948). A recent, smaller work which takes up a theme that demands working across the boundaries of rabbinic and patristic literatures (and considers Roman legal codes and epigraphy) is Louis Feldman, "Proselytism by Jews in Third, Fourth and Fifth Centuries," *Journal for the Study of Judaism* 24 (1993) 1–58.

tion here between polemic and dialogue is largely one of attitude. Polemic presumes the other is Other, in opposition, to be refuted. Dialogue, that rarest of religious discourses, presumes mutual progress can be made toward understanding of a verse, an issue, a point of theology, perhaps even one another. It is never easy to discern when a two sided approach will reveal polemic, when dialogue. Unfortunately, it's a reasonably safe bet methodologically to assume that the literatures are polemicizing against one another.[25]

The question of dialogue and polemic is only one side of a larger question in the comparison of rabbinics and patristics. The existence of parallels between the literatures raises vexing methodological questions. Although there are many kinds of parallels which may be considered, only larger units of parallel traditions are dealt with in these studies.[26] Further, the precise usefulness of such parallels needs to be considered.[27] Although Tertullian was kvetching about "a mottled Christianity of Stoic, Platonic and dialectic composition," his question may well be asked regarding the comparison of patristic with rabbinic literatures, "What indeed has Athens to do with Jerusalem?"[28]

Often in the past, studies of parallels focussed on the question of direction or who borrowed from whom. There is little doubt that this is an important contribution to knowledge in general, and the consequence of influences must not be overlooked. Indeed, my assertion above that the Rabbis were Hellenists much as were the Church Fathers, can only be made due to a century of research tracing hellenistic influences into

---

[25] Scholars must also recognize their own biases. In doing so it may be possible for study of ancient polemic to lead to modern dialogue. This admission of hope is part of my disclosure of bias, necessary for (though readily apparent to) the readers of these essays. I write in the hope of dialogue, even as I write as a scholar who pretends to objectivity and dispassionate scholarship. There is no disguising my position as a scholar of rabbinics, first and foremost. The work of this volume, while it considers rabbinic and patristic literatures together to be mutually illuminative, has as a primary goal the exegesis of rabbinic literature. Finally, I am an ordained Conservative rabbi, writing in the late twentieth-century United States. The openess to ecumenism in America, my position as a tenured faculty member at the Jewish Theological Seminary of America and the title of the chair I hold there: Appleman Associate Professor of Midrash and Interreligious Studies, my status as visiting faculty in the past decade at Union Theological Seminary, Princeton Theological Seminary, Oxford and Cambridge Universities, all these and more attest to the earnestness with which I undertake this volume (published by a German house, under the combined editorship of Protestant and Catholic scholars). This bias cannot help but be writ large throughout these pages.

[26] Morton Smith, *Tannaitic Parallels to the Gospels* (Philadelphia, 1951) makes a variety of distinctions among types of parallels which remain useful guidelines in comparative studies.

[27] Samuel Sandmel, "Parallelomania," *JBL* 81 (1962) remains a useful starting point for any discussion of this issue.

[28] De Praescr. Haer. 7. I am using the felicitous translation of H. A. Wolfson, *The Philosophy of the Church Fathers* (Cambridge, Mass., 1956), 102.

rabbinics by means of parallel traditions. Yet the very literature on the subject[29] teaches us caution in using parallels to trace influences. Often the bias of a researcher affects his or her conclusions in this regard. Saul Lieberman's famous studies on the relationship of hellenistic hermeneutic devices to rabbinic modes of exegesis were marred by his reluctance to admit outright that certain rabbinic halachic norms were derived from hellenistic practice.[30]

In comparisons between Judaism and Christianity, a variety of biases have been indulged. Parallels have been adduced to show Jewish origins for many Christian institutions or Christian origins for later Jewish ones.[31] Paul Billerbeck's *Kommentar zum Neuen Testament* uses parallels selectively to portray rabbinic Judaism as the natural inheritor of the doomed works righteousness Pharisaism Matthew descries and John condemns. All in all, the question of "Who Borroweth?" or "Which Came First?" produces results which confirm the prejudices of the biased researcher. This is not to say that there are not some few studies that genuinely attempt to trace the history of a religious idea without parochialism. Modern historiography, however, would have us err to the side of caution.

What, then, may be gained by the comparative study of rabbinic and patristic literatures? What can parallels in the varied *opera* teach us? First and formost, the existence of parallels is indicative of a general milieu. This is not to say that one text necessarily provides "background" for another. It does, however, give a generally impressionist viewpoint of the era in question. Scholars are a bit like lepidopterists, requiring – in the interests of good method – that the butterfly be pinned down for proper study. However, there genuinely are occasions when all one can do is identify what's there, floating in the air, without pinning it down. It isn't exact scholarship, but it teaches us how to view the field of butterflies. That's why I use the term impressionist. When we get up close the picture we thought we were looking at dissolves into a field of dots. Knowing the limitations of the research is as important as caution in the exercise of method.

There is more, yet, that parallels can teach us. How the traditions are used, how they are reshaped, *mutatis mutandis*, by rabbinic Judaism and Christianity teaches us a good deal about the tendencies of the redactors of the traditions. Jews and Christians will, necessarily, treat a tradition about

---

[29] Cited in brief above, n. 8.

[30] *Hellenism in Jewish Palestine* (New York, 1962) 47–82. Lieberman was willing to state that aggadic exegetical devices were borrowed by the rabbis from the Greeks. He exercised excessive scholarly caution, however, for halachic norms and could not bring himself to conclude (though adducing better evidence than he had for aggadic materials) that the rabbis borrowed certain means for determining Jewish law.

[31] S. Spiegel, *The Last Trial* (New York, 1967), an English translation of the Hebrew original, 1950, carries wonderful examples of both types of triumphalism.

the advent of the Messiah in a very different way. Using the common tradition, we can observe the differences. It is in that observation (and not in the mere commonality) that the history of religions may be written. Or, there may be a common story (chria) about a pagan who wishes to convert. How the story has the pagan characterize the pinnacle of grandeur in the given religion tells us how the story-tellers of an era viewed their grandees and spun myths about them.[32] In other words, the very methods that redaction critics use to analyze the traditions history of a story within Judaism *or* Christianity can be profitably employed to analyze a tradition in both Judaism and Christianity.

Rabbinic and patristic literatures share certain methodologies, both in their exegetical approach to Scripture as well as in their individual units of didactic literature, the lives of their saints. As mentioned above, the genre of the hellenistic chria assures that a certain commonality of form will be observed.[33] When St. Jerome grumbles about the temerity of Praetextatus who offended Pope Damasus by teasing him, "Make me bishop of Rome and I will at once be a Christian," he uses the chria to express his pique. It is not surprising to find a parallel chria in a story of Hillel and a would-be convert.[34]

Pagans, Christians and Jews looked upon their leadership as a source of wisdom, privileged lineage and enviable wealth. As St. Augustine observes, "jealousy boils up only against clergy, especially bishops, whose authority is seen to bulk the largest and who are thought to use and enjoy church property as if they owned it themselves."[35] In rabbinic circles, Hillel − a mythic founding father *par excellence* − is of good lineage,[36] but famous for his poverty.[37] Even after he became the great leader/scholar, he remained poor.[38] This points up the reality in both synagogue and church that wealth and lineage were sought as qualifications for − and not as consequences of − ecclesiastical office. As Ramsay MacMullen puts it, "considerations of a material sort ... often appear to have been decisive in the selection of late Roman church leaders ... judged to be of the right

---

[32] See the discussion in "Hillel, Hieronymus and Praetextatus." See, now, on Praetextatus, L. Michael White, "Finding the Ties that Bind: Issues from Social Description," *Semeia* 56 (1991) 3−22.

[33] The basic work on the chria in rabbinic and greco-roman rhetoric is by Henry Fischel and may be found in the collection he edited, *Studies in Greco-Roman and Related Talmudic Literature*.

[34] See below, "Hillel, Hieronymus and Praetextatus."

[35] Ep. 125; here using the translation of Ramsay MacMullen, *Christianizing the Roman Empire* (New Haven, 1984), 53. His description is a major source for what follows.

[36] p. Taanit 4: 2 (68a), where R. Levi reports him to be of Davidic descent.

[37] b. Yoma 35b

[38] b. Sotah 21a.

circles, eloquence, vigor, and place in the world."[39] He further notes, "In eastern episcopal elections ... candidates were promoted ... on the basis of their pedigree or money, γένος and πλουτος."[40]

This is underscored by a well known rabbinic legend about the knotty problem of replacing a deposed patriarch.[41] The Babylonian Talmud[42] characterizes the deliberations:

> With whom shall we replace him? Shall we replace him with Rabbi Yehoshua? He is a plaintiff in the incident [that led to the deposing of Rabban Gamaliel II]. Shall we replace him with Rabbi Aqiba? Perhaps he will suffer harm since he is not of proper lineage. Rather, let us replace him with Rabbi Elazar ben Azariah, for he is wise, he is rich and he is a tenth generation descendent of Ezra. He is wise − so if there are [legal] difficulties raised he can solve them. He is rich − so if he is called upon to provide service to [i. e., bribe] the Imperial house he can do so. He is a tenth generation descendent of Ezra and thus has proper lineage and it is difficult to harm him.

Elazar ben Azariah seems to have all the qualifications to be a late antique bishop: lineage, wealth and, as an added bonus, wisdom. He wouldn't have been the first person drafted to be bishop who was lacking the qual- ification of being well schooled in Christianity.[43] But Elazar is made, however briefly, the patriarch of the Jews. It is tempting to see in these stories or in the ones of Hillel and Jerome cited above, a certain common- ality betwen Church and Synagogue. One might make a case that in the monotheistic or biblical establishments of Palestine certain forms were fol- lowed, expectations met. Patriarchs and bishops were chosen by the same criteria, conversions from paganism followed similar patterns. Or, being methodologically more cautious, one might assert that at least the stories told about such events, the literary transmission of myth and legend, the didactic narrative which became the lives of the saints, these were cut from the same mold.

But even this is insufficient methodological caution. It is here that the hellenistic milieu in which both church and synagogue flourished must be brought to the fore. Stated simply, regarding methodology in the com- parative study of patristics and rabbinics, hellenistic rhetoric causes distur- bances in the field. An unavoidable interference emanates from hellenistic

---

[39] MacMullen, ibid. 35.

[40] MacMullen, ibid., 142, n. 3. See, too, Peter Brown, *Augustine of Hippo* (Berkeley, 1967) 193−99, on the bishop as public figure and patron.

[41] On the following story see the exemplary article by Robert Goldenberg, "The Depo- sition of Rabban Gamaliel II: An Examination of the Sources," *JJS* 23 (1972) 167−90. References to the parallel versions in rabbinic texts as well as other related texts are found there.

[42] b. Berakot 27b.

[43] See MacMullen, ibid., and see Robin Lane Fox, *Pagans and Christians* (New York, 1987), 493−545, "'Bishops and Authority," esp. 503−517.

education that contaminates the "purity" of any comparative research. In the story of Hillel, Hieronymus and Praetextatus both the form of the *chria* and the expectations of the plutocratic ol' boys network confound our ability to hold Christianity and Rabbinic Judaism side by side for comparison. The hellenistic background intrudes into the foreground. In the case of Elazar ben Azariah and his Church colleagues, again, the plutocrats get in the way. One need not be electing a bishop or a patriarch to expect leadership to have wealth, wisdom and family. It is a leadership model well known to the pagan equestrians and senators of antique culture.[44] It is not unknown among a similarly horsey, private school senatorial class, even today. So, although the comparison of Elazar ben Azariah to the bishops is tempting, even suggestive, it's hardly big news.

Other forms of comparison appear, at first blush, a bit more immune to disturbances in the field. It would seem unlikely that a common exegesis of Scripture could be anything other than shared, perhaps even borrowed, and thus ripe for "pure" comparison. One such case in point is found in the Apostolic father, Barnabus, who when pondering the mysteries of the cross, turns to two successive images from the Torah.

> And he says again to Moses, when Israel was warred upon by strangers ... the Spirit speaks to the heart of Moses to make a representation of the cross, and of him who should suffer, because, he says, unless they put their trust in him, they shall suffer war forever. Moses therefore placed one shield upon another in the midst of the fight, and standing there raised above them all kept stretching out his hands, and so Israel began to be victorious; then whenever he let them drop they began to perish. Why? That they may know that they cannot be saved if they do not hope on him ... Again Moses makes a representative of Jesus showing that he must suffer, and shall himself give life ... Moses therefore makes a graven serpent, and places it in honour and calls the people by a proclamation. So they came together and besought Moses that he would offer a prayer on their behalf for their healing. But Moses said to them, "Whenever one of you," he said, "be bitten, let him come to the serpent that is placed upon the tree, and let him hope, in faith that it though dead is able to give life, and he shall straightaway be saved." And they did so ...[45]

It has long been noted that Barnabus has affinities with Jewish and specifically rabbinic literature.[46] Yet while this passage draws on the pentateuchal

---

[44] Robin Lane Fox, op. cit.; Ramsay MacMullen, *Roman Social Relations* (New Haven, 1974), *Corruption and the Decline of Rome* (New Haven, 1988), *Changes in the Roman Empire: Essays in the Ordinary* (Princeton, 1990), 13–24, 190–97; and Peter Brown, *Augustine of Hippo* (Berkeley, 1967), *Religion and Society in the Age of St. Augustine* (London, 1977), and idem, in Paul Veyne, ed., *A History of Private Life: From Pagan Rome to Byzantium* (Cambridge, Mass., 1987) 239–85; finally, Lee I. Levine, *The Rabbinic Class of Roman Palestine in Late Antiquity* (Jerusalem, 1989).

[45] Barnabus XII 2–7, the translation here is Kirsopp Lake, *The Apostolic Fathers* I 383– 385 (Loeb Classic Library).

[46] R. A. Kraft, *The Apostolic Fathers: A New Translation and Commentary. Vol. 3,*

text, it is a classic example of Christian typology.[47]   One is, as a result, tempted to locate the exegesis in a purely Christian framework, with some nod to the origins of typology in pagan Alexandrian grammar and rhetorical schools of exegesis. But, heads can be turned toward a comparison with rabbinic literature when one reads the Mishnah to Rosh HaShana 3: 8, citing the same two Biblical passages:

> Then, *whenever Moses held up his hand, Israel prevailed* … (Ex. 17: 11). Do Moses' hands then make or break a war? Rather this passage is meant to tell you that whenever Israel looked on high and subjugated themselves to their Father in Heaven they were victorious, and if not, they fell.
> Similarly you find, *Make a seraph figure and mount it on a standard. And if anyone who is bitten looks at it, he shall recover* (Num. 21: 8). Does a serpent give death or life? Rather, when Israel looked on high and subjugated themselves to their Father in Heaven they were healed, and if not, they fell.

Here, then, is the dilemma. Both Barnabus, writing in early second century Alexandria,[48] and the Mishnah, redacted in late second-century Palestine, take up two scenes in the Hebrew Bible with troubling overtones of magic and treat them with virtually the same exegetical method. It makes one terribly tempted to assume some nexus between the two works – either Barnabus' tradition was adopted by Palestinian rabbis – or an early Jewish, proto-Mishnaic tradition was available to Barnabus. A tempting nexus, but not a necessary one. It is clear that typology has its origins in hellenistic method. It is equally clear that much of rabbinic hermeneutic has its roots in hellenistic, particularly Alexandrian technique.[49]   Further, a careful perusal of Barnabus shows that he intersperses references to Isa. 65, Deut. 27 and Num. 13 in his (far broader) treatment of the passages.

Barnabas and Didache (Toronto, 1965); Birger Pearson, "Christians and Jews in First Century Alexandria," in G. Nickelsburg and G. MacRae, edd., *Christians among Jews and Gentiles: Essays in Honor of Krister Stendal* (Philadelphia, 1986) 206–216, esp. 212–214; L. W. Barnard, *Studies in the Apostolic Fathers and their Background* (New York, 1966) 41–72; idem, "Judaism in Egypt, AD 70–135," *Church Quarterly Review* 160 (1959) 320–34; Karen Chandler, "The Rite of the Red Heifer in the Epistle of Barnabas and Mishnah Parah," in W. S. Green, ed., *Approaches to Ancient Judaism* V (Atlanta, 1985) 99–114; M. B. Shukster and P. Richardson, "Temple and Bet Ha-midrash in the Epistle of Barnabas," in S. Wilson, ed., *Anti-Judaism in Early Christianity* (Waterloo, 1986) 17–31. My thanks to Dr. Bruce Neilsen for some of these references.

[47] The classic here remains K. J. Woollcombe, "The Biblical Origins and Patristic Development of Typology," *Essays on Typology* (Naperville, 1957).

[48] See above, n. 46.

[49] Here the citations above to Fischel and Lieberman are particularly apposite. I would add to these references the seminal work by Zacharias Frankel, *Über den Einfluß der palästinischen Exegese auf die alexandrische Hermeneutik* (Leipzig, 1851) which set the ball rolling; and the still influential articles of David Daube, "Rabbinic Methods of Interpretation and Hellenistic Rhetoric," *HUCA* 22 (1949) 236–64; idem, "Alexandrian Methods of Interpretation and the Rabbis," *Festschrift H. Lewald* edd., M. Gerwig, et al (Basel, 1953) 27–44. My own "Jots and Tittles," below, is a modest addition to an already well established literature.

Given that both Barnabus and (if we may presume the redactor to be the
author) Rabbi Yehuda HaNasi 1) read roughly the same Bible, 2) shared a
similar enough monotheism to be uncomfortable with texts that smacked
of magic and 3) were schooled in the same hellenistic hermeneutics, it
would be surprising if they had *not* attempted similar solutions to the two
(forgive the pun) cruxes. There need be *no* dependence for there to be
common hellenistic milieu.

The case of Barnabus is exacerbated, however, by yet another parallel
of traditions that rely on similar methodology to solve another biblical
conundrum. In Genesis 14:14 we read how Abraham rides out to rescue
his nephew Lot, a captive in the War of the Four Kings vs. the Five
Kings.[50] As the Torah tells it, Abraham musters his household retainers,
eighteen and three hundred by number, and deploys by night to assure a
suprise victory. The passage is surprising for there is no previous hint of
Abraham's military prowess. Where does he get a platoon to command?
How is it that Abraham plays the part of noble warrior instead of father of
faith? Jewish and Christian commentators try to harmonize these images.
Barnabus comments,

> Notice that he first mentions the eighteen, and after a pause the three hundred.
> The eighteen – *iota* (= ten) and *eita* (= eight) – you have Jesus – and because
> the cross was destined to have grace in the τ (= 300) he says *and three hundred*.
> So he indicates Jesus in the two letters and the cross in the other.[51]

By a very clever reading of the numbers Barnabus translates Abraham's
warriors into faith in the crucified Jesus. So, Abraham remains father of
faith and victorious warrior – all in all a model Christian. Barnabus' exegesis seems astonishing, it certainly is an unusual way of interpreting a
crux – the numbers are not numbers at all, but letters symbolizing something else entirely. Barnabus acheives this *coup* through a quirk of Greek
annotation; numbers are represented by letters of the alphabet. Thus every
number can be expressed alphabetically and every word, conversely, has a
numerical value. It is possible to equate words with the same numerical
value – this technique is called *isopsephie* or *geometria*.[52]

This latter term is well known as an exegetical technique in rabbinic
literature, where it is usually transliterated as *gematria*. Indeed, it has

---

[50] On the passage see Y. Muffs, "Abraham the Noble Warrior: Patriarchal Politics
and Laws of War in Ancient Israel," *Journal of Jewish Studies (Essays in Honour of
Yigael Yadin)* 33 (1982) 81–107, now reprinted in Muffs' *Love & Joy: Law, Language
and Religion in Ancient Israel* (New York, 1992) 67– 95.

[51] Barnabus 9:8, following LCL, *Apostolic Fathers* I 372–3.

[52] See S. Lieberman, *Hellenism in Jewish Palestine*, 69, n. 173 and pp. 72f, nn. 198–211.
See now H. L. Strack and G. Stemberger, *Introduction to the Talmud and Midrash* (Min-
neapolis, 1992) 32–3, who cites S. Sambursky, "On the Origin and Significance of the
Term Gematria," *JJS* 29 (1978) 35–38.

been noted[53] that *gematria* is used by the rabbis in much the same way to solve the crux of the three hundred eighteen warriors of Genesis 14. The oft repeated midrashic solution: "Rabbi Shime'on ben Laqish quoted bar Qappara, It was [Abraham's servant] Eliezer, by himself, for the [numerical value of] the name Eliezer is *eighteen and three hundred* (ibid.)."[54] Like Barnabus, Resh Laqish has reconciled the image of Abraham as father of faith with that of noble warrior. Now, instead of leading a platoon into battle, Resh Laqish imagines Abraham and his faithful servant, Eliezer, playing out the roles of Don Quixote and Sancho Panza as they go tilting into battle to save Lot – their faith in God as their banner.

A comparison of Barnabus and Rabbi Shime'on is instructive. First – as in the case of Moses, Amalek and the Brazen Serpent – Barnabus' reading of Scripture is being compared with a rabbinic text of a century or more later.[55] It is possible that a very late Tanna or early Amora (that is to say, roughly contemporary with the redaction of the Mishnaic tradition, above) knew Barnabus or knew the either proto-rabbinic or early Christian tradition Barnabus made use of. Second, we would do well to point out that despite the common *gematria*, the conclusions point to very different world views. Barnabus once again has Christ as his referrent. Although he uses numerological norms, his hermeneutic approach is, in general, typological. Rabbi Shime'on, unlike the exegesis of the Mishnah, does not rely on reference to God to mitigate the dissonance the 318 warriors impart; he turns instead to another biblical personality.[56] For Resh Laqish, midrash triumphs over typology. One need not turn to God to harmonize all biblical irritants.

This very difference in *Weltanschauung* may well be the stuff comparisons between rabbinics and patristics is meant to reveal. On the other hand, it may, along with the anachronism inherent in these comparisons, give us occasion to look further. It must be pointed out that methodologically, Barnabus and Resh Laqish are not quite doing the same thing. R. Shime'on does simple numerical equivalency: the letters in Eliezer add up to 318. Barnabus has a different approach. In Greek, 318 would be

---

[53] Lieberman, ibid., 69, Strack, Stemberger, ibid.

[54] Pesikta DeRav Kahana 8:2 (ed. Mandelbaum, 139). R. Shime'on fl. early third century. Bar Qappara fl. late second cent. Parallels in Lev. R. 28:4 and Gen. R. 42 (43):2 (ed. Theodor, 416, and see the notes there for full citation of all the parallels), only cite R. Shime'on ben Laqish.

[55] This depends on the reliability of attribution. Assuming the attributions to be accurate, there remains the question of whether to credit the rabbinic tradition to R. Shime'on or to bar Qappara. If the traditions are pseudepigraphical, they can at best be dated to the redactive dates of the midrashim, viz. fifth century at the earliest.

[56] This technique is a version of what Isaac Heinemann calls "flight from anonymity," wherein an anonymous biblical character is identified midrashically with a known one. See, *The Methods of Aggadah* [Hebrew] (3rd ed., Jerusalem, 1970) In our case, an entire group is so identified through the vehicle of *gematria*.

represented as τιη. Barnabus relies on the biblical ordering of the numbers to help make his point. In Hebrew and in Greek the eighteen comes first. So, Barnabus leads with Jesus, whose name begins with the *iota eita* that also signifies eighteen. He ends with *tau* the Greek letter that symbolizes three hundred and the cross.[57] In neither case do the signifieds have the numerical equivalancy of the numbers which serve as their signifiers.

Not only are Barnabus and the midrash not engaging in the same activity, but again, hellenism complicates the possibility of dependence upon one another or even upon a common exegetical source. Half a century ago Prof. Saul Lieberman pointed to *gematria* as "one of the most important components of the *onirocritica*."[58] He cites Artimedorus as a common source for *gematria* interpretations of dreams. It is no suprise to learn that Artemidorus wrote just around the time of bar Qappara, Barnabus and R. Shime'on ben Laqish.[59] In a more recent study, S. Sambursky traces the origins of the term *gematria* first to the works of the fifth century (CE) commentator to the *Timaeus*, Proclus, and through him to Theodorus of Asine, a disciple of Iamblichus. Iamblichus argues against the numerological exegeses of Amelius and of the somewhat earlier scholiast, Numenius. Again, we find dates for *gematria* varying from the second century CE (Numenius) through mid-third (Amelius, ca. 246–270 CE) and early fourth (Iamblichus, 250– 325 and his student and contemporary, Theodore). What we have here, then, is hellenistic interference from contemporary sources. In general *gematria* seems best suited to the late second or early third century,[60] another product of the Second Sophistic.[61] Mention of the Second Sophistic touches on the cause of hellenistic interference in patristic and rabbinic circles. The Church was equally comfortable in both the worlds of philosophy and of rhetoric from the time

---

[57] The *tau* shaped cross is associated in later Christian art with other Old Testament scenes: it is the form used by the Israelites to mark their doorposts in Egypt with paschal blood and was the form of the standard upon which the brazen serpent was raised. See G. G. Sill, *A Handbook of Symbols in Christian Art* (New York, 1975) s. v. Cross.

[58] S. Lieberman, *Hellenism in Jewish Palestine*, 72.

[59] Late second century, according to *Oxford Classical Dictionary*, s. v. Artemidorus.

[60] See, too, W. Bacher, *Die exegetische Terminologie der jüdischen Traditionsliteratur* (Leipzig, 1899) s. v. notarikon. Now it is true that one rabbinic source quotes an earlier sage, ben Azzai, doing something like *gematria*. He suggests that the word *eikah* with which Lamentations begins, should be read to mean that the Jews were exiled only when "they denied the One (*alef*) God, the ten (*yod*) commandments, the law of circumcision given after twenty (*kaph*) generations, and the five (*he*) books of the Torah" (apud Strack, Stemberger, op cit., 33, where there is further citation of secondary literature on *gematria*) But Lamentations Rabbah is at earliest a fifth century work, and ben Azzai nowhere uses the term *gematria* in his *notarikon* style exegesis.

[61] Basic introduction and bibliography may be found in G. W. Bowersock, ed., *Approaches to the Second Sophistic* (University Park, Pa., 1974).

of Tertullian,[62] through Augustine and the Cappadocian fathers.[63] The rabbis, for their part, paid little attention to philosophy beyond the standard Stoicism of the era. Rhetoric *was* hellenism in rabbinic culture. The overlap in content between rabbinic *aggada* and the legends in Philostratus' *Life of Appolonius of Tyana* merely serves to underscore the common rhetoric the rabbis share with the Second Sophistic.[64] In other words, the increased interest in philosophy and particularly in rhetoric, which were the earmarks of the revival of Greek culture in the eastern Empire known as the Second Sophistic, affected the development of both rabbinic and patristic literatures. It was these disturbances in the field which account for a large share of commonality in rabbinics and patristics. While such hellenistic interference has been charted in a variety of studies for each religious literature separately, it is equally necessary to consider hellenistic influences and background in comparative studies.[65]

The essays in this volume try to keep an eye on the common hellenistic heritage shared by the fathers of the world. Two articles explicitly draw upon hellenistic traditions to aid the comparative process.[66] In the remainder of the chapters, the assumptions of common rhetorical training and hellenistic milieu are taken as a given. All of the articles collected here were written with the intention of collecting them together as a book. Before the very first article was written, almost a decade ago, a broad general outline of the contents was drawn. It was my intention for these studies to explore a variety of scholarly issues. Methodology was a clear concern. This led to a consideration of both topical issues (e. g. Mortal Sins), form critical issues (e. g. Hillel, Hieronymus and Praetextatus), exegetical issues (e. g. Three Syriac Cruxes) and polemical issues (e. g. Anti-Christian Polemic in Leviticus Rabbah). Where it was considered necessary, basic groundwork was laid (e. g. Prolegomenon to the Study of Jewish-Christianities in Rabbinic literature). The reviews included in this book demonstrate, again

---

[62] See T. D. Barnes, *Tertullian* (Oxford, 1971) where the Church father is referred to as a "Christian sophist."

[63] For Augustine, see Peter Brown, *Augustine of Hippo* (Berkeley, 1967) who underscores both Augustine's relationship to philosophy and his professorship of rhetoric at Milan. The Cappadocian fathers studied rhetoric with Libanius in Antioch.

[64] As with the case of a general monograph on greco-roman rhetoric and rabbinic hermeneutic, there is a need for at least some articles, if not a full length study on rabbinic aggada and the works of Philostratus. I hope to return to these both at a future occasion.

[65] This section on "Disturbances in the Field: Greco-Roman Rhetoric as Interference in the Comparative Study of Rabbinic and Patristic Literatures," was read as a paper to the Rhetoric and the New Testament Section of the Society of Biblical Literature, in convention in Washington, D. C., November, 1993.

[66] See "Mortal Sins," and "Hillel, Hieronymus and Praetextatus," below.

and again, my insistence on attention to methodology and the dictates of chronology in comparative studies.

I conceived of this project like an archeological excavation. The various studies are but soundings, trenches cut in a field in an attempt to uncover a past civilization. Of course, even with a complete excavation, only so much may be learned about earlier eras. Only the bare bones may be exposed, while the flesh and blood – the very quickening necessary to animate history – this is left somewhere between the scholar's writing and the imagination of the reader. Doing archeology of literature does not even really expose the bones, it only exposes other, older scholars' descriptions of the phenomena we are all trying to enflesh. God's challenge to Ezekiel echoes in our ears, "Son of man, can these bones live?"

In an attempt to breathe some life into the ancient words of the fathers of the world, heed was given to the variety of languages they spoke (and the barriers these varied languages may have imposed). The studies here all presume rabbinic fluency in both Hebrew and Aramaic. To a lesser extent it assumes that some Palestinian rabbis knew some Greek. Nevertheless, care was also taken to assay the Latin fathers, particularly those like Jerome, who lived in Palestine and claimed some familiarity with both Hebrew and Jewish traditions. Where a towering figure like Augustine is concerned, his correspondence with Jerome and his general influence over Church doctrine suggested that he be considered rather than excluded. Syriac, an Aramaic language of the Church, was taken as a given for comparative studies between Rabbinics and Patristics (although not all Patristics scholars range far enough east linguistically to include Syriac works in their own studies).

On the Church side, then, there is a mixture of Greek, Latin and Syriac fathers. Chronologically, these fathers cover the range of the patristic period, from the apostolic fathers in the late first and early second century through the fall of Rome in the early fifth century. This brings us up to the time of the Pelagian heresy (a movement notable not only for its affinities with rabbinic theology, but notable in that Jerome and Augustine accuse its followers of Judaising[67]). The fathers considered in these pages range geographically from western Europe to the eastern borders of the Roman Empire and beyond, to the Tigris and Euphrates. They occupy a broad range of time and territory reined in by consideration of the specific rabbinic texts with which they are compared. In other words, fathers from the West are only compared to Palestinian or Babylonian rabbis with some methodological cause.

---

[67] Alas, an essay on aspects of Judaising in Pelagianism will have to await a later occasion.

Mention of both Palestine and Babylonia brings up the thorny issue of control over rabbinic sources. For the most part I am cautious about attributions in rabbinic literature and prefer to deal with redactional dates rather than assuming specific rabbis stated certain traditions. However, where due methodological caution allows for the possibility of more specific attribution and the comparison with a given father of the church benefits from it, there are instances where specific assignment of a tradition to a given rabbi has been undertaken. As well, problems in rabbinic chronology (a notoriously difficult problem in comparisons with New Testament material), even though eased by comparison with contemporary literature, are by no means ignored. These factors are primarily discussed in the notes, but fair warning must be given here: chronology and accurate dating of rabbinic traditions remains a methodological crux.

A final caveat in the overall treatment of rabbinic texts remains to be sounded. Scholars traditionally distinguish between the Land of Israel (a.k.a. Palestine in the Roman era) and the diaspora. In our studies, diaspora generally refers to Babylonia of rabbinic tradition – although comparison with the church fathers often invites forays into Europe, Asia Minor and North Africa. I am not at all clear exactly what scholarly benefit is gained in making the distinction between Holy Land and diaspora, especially since most of the areas mentioned were part of the same Roman Empire. The notable exception is Babylonia (and areas of the Syriac church), where customs and even canon differed. On the rabbinic side, most of the traditions from the Babylonian literature (primarily the Talmud) cited in this volume speak of Palestinian rabbis and traditions. To the extent that the Babylonian Talmud accurately preserves Palestinian traditions (and wherever possible, parallels are adduced from Palestinian literature), one assumes we are speaking of Palestinian Judaism. In one case (Mary Maudlin Among the Rabbis) where the traditions speak of Babylonian rabbis and have no parallels, Church traditions are cited from as nearby as possible – either from the Greek East or Syriac speaking enclaves. So, where controls may be exerted attention has been paid to both chronology and geography in my treatment of rabbinic traditions.

The essays in this volume cover a broad range of issues in the comparative study of Rabbinic and Patristic literatures. The opening two essays are comparative in the broadest sense, they take topics such as exegetical parameters or hamartology and examine the rabbinic and patristic attitudes in light of one another. In "Jots and Tittles," both Church and Synagogue are found to have similar misgivings about extreme allegory. Neither church fathers nor rabbis were prepared to utterly obliterate the contextual meaning of a verse of Scripture no matter how profitable the allegorical replacement of meaning may have been. In both Church and Synagogue, the *peshat* or *historical* meaning was maintained, even as hermeneutical hay was made through *derash*, typology or allegory. "Mortal Sins" finds that throughout the hellenistic world there was a common consensus regarding actions considered beyond the pale. Although pagans, Jews and Christians reacted differently to the variety of unacceptable sins, all agreed that certain acts were unacceptable and occasionally, unforgivable.

The following four essays all consider aspects of interreligious polemic. "Trinitarian Testimonies" opens with my oft stated warning, rehearsed above, that rabbinic literature cannot glibly provide "background" to the New Testament. I offer a way of reading a Pauline passage, long compared with rabbinic texts, in light of the interpretation the Church Fathers gave to it. Once Paul is seen through the lens of patristic concerns for trinitarian doctrine, the rabbinic text which parallels the Pauline passage can be understood as anti-trinitarian polemic. This not only furthers understanding of both the rabbinic and patristic passages adduced, but shows the rabbis to be familiar with contemporary Church issues and arguments. Just as rabbinics scholars have long lamented the Church's inability to see Judaism beyond the "Old Testament," it behooves those same scholars to see the Church and its issues beyond the New Testament.

The polemic considered in "Overturning the Lamp," is of a different nature. It begins by focussing on an inner-Christian polemic. Surveying the name- calling and mud-slinging that was common in Church disputes over eucharist and other tests of orthodoxy, the article demonstrates how Jews and pagans repeated the charges Christians made about one another. Of course, Christians of old were quick to blame outsiders for the scurrilous rumors, but the point remains that nothing was being said about Christians by others that they weren't saying themselves. If any lesson is to be learned from this essay it is this: be careful what you say about one another, others less generous will be sure to repeat and embellish it. The best proof of the effectiveness of these canards of old is that they are still taken as fact by historians of today.

"Mary Maudlin Among the Rabbis" is unique among the essays in this collection for a variety of reasons. It is the most recently written and was conceived after the plan of the whole volume was designed. Further, it treats of Babylonian Jewish traditions exclusively. Since my scholarship concentrates on Palestinian rabbinic literature it is an unusual departure. It surveys rabbinic sayings about Mary and in so doing only incidentally considers patristic traditions about her. This is to say that the essay is not properly comparative, but enlists contemporary church literature to untangle the meaning of the rabbinic texts. The essay was undertaken at the invitation of Prof. Phyllis Trible to me to be the token male author in a feminist volume on Miriam and Mary. The privilege of joining such company led me to write on rabbinic views of Mary rather than the more predictable essay on Miriam.[68] The missionary zeal of the feminist volume also led to the article's apologetic and eirenic tone in an essay about patently polemic literature.

The final of this group of essays undertakes to survey the anti- Christian material in a very important work, Leviticus Rabbah. Since that midrash was one of the first self-consciously composed books of the rabbis,[69] and the book's redaction comes well into the era of Christian dominance of Palestine, one might have expected a consistent and well-aimed argument against Christianity. Instead, "Anti-Christian Polemic In Leviticus Rabbah," finds that the redactor of that work only addressed Christianity as occasion called for. When he stumbled upon Christian issues in pursuit of his rabbinic agenda, he addressed them. In light of the well known rabbinic penchant for organismic rather than systematic thinking, this finding is not surprising.[70] Although a concentrated polemic is not evident, again it is clear that the rabbis were aware of current issues in Church theology and unafraid of attacking or parodying them.

At this juncture in the volume, four shorter essays appear, each of which originally was published as a book review. In these reviews the themes layed out in the first half of the volume will be evident. "Text, Translation, Targum," has as its focus a variety of recent works in the field of Targum literature. I take to task those scholars (particularly Christian) who fall prey to anachronism in their quest for recovery of some element (in this case, Aramaic language and literature) of the historical Jesus. I point out that Targums as we have them are notably late, often post-Islam. One may as well rely on Syriac literature to recover Jesus' Aramaic. Nevertheless, there is a good deal to be gleaned from Targum studies, particularly when methodological controls are applied and the limits of the literature realized.

The same problem of anachronism is evident in Samuel Lachs' *Rabbinic Commentary on the New Testament*. Methdologically it represents no advance whatsoever over Billerbeck's *Kommentar*. Lachs does treat rabbinic traditions with considerably more affection, but jumbles together early and late, as though a rabbinic text first composed a millenium after the Gospels sheds more light on them than a Church commentary, simply by virtue of having been written in Hebrew. Equally guilty of anachronism is Alan Segal's *Rebecca's Children*, which also lacks any coherent methodology or control over rabbinic texts. Although Segal's sociological method is

---

[68] An excellent essay on the character of Miriam in rabbinic narrative was planned for the volume by reproducing Devorah Steinmetz's "A Portrait of Miriam in Rabbinic Midrash," *Prooftexts* 8 (1988) 35–65.

[69] While posing as commentary, Leviticus Rabbah actually takes up a thematic treatment of the rabbinic agenda (as opposed to the agenda of Leviticus).

[70] On organismic thought see Max Kadushin, *The Rabbinic Mind* (New York, 1965, 2nd ed.).

provocative and even promising, the sheer sloppiness of his use of rabbinic texts precludes any serious profit from the work. This, combined with the problem of comparing rabbinic and New Testament literature produced a frustrated review. I would welcome application of Segal's sociological model and keen mind to a comparison of contemporary rabbinic and patristic texts.

The last of the reviews presented covers two distinct types of work: Judah Goldin's elegant essays and Jacob Neusner's controversial insights. Goldin's essays offer readers of this volume a useful model for exegesis of rabbinics, particularly in light of hellenistic background. Again and again the erudite scholar calls upon a greco-roman source to explicate a rabbinic text. The exegeses in Goldin's essays are masterful and inspiring. Jacob Neusner is simply too hurried to be thorough. It does not, however, preclude him from being inspiring. Christian scholars attend to Neusner's works on rabbinics far more than do Jewish scholars who specialize in them. I think the attention afforded to Neusner is a product of his sheer volume. Nevertheless, in all the flurry of chaff there are golden kernels of wheat. Neusner offers a simple idea which once stated seems obvious. This is sufficient guarantee of genius, particularly so since there is only assertion, no evidence to butress his claim. Neusner suggests that post-325, rabbinic texts turn to the agenda of responding to Christianity. The proposition makes excellent intuitive sense, and I give it more credit now than I did when I reviewed the work half-a decade ago. However, the hypothesis must be subjected to strenuous testing, and if my findings on Leviticus Rabbah are any indication, will be difficult to prove.

Following the section of reviews, three varied essays remain. In the first, "Prolegomenon to the Study of Jewish-Christianities in Rabbinic Literature," I map the field and the problems inherent in it. I remain pessimistic about how much clear progress can be made in what is, by definition, an unclear area of study.[71] Nevertheless, the very existence of Jewish-Christianity demands attention from scholars in the field. Granted, it is and will remain a grey area where clear lines and distinctions cannot be drawn. Nevertheless, anyone working in the field of rabbinics and patristics must consider what was surely one of the sorest points of contact between the two religious communities.

---

[71] Recently Wolfram Kinzig expressed more optimism, *Vigiliae Christianae* 45 (1991) 27–53. However, this work should be read in light of other recent attempts to narrow the definition of Jewish-Christianity even more severely. See Joan E. Taylor, "The Phenomenon of Early Jewish- Christianity: Reality or Scholarly Invention?" *VC* 44 (1990) 313–34 and now, idem, *Christians and the Holy Places. The Myth of Jewish-Christian Origins* (Oxford, 1993). Equally narrow (and to my view, equally unsuccessful) Ray Pritz, *Nazarene Jewish-Christianity* (Jerusalem, 1988) and see the review by A. F. J. Klijn, *VC* 43 (1989) 409– 10.

An essay on some interfaces between Syriac and Rabbinic literature follows. It is a wonder why more work has not been done comparing two religious communities which were contemporary, shared a common language and for the most part a common geography. On the whole, Church scholars ignore the Syriac church. It is not part of the Great Church and it's language is Semitic, not Greco-Roman. Nevertheless, there are many significant studies in place and more being produced daily.[72] I offered my "Three Syriac Cruxes" to add to a trend in the right direction. Finally, I explore the phenomenon of conversions from paganism in "Hillel, Hieronymus and Praetextatus." There, I show that the pagan rhetorical form of *chria* controls the telling of tales about such conversions. On the Christian side, St. Jerome tells a snide story about the very powerful and successful pagan Vettius Agorius Praetextatus' would-be switch, if only he could be bishop of Rome. On the Jewish side, a similar tale is told of Hillel and a potential proselyte. The Hillel *chria* is adumbrated with a report of a *keldon*, much like the voice St. Augustine hears in the process of his conversion. Here, the comparison of both form and content shows us how popular tales of the rich and famous were in Late Antiquity. The Lives of the Saints, Jewish and Christian, were subject to the same laws of gossip that govern every society in every age.

All told, these essays are driven by exegesis. I come as a midrash scholar attempting to understand the flow of rabbinic texts. When it seems necessary, I invoke Christian texts. Since midrash is the most notable public face of rabbinic tradition, it is not unreasonable to rely upon an understanding of Christianity and the greco-roman milieu to read between the lines of such texts. Along the way, I learned a great deal about Christianity and learned that the rabbis of old had troubled themselves to do so, too. If the comparative studies in this volume offer clear exegeses of rabbinic texts, I have achieved my scholarly goal. If they also make a modest contribution to the social history of Late Antiquity, or to the understanding of the development of the two sister religions as Greco-Roman phenomena, I should be delighted. In any case, my work could not be accomplished without certain basic bibliography in the field. Rather than presume it, it will be briefly surveyed with some attention to works of the last decade.

---

[72] In addition to the works I cite in the article, some studies of recent interest include, e. g., Han Drijvers, "Jews and Christians at Edessa," *JJS* 36 (1985) 88–102; A. P. Hayman, "The Image of the Jew in the Syrian Anti-Jewish Literature," in edd. J. Neusner and E. Frerichs, *To See Ourselves as Others See Us: Christians, Jews, "Others" in Late Antiquity* (Chico, 1985) 423–441; and S. T. Benin, "Commandments, Covenants and the Jews in Aphrahat, Ephrem and Jacob of Serugh," in ed. David Blumenthal, *Approaches to Judaism in Medieval Times* (Chico, 1984) 135–56. My thanks to Dr. Bruce Nielsen for these citations.

Almost a century ago, the great Talmudist, Louis Ginzberg, began publishing his series of studies *Die Haggada bei den Kirchenvätern.*[73] The ease
with which Ginzberg worked in rabbinic and patristic sources set a daunt-
ing standard for all who followed. No one since that time has covered the
breadth of the material or plowed it so thoroughly. Of course, the methods Ginzberg used are now a century out of date and even his prodigious
knowledge of rabbinics has been advanced through the discovery of the
Cairo Geniza materials. Nevertheless, his articles remain the place for all
comparative work on these literatures to begin, no matter what its focus.[74]
Another major contribution to the field came on the heels of World War
II – Marcel Simon's *Verus Israel: Etude sur les relations entre Chretiens et
Juifs dans l'empire romain (135– 425).*[75] The work remains a model study,
although there could be quibbles about both the lower critical methodology as well as the higher. Simon's reliance on standard printed texts and
his post-war methodologies are readily understandable – methods have
changed in the last half century and texts were largely unavailable at the
time Simon wrote the work. *Verus Israel* is both an historic as well as
scholarly achievement.

In 1961, Yitzhak Fritz Baer wrote a review article, "Israel, the Christian
Church, and the Roman Empire from the Time of Septimus Severus to
the Edict of Toleration of 313."[76] Baer was writing history and admirably
made use of both patristic and rabbinic sources to arrive at a more or less
synthetic overview of the period.[77] Half a decade later, from the Christian
side of the field, Emilien Lamirande published a bibliographic essay in the

---

[73] Ginzberg's first publications were in *Monatschrift für Geschichte und Wissenschaft
des Judenthums* 42 (1898) and 43 (1899) which was reprinted in Berlin, 1990. His
Inaugural Dissertation was printed in Amsterdam, 1899. Other volumes trickled out
over the following decades until the sixth part was finally published in 1935. Updating
of the material can be found scattered through the notes of his *Legends of the Jews* 7
vols. (Philadelphia, 1909–1938). For a full bibliographic listing of the *Kirchenvätern*
articles see Baskin, cited below.

[74] There were earlier works such as Moritz Friedlander's *Patristische und Talmudische
Studien* (Wien, 1878); D. Gerson, "Die Kommentarien des Ephraem Syrus im Verhältnis
zur jüdische Exegese," *MGWJ* 17 (1868); A. H. Goldfahn, *Die Kirchenväter und die
Agada* (Breslau, 1873); H. Graetz, "Haggadische Elemente bei den Kirchenvätern,"
MGWJ 3 (1854); S. Krauss, "The Jews in the Works of the Church Fathers," *Jewish
Quarterly Review* O. S. 5 (1893); and a variety of articles by M. Rahmer, C. Siegfried,
and Wilhelm Bacher (see the listings in Baskin); yet none of these had the systematic
breadth and depth of Ginzberg's studies. For a more thorough review of the early works
in the field see the Introduction to Jay Braverman's *Jerome's Commentary on Daniel: A
Study of Comparative Jewish and Christian Interpretations of the Hebrew Bible* (CBQ
Monograph Series 7: Washington, 1978).

[75] Paris, 1948. English Translation, London, 1986.

[76] *Scripta Hierosolymitana* 7 (1961) 79–149.

[77] Like many Israeli historians, Baer was credulous regarding rabbinic texts and unduly
suspicious of Christian texts. The resulting rabbinocentric history is not surprising.

journal *Vigiliae Christianae*.[78] The brief work particularly surveys nine-teenth century Jewish historiography that is relevant to patristic studies.

N. R. M. de Lange's *Origen and the Jews*[79] was published in 1976 and heralded a small explosion of studies in the field. In part, de Lange led the way with a study of a seminal figure, long acknowledged to make use of Jewish sources. In part, publication of the work by a prestigious aca-demic press brought it wide attention in the scholarly community. In part, de Lange's work at Oxford and Cambridge guaranteed that the primary locus for patristic scholarship would take some notice of rabbinics. Fi-nally, de Lange's own sure scholarship in both fields[80] assured a careful and balanced study. Indeed, Christian scholars began to look to rabbinic sources in their own work. E. P. Sanders, who had just mastered rabbinic literature to write his *Paul and Palestinian Judaism*,[81] edited a series of three volumes on *Jewish and Christian Self-Definition* which, while treat-ing Judaism, Christianity and paganism separately, nevertheless considered rabbinics and patristics within the context of the Greco-Roman world.[82]

A similarly welcome work was produced in collaboration in 1978 when Wayne Meeks (a New Testament scholar) and Robert Wilken (a patristics scholar) joined together to study *Jews and Christians in Antioch*.[83] Al-though the work was not particularly strong on rabbinics, it did gather Greek sources together with archeological reports to paint a clear histor-ical picture. The background they drew there was helpful to Wilken in his subsequent study on *John Chrysostom and the Jews*.[84] David Rokeah, meanwhile working in Jerusalem, produced *Jews, Pagans, and Christians in Conflict*.[85] The work is notable for having been produced by a Jew, in Israel, as the result of doctoral studies. It is not, however, any method-ological advance over Baer's work two decades earlier.

Doctoral studies were responsible for two American Jewish works which took up biblical characters and studied them in light of subsequent post-

---

[78] "Etude bibliographique sur les Peres de l'Eglise et l'Aggadah," *VC* 21 (1967) 1–11. See Baskin's comments, p. 53 of her survey.

[79] *Origen and the Jews: Studies in Jewish-Christian Relations in Third-Century Palestine* (Cambridge, 1976).

[80] He is lecturer in Rabbinics at the University of Cambridge, yet publishes and re-searches regularly in patristics.

[81] *Paul and Palestinian Judaism: A Comparison of Patterns of Religion* (London and Philadelphia, 1977).

[82] E. P. Sanders, et al., edd., *Jewish and Christian Self Definition* 3 vols. (Philadelphia, 1980–83).

[83] *Jews and Christians in Antioch in the First Four Centuries of the Common Era* (Mis-soula, 1978).

[84] (Berkeley, 1983). See also Wilken's *Judaism and the Early Christian Mind* (New Haven, 1971) and most recently, *The Land Called Holy: Palestine in Christian History and Thought* (New Haven, 1992).

[85] (Jerusalem and Leiden, 1982). The original Hebrew was Rokeah's doctoral disser-tation at the Hebrew University.

biblical traditions. The earlier, by Judith Baskin, particularly focusses on rabbinic and patristic literatures.[86] The latter, by Steven Fraade, takes not only rabbinics and patristics, but also treats Apocryphal, Pseudepigraphal, Hellenistic Jewish, Samaritan and Mandaen traditions.[87] Baskin's work also led her to publish a very important bibliography specifically in this field. It remains the most useful bibliographic guide extant and covers far more ground, far more thoroughly, than any other writing comparing rabbinic and patristic literatures. My own work presumes and depends on her bibliographic essay throughout − to avoid redundancy, I often do not cite works which I know to be available in Baskin's article. "Rabbinic-Patristic Exegetical Contacts in Late Antiquity: A Bibliographical Reappraisal," must be consulted by anyone working in rabbinic or patristic literatures.[88]

In 1986 a Jewish and a Christian scholar teamed up to write extended essays which were produced bound together as *Early Biblical Interpretation*.[89] The work is remarkable in that each scholar essentially writes apologetic for his own religion's exegetical traditions. Kugel first traces rabbinic midrash as a direct outgrowth of inner-biblical interpretation already found in Hebrew Scripture. Greer then follows showing how patristic interpretation was a natural consequence of the notion of a Christian Bible. That the two disparate essays are in the same volume is a testimony both to the ingenuity of Wayne Meeks, the series editor; and to the ecumenism of Westminster Press, the publisher. Two years later M. J. Mulder edited a much broader compendium on interpretation of Scripture as part of the series Compendia Rerum Iudaicarum ad Novum Testamentum. Although the series title may lead one to expect Christian bias, the series as a whole is well balanced. Mulder's volume is called *Mikra: Text, Translation, Reading and Interpretation of the Hebrew Bible in Ancient Judaism and Early Christianity*.[90] The twenty chapters and more than nine hundred pages are exhaustive, and include a workmanlike essay on Rabbinic Literature by Rimon Kasher and a magisterial chapter on the Church Fathers by William Horbury.[91]

Recently, we have been graced by a study specifically devoted to the comparison of rabbinic and patristic literatures, *Mikra and Midrash: A Comparison of Rabbinics and Patristics*.[92] Marc Hirshman undertakes to

---

[86] *Pharoah's Counsellors: Job, Jethro and Balaam in Rabbinic and Patristic Tradition* (Chico, 1983).

[87] *Enosh and His Generation: Pre-Israelite Hero and History in Postbiblical Interpretation* (Chico, 1984).

[88] The essay is published in William S. Green, ed., *Approaches to Ancient Judaism vol. 5: Studies in Judaism and Its Greco-Roman Context* (Atlanta, 1985), 53−80.

[89] James L. Kugel and Rowan A. Greer (Philadelphia, 1986).

[90] (Assen/Maastricht and Philadelphia, 1988).

[91] See my review of the entire volume in *Shofar* 8 (1990) 95−96.

[92] המקרא ומדרשו: בין חז"ל לאבות הכנסייה (הקיבוץ המאוחד, 1992).

compare, contrast and analyze rabbinic and patristic traditions in each of his nine chapters and appendix. He focuses on exegesis, genre and, occasionally, polemic. Hirshman sets the exegesis of the fathers and the rabbis in the Church and Synagogue, in the *Sitz im Leben* of homily and sermon. His genre studies include an understanding of the differences between the two literatures, particularly between Church commentaries and rabbinic homilies. Yet, Hirshman does not give enough attention to the problem of written sources as all we have of extant rabbinic material. While he does account for considerable patristic editing even of their orally delivered sermons, he could have provided a more literary model for the rabbinic texts and thus sidestepped the problem of obscure transmission history.[93] This quibble aside, Hirshman's work is a very important step forward in the field and we look forward to an English sequel.

Three very recent works deserve mention to round out this survey, although none of them specifically deals with comparative study of rabbinic and patristic literatures. Each, however, is commendable for its willingness to assume such comparison as the basis for the essays in the volume. All three are anthologies of articles: Hershel Shanks, ed., *Christianity and Rabbinic Judaism*; Judith Lieu, John North and Tessa Rajak, edd., *Jews Among Christians and Pagans*; and finally, Everett Ferguson, ed., *Studies in Early Christianity: A Collection of Scholarly Essays*.[94] Again, the tendency of these works is to take rabbinics and patristics in tandem, studying them separately rather than comparatively. But, the inclusion of both literatures together in so many volumes, bodes well for comparative studies in the future.

The foregoing study of secondary literature is by no means exhaustive. I hope, rather, to provide some signposts on the road which indicate some direction for the future. The articles which follow this introduction provide, I hope, some further indicators for methodologies and avenues which may be profitable to research. In the decade I have been working in the area of comparison of rabbinics and patristics I have been reminded again and again of the centrality of the legacy these fathers have left us. Our culture and literature, both religious and secular, is infused with the ideas, language, categories and morality of both Church and Synagogue. As our modern history grows ever more fratricidal and fractious it is to our benefit to recall that we are all children of the same fathers of the world.

---

[93] As does David Stern, *Parables in Midrash: Narrative and Exegesis in Rabbinic Literature* (Cambridge, Mass., 1991), see my review in *CBQ* 55 (1993) 183–84.

[94] Shanks, (Washington, D. C., 1992); Lieu, et al., (London, 1992); Ferguson, (New York, 1993).

Jots and Tittles

On Scriptural Interpretation in Rabbinic and Patristic Literatures

Rav Yehuda quoted Rav:[1]
When Moses ascended to the Heights [to receive the Torah] he found God sitting and drawing crownlets upon the letters.[2] Moses said to God, "Master of the Universe, what is staying Your hand [from giving me the Torah unadorned]?"
God replied, "There is a man who will arise many generations in the future, his name is Akiba b. Yosef. He will exegetically infer mound upon mound of *halakhot* from each and every tittle."[3]
Moses requested, "Master of the Universe, show him to me." God said, "Turn backwards [and you will see him]."
Moses [found himself in R. Akiba's classroom where he] sat at the back of the eighth row.[4] He didn't understand what they were talking about and felt weak. Then, they came to a matter about which the students asked Akiba, "Rabbi, how do you know this?" He told them, "It is the [oral] law given to Moses at Sinai." Moses felt relieved.
He returned to God and said, "Master of the Universe, you have a person like this and [still You choose to] give the Torah through my hands?"
God replied, "Silence! This is according to My plan."
Moses said, "Master of the Universe, you've shown me his teaching (Torah), show me his reward." God said, "Turn [backwards and you may see it]. Moses turned around and beheld [the Roman torturers] weighing his flesh on the market scales. He said to God, "Master of the Universe, that was his Torah and this is his reward!?"
God said, "Silence! This is according to my plan."

This remarkable legend has many aspects which demand both commentary and consideration. As it has been redacted in the Babylonian Talmud, it is a kind of Jobian theodicy which seems to suggest that even Moses, who was granted face to face communion with God and had the merit

---

[1] B. Menaḥot 29b. Rav Yehuda d. ca. 300, Rav d. ca. 250.

[2] Cf. b. Shab. 89a where the same tradition is reported in the name of the Palestinian, R. Yehoshua b. Levi (d. ca. 250). The crownlets are calligraphic adornments added atop a number of the letters in a Torah scroll written in the square, Aramaic script. These are probably the tittles (literally horns or rays) of Mt. 5: 18.

[3] "Exegetically infer" (*lidrosh*) literally means to search out. "Each and every tittle" (*kol qots veqots*) literally means each thorn and thorn.

[4] The smartest students sat in the first row, less intelligent students sat in the back.

of having the Torah revealed through his person, even Moses was not made privy to the reasons why God allows His saints to be martyred.[5] At the same time, the legend gives rise to the notion, found elsewhere in rabbinic literature,[6] that Moses had all future Torah revealed to him at Sinai — especially oral Torah — whether he understood it or not. However interesting and important these points may be, we wish here to concentrate on a third aspect of the legend, concerning R. Akiba's exegetical abilities. God tells Moses that for each and every tittle in the Torah, Akiba will perform exegesis that will yield mounds of laws. Even for the Yavnean era this must be accounted an impressive performance of exegetical skill!

The talmudic legend underscores a dispute in the late-first and early-second centuries between the more prominent proponents of exegetical activity in the rabbinic academies, R. Akiba and R. Yishmael. The latter had systematized his hermeneutic methodology into a list of thirteen exegetical norms.[7] Supposedly, Akiba and Yishmael had each adopted his system from the earlier norms of the sage Hillel, though Akiba's norms are nowhere systematized and the attribution of seven norms to Hillel is much later than that sage or his school.[8] Further, for all that R. Akiba employs unusual methods of exegesis, he is nowhere reported actually deriving Jewish law from a crownlet on a letter.

Before entering further into the fray of late-first century rabbinic exegesis, it is worth taking a step back to see what the other third-century contemporaries of our rabbinic legend spinners (R. Yehuda, Rav and R. Yehoshua b. Levi) had to say about exegesis of jots and tittles. One naturally looks to their Palestinian counterpart in the Church, the most prolific and perhaps greatest of all scriptural interpreters, Origen.[9]

---

[5] My thanks for this point goes to my students in my 1984—85 Seminar on Critical Methodologies in the Study of Midrash at the Jewish Theological Seminary of America. There are other, contradictory legends of Akiba's martyrdom; see, e. g., Midrash Mishle, ch. 9.

[6] Cf. j. Pe'ah 2:6 (17a) and parallels.

[7] Preserved in the introduction to the Sifra (on Leviticus) and the Mekilta of R. Shime'on b. Yohai to Exod. 21:1, both works attributed to the Akiban school. For a balanced view of the "schools" of Akiba and Yishmael and the works each school purportedly produced, see M. D. Herr, "Midreshei Halakha," *Encyclopaedia Judaica* 11:1521ff. and the bibliography there.

[8] Hillel's norms in t. San. ch. 7 (end), introduction to Sifra, Aboth De Rabbi Nathan A ch. 37, cf. j. Pes. 33a and t. Pes. ch. 4. Herman Strack, *Introduction to the Talmud and the Midrash* traces the relationship of Yishmael's list to Hillel's norms. Akiba's methods will be discussed in more detail, below. See Isaac Heinemann, *Darkhei ha'aggadah* [The Methods of the Aggadah] (Jerusalem, 1964), 96ff. on rabbinic attention to jots and tittles.

[9] The relationship of Origen's methods of exegesis with the rabbis' methods is admirably catalogued in N. R. M. de Lange, *Origen and the Jews* (Cambridge, 1976). G. Bardy, *Revue biblique* 34 (1925): 217—52 lists the passages where Origen's "Hebrew" teacher is mentioned. A. von Harnack, *Der Kirchengeschichtliche Ertrag der exegetis-*

For the sake of determining Origen's attitudes toward scriptural interpretation, we may profitably turn to the anthology of his works, compiled
a century or so after his death, called the Philocalia. The first part of
this work is particularly concerned with Origen's hermeneutic norms and
preserves important comments which were otherwise lost when his many
other works suffered the ravages of censorship and time.[10]

There, Origen echoes the legend told by his Palestinian and Babylonian
contemporaries about Akiba:

> I suppose that every letter, no matter how strange, which is written in the oracles
> of God, does its work. And there is not one jot or tittle written in the Scripture,
> which, when men know how to extract the virtue does not work its own work
> ...
> The saint is a sort of spiritual herbalist who culls from the sacred Scriptures
> every jot and every common letter, discovers the value of what is written and its
> use, and finds there is nothing in the Scripture superfluous ...[11]

This pronouncement is repeated (no doubt following Origen), by later
Church exegetes. So, Gregory Nazianzen:

> We however, who extend the accuracy of the Spirit to the merest stroke and
> tittle, will never admit the impious assertion that even the smallest matters were
> dealt with haphazard by those who have recorded them ... on the contrary, their
> purpose has been to supply memorials and instructions for our consideration
> under similar circumstances.[12]

Or more succinctly, Jerome, "In the divine Scriptures every word, syllable,
accent (*apices*) and point is packed with meaning."[13] Finally, returning to
Origen for one last comment on the matter,

---

chen Arbeiten des Origens (= *Texte und Untersuchungen* 42) 3: 22–29, 47–51 and 4:
4–34, 81–87 writes of Origen's "Hebrew" teacher and generally about Jewish influence.
J. Daniélou, *Origène* (Paris, 1948) seems ignorant of rabbinic exegesis. I have not seen
B. Murmelstein, "Aggadische Methoden in den Pentateuchhomilien des Origenes," *Zum
40jaehrigen Bestehen der Israelitisch-theologischen Lehranstalt* (Wien, 1933), pp. 13–122.
R. Kimelman, "Rabbi Yoḥanan and Origen on the Song of Songs: A Third-Century
Jewish-Christian Disputation," *Harvard Theological Review* 73 (1980): 567–95 should
be added to the thorough bibliography in de Lange.

[10] For the Philocalia I am using the new critical edition by N. R. M. de Lange with
French translation and commentary by M. Harl (*Sources Chrétiennes* #302, 1983) and
the older English translation of G. Lewis (Edinburgh, 1911).

[11] Philocalia X 1, X 2, each quote from *in Jer. hom.* 39. For "nothing superfluous,"
see below.

[12] *Or.* 2: 105, trans. *Ante-Nicene Fathers*.

[13] *In Eph.* 2 (3,6), Patrologia Latina 26, 481, translated by J. N. D. Kelly, *Early Christian
Doctrines* (London, 1958), p. 62, n. 2. See too, John Chrysostom, *In illud, Sal. Prisc. et
Aquilam* (Rom 16: 3) *Sermo* I (Patrologia Graeca 51, 187): "In Scriptura nihil superfluum
... ut in sacris Scripturis nihil supervacaneum esse intelligatis et non necessarium, sive
unum iota sit, sive apex unus." For more on the Antiochenes, see below and Kelly,
pp. 72–76.

Not a single tittle of the sacred Scriptures is without something of the wisdom of God; for He Who gave me a mere man the command, "Thou shalt not appear before me empty," how much more will He not speak anything "empty."[14]

Here, Origen sounds particularly rabbinic, reasoning *a fortiori* from Deuteronomy 16:16. This type of reasoning is known to the rabbis as *qol vaḥomer* and is the first of R. Yishmael's thirteen norms of exegesis. It must be noted, however, that one hardly need be a rabbi to read the Bible, nor need one be a rabbi to reason from minor to major.[15]

Still, such reasoning was far from alien to Akiba and Yishmael. In addition, they are recorded using and disputing other means of exegesis which might by some be considered "empty." At issue here is the notion, expressed by Origen above, that nothing in Scripture is superfluous. Hence the Hebrew particle *et*, which introduces the object of God's creative efforts in Genesis 1:1 and which is usually ignored by translators, becomes subject to debate;

> R. Yishmael asked R. Akiba, "Since you served a discipleship with Nahum of Gimzo for twenty-two years [and he taught you his exegetic principle that] *akh* and *rak* serve to limit [the meaning of the text, while] *et* and *gam* serve to expand [the scriptural scope], what does this *et* written here (Gen. 1:1) mean?"
> Akiba said, ["And what do you take it to mean"]?[16]
> [He said,] "If the Bible had said, 'In the beginning created God[s]: Heaven and Earth,' we might have said that Heaven and Earth are also gods."
> He said, "*For it is no empty thing for you* (Deut. 32:47) and if it is empty, for you are to blame, for you know not how to interpret! *Et hashamayim* [*and the heaven*] includes the sun, moon, stars and constellations. *V'et ha'arets* [*and the earth*] includes trees, weeds and the Garden of Eden."

Akiba is consistent in his use of extraneous words of text as pegs for exegesis (eisegesis?). His use of Nahum's principle of inclusion is found in the tannaitic literature (ca. 70– 200),[17] as is his inference of laws from the mere juxtaposition of scriptural portions.[18] Akiba learns from the repetitions of the Bible, be they doublets[19] or infinitive absolutes. Again,

---

[14] Philocalia 1:28, *in Jer. hom.* 39.

[15] For *qol vaḥomer* see n. 7, particularly in the Sifra, ed. Finkelstein (New York, 1984). For *a fortiori* as a Greco-Roman hermeneutic device see, S. Lieberman, *Hellenism in Jewish Palestine* (New York, 1962), 47ff.

[16] Genesis Rabbah 1:14. The reading is difficult and must be emended if Akiba is to employ the norms he learned from Nahum. For this reconstruction I follow the suggestion of H. Graetz in J. Theodor's commentary in his edition of this text, Genesis Rabbah 1:14. Cf. Genesis Rabbah 53:15, where the redactor repeats this form in a constructed debate between Akiba and Yishmael over Gen. 4:1 and Gen. 21:20.

[17] E. g., m. Sheb. 3:5. For more on Akiban exegesis see Strack, *Introduction* and the other standard handbooks and encyclopedias.

[18] E. g., Sifre Numbers #131 (p. 169).

[19] See m. Sotah 5:1 where the doublet seems to be the point of his exegesis. This passage probably does not illustrate Akiba's use of the letter *vav* as an hermeneutic

Yishmael debates this latter type of exegesis, and in so doing formulates his own rule of thumb for scriptural interpretation,

> "*That person shall be utterly cut off* (*hikaret tikaret*) (Num. 15:31). Cut off (*hikaret*) in this world and cut off (*tikaret*) in the world to come," so R. Akiba. R. Yishmael said, "Since elsewhere in Scripture we are taught that *he should be cut off*, am I to infer being cut off from three worlds? What is the point of "utterly cut off (*hikaret tikaret*)"? [Simply that] the Bible uses human expressions [and nothing more may be inferred from the repetition]."[20]

Now Origen, who for the sake of scriptural exegesis is himself not above using an infinitive absolute[21] or a solecism confusing singular and plural verbs,[22] takes exception to R. Yishmael's principle. He repeatedly makes the point in his work *First Principles*:

> Think of the words of the Holy Spirit as not to deem the language the ornate composition of feeble human eloquence, but to hold, according to the scriptural statement that "all the glory of the King [sic] is within," [Ps. 45:14] and that the treasure of divine meaning is enclosed within the frail vessel of the common letter.[23]
>
> Our weakness cannot in each phrase approach the hidden glory of the truths concealed in poor and contemptible language. For we have a treasure in earthly vessels, that the exceeding greatness of the power of God may shine forth, and not be thought to come from us men.[24]

Or most simply, "What we believe to be the words of God are not human compositions."[25] Quite unlike R. Yishmael, Origen believes that the Torah does not speak in human language. Apparently agreeing with R. Akiba (who nowhere articulates the principle), Origen holds the Scripture to be a kind of divine code which the exegete can solve. This notion is, of course, not new with Origen. His guru of allegoric exegesis, Philo of Alexandria, makes the case repeatedly.[26] It was Philo who taught Origen that each word was fair game for exegesis, even the repetitions of the infinitive absolute. "Well knowing that he never puts in a superfluous word, so vast is his desire to speak plainly and clearly, I began debating with myself why he said that the intentional slayer is not to be put to

---

hook; see M. Chernick, *Proceedings of the American Academy for Jewish Research* 49 (1982), Hebrew Section, 105–22.

[20] Sifre Numbers #112 (p. 121).

[21] Comment on Exod. 15:1, *In Exod. hom.* 6,1 (*Die Griechischen christlichen Schriftsteller* vi 193.2), in de Lange, *Origen*, p. 111, n. 43.

[22] Philocalia VIII 1.

[23] *De princ.* IV 26 (Latin).

[24] *De princ.* in Philocalia I 7.

[25] *De princ.* in Philocalia I 6. Cf. *De princ.* IV 9 in Philocalia I 9.

[26] Particularly in *De conf. ling.* 14 (V).

death only but *by death to be put to death.*[27] At first blush, one might find some solace for R. Yishmael in Philo's comment about God's "vast ... desire to speak plainly and clearly." But the Akiban attitude prevails when Philo employs an infinitive absolute for exegesis[28] and states quite explicitly "that he never puts in a superfluous word."

Origen takes this Alexandrian perspective to heart. "There is nothing in the Scriptures superfluous," he exclaims. "Nothing is idle with God."[29] "Holy Scripture never uses any word haphazard and without purpose."[30]

The trouble with this exegetical point of view is that Scripture often taxes even the most fertile imagination to offer reasonable interpretation of its many cruxes. Even Origen, with all the tools of the allegorist at hand, seemed on occasion to despair of getting the meaning right, when he warned, "There are certain things which cannot be unfolded at all by any words of human language, but are made known more through simple apprehension than by any properties of words."[31] No doubt there are many undergraduates and even professors who can empathize with this view; particularly in regard to biblical interpretation. For Origen, however, the case was not one of feeling the meaning of a passage yet being unable to express it. He was wedded to the absolute necessity of wrenching sense from the text.

> Inasmuch as the solecisms in Scripture, if literally taken, often confuse the reader, so that he suspects the text to be neither correct, nor in accord with propriety of reason; and this is to such an extent, that some persons by way of correction, even venture to make alterations and substitute another meaning for that of the seemingly inconsistent passages, I fear something similar may befall the language of the passages before us; we are therefore bound to see what their hidden meaning is.[32]

Since it is quite clear that Origen does not take this course out of any fear of textual criticism, there must be other reasons for his insistence on his exegetical technique. If Scripture, as R. Yishmael would have it, speaks

---

[27] *De Fuga* #54 (On Flight and Finding, trans. Loeb). For the relationship of Philo and the Alexandrian school with rabbinic exegesis, the best recent treatment remains I. Heinemann, 180ff.

[28] Both Philo and Origen might be forgiven for attaching special emphasis to the infinitive absolute construction, given their Greek-speaking perspectives. In Akiba's case, the insistence on treating the inf. abs. as a superfluity for exegesis must be taken as an instance of hermeneutical stubbornness.

[29] Philocalia X 2, *in Jer.* hom. 39; in *Num.* hom. XIV 2, cf. John Chrysostom above, n. 13 and idem., *in illud Vidi Dominum* II 2 (PG 56, 110), Scriptura nihil habet supervacuum."

[30] *In Cant.* hom. I 8 (trans. *Ancient Christian Writers*), cf. Gregory Nazianzen above, n. 12.

[31] *De Princ.* IV 27 (Latin).

[32] Philocalia VIII 1, *Comm. in Hos.*

human language, then every verse and chapter should be immediately understood. If the passage cannot be understood, then it may, perhaps, like other vague human discourse, be safely ignored or forgotten. This attitude is quite unacceptable to Origen:

> Let us not then weary when we hear Scriptures that we do not understand; but let it be unto us according to our faith, by which we believe that all Scripture being inspired by God is profitable. For as regards these Scriptures, you must admit one of two things: either that they are not inspired because they are not profitable ... or you must allow that because they are inspired they are profitable.[33]

The simple either/or proposition Origen formulates leaves him no choice but to rely on allegory and the many other exegetic techniques he employs to make sense of inspired Scripture. In general, this is the hallmark of the "Alexandrian school" of exegetes, and this "predilection for allegory" infected the Palestinian and Cappadocian fathers as well.[34]

In the late fourth and early fifth centuries, the Antiochene opponents of allegorical interpretation nevertheless could agree with Origen's either/or proposition. They, too, held Scripture to be inspired and therefore profitable. Where they differed with the Alexandrians was only in regard to the legitimacy of allegory as a hermeneutic device. The Antiochenes, rather, had a "passion for literalism." They concurred wholeheartedly with Alexandrian use of typology, limited though it may be in precise application. But the Antiochenes preferred the insights of *theoria* to the unreliable means of allegory in the solution of scriptural cruxes.[35]

It is tempting to simply identify the Akiban method with the Alexandrian and then to group Yishmael with the literalist Antiochenes. This is much too simple, however. In real, physical terms, rabbinic tradition records Akiba visiting Antioch,[36] exactly the opposite place one might expect given his exegetical position. The dubious historicity of this rabbinic tradition aside, the problem is much more complex. As alluded to above, the Antiochenes and Alexandrians agreed on more matters than they disagreed regarding scriptural interpretation. And the rabbis weren't so tidily divided into isolated schools, nineteenth-century German Jewish historiographers to the contrary. There are numerous instances of Yishmael invoking Akiban norms and Akiba employing Yishmaelean norms to prove a point.[37] As noted above, Yishmael's list of thirteen norms of

---

[33] Philocalia XII 2, *in Josh hom.* 20.

[34] Kelly, 74.

[35] Kelly, 72–78.

[36] Akiba in Leviticus Rabbah 5: 4.

[37] e. g., Sifra, at the start of *aharei mot.*

exegesis is preserved in a commentary presumably issuing from Akiba's school.[38]

Although this refusal of the ancients to be simply categorized is annoying to scholars who prefer neat labels and tidy storage boxes, it very much proves a point about exegetes. Hermeneutic theory or exegetical ideology comes second to theology and textual demands. In short, the exegetes used the text (O. T. and N. T.) as a pretext for promoting their own theological agenda and viewpoints. If one required allegory on occasion to work a point into Scripture, so be it. If one must employ an Akiban norm to press home a halakhic point, so be it. At a certain juncture the very integrity of the scriptural text was threatened by the rage to read rabbinic and patristic notions into the verses, words, and letters of the Bible. When entire theologies or legal theories might be hung upon a jot or tittle, when "mountains may be suspended by a hair," as the rabbis so aptly put it, then there must be some reaction.

The Antiochene "school" of exegesis put forth *theoria* as a reaction to what it perceived as the "unreliable, indeed illegitimate" use of allegory as a means of scriptural interpretation.[39] It decried the extremities of allegorism, but carefully replaced it with *theoria* so that the enterprise of exegesis might continue apace. The issue was not interpretation or even reading theology into Scripture, but the radical nature of the method. One simply could not do violence to the text in the fashion of the allegorists. For in allegory, the verse of Scripture loses all meaning at face value. The simple sense of Scripture is not merely subordinated to the interpretation, it is obliterated by making each part of a verse refer to something else entirely. What was to the allegorists an ingenious method for preserving the profitability of an otherwise incomprehensible text was too extreme for the Antiochenes. They preferred to find their theological points through an exegesis that was offered *in addition* to the "literal" sense of Scripture, what they called the historic facts of the text.

Severian of Gabbala, writing at the outset of the fifth century, puts it like this: "It is one thing to force allegory out of the history, and quite another thing to preserve the history intact while discerning a *theoria* over and above it."[40] The distinction between how the Antiochenes perform an exegesis and how the Alexandrians "abuse" the text is neatly put by Diodore of Tarsus, mid-fourth century: "We must be on guard against letting the *theoria* do away with the historical basis, for the result would be then, not *theoria*, but allegory."[41]

---

[38] See M. D. Herr, above, n. 7.

[39] Kelly, 76. See now, Rowan Greer in J. Kugel and R. Greer, *Early Biblical Interpretation* (Philadelphia, 1986), pp. 175–199, esp. p. 195.

[40] *De creat.* 4: 2 (PG 56, 459) translated in Kelly, 76.

[41] *Praef. in pss.* translated in Kelly, 77.

So long as the "historical basis" remains intact, that is to say the simple, literal sense is not violated or obliterated, then the exegesis qualifies for *theoria*. Once the simple meaning is completely swept from view in favor of a whole new meaning for the verse, entirely free of scriptural context, and even independent of the language used in the original, then the sin of allegory has been committed. In Antiochene terms this was no longer exegesis, it was invention, novelty, and therefore untenable.

Such a reaction against the extremes of exegesis was becoming apparent in the rabbinic academies around the same time. Early on, particularly in the tannaitic era, there were Sages who made little distinction between their interpretations and the simple meaning of Scripture. At best, the simple meaning of the text (*peshat*) and its rabbinic exegesis (*derash*) are on a continuum of hermeneutic readings and the distinction between them is not clearly demarcated. But, by the fourth century, it was clear to most rabbinic exegetes that somehow there was a difference between the two readings of Scripture. As with the Antiochenes, it was no longer acceptable to obliterate the simple, literal meaning of the text. This is neatly summarized by the Babylonian Mar, son of Rav Huna, in a very telling dialogue,

> He (Mar) said, "Scripture cannot lose its literal sense (*peshuto*)."
> Rav Kahana replied, "I am eighteen years old and have studied all six orders [of the Mishnah] yet I did not know that Scripture cannot lose its literal sense until now."
> What does this story teach us [asks the talmudic redactor]? That one should study [by rote] but afterwards must learn the logic behind what he has memorized.[42]

That Rav Kahana, clearly an adept in rabbinics, could have memorized all of Mishnah with its occasional exegeses, and presumably had heard hundreds of exegetical discourses in the academy and synagogue and yet still not realized that Scripture could not lose its plain sense, indicts certain attitudes toward exegesis in the rabbinic world. Much as for the Alexandrians, the simple meaning of Scripture was left far behind in favor of rabbinic interpretations. Mar, son of Rav Huna, objected in the same fashion as the Antiochenes – he preferred midrash to be like their *theoria* and the plain sense of Scripture to preserve its integrity. Rabbinic sermons and halacha were fine, so long as they did not obliterate *peshat*.

A certain caution must be exercised at drawing too fine a conclusion about the parallel development of the exegetical dialectic in Church and Synagogue. While the reactions of the Antiochenes and Mar, son of Rav Huna are quite similar, they need not have been borrowed one from another. It is conceivable that lines of communication between Tarsus and Palestine,

---

[42] B. Shab. 63a.

Gabbala and Jewish Babylonia were humming with mutual indignation at those exegetes who had pushed their methods far enough to leave the Bible well behind them. It is just as likely, however, that we are merely witnessing a common development in both sets of exegetical workshops. Given the perceived excesses of their predecessors, the independent stirrings of protest against too much attention to the jots and tittles of Scripture was a wholly natural development in both patristic and rabbinic literatures. And considering the individual styles of particular exegetes in both camps, the persistence of exegesis of jots and tittles concomitant with the reaction against it is also to be expected.

The independence of this parallel development may be perceived, in fact, by a closer look at the third-century sources of the "jots and tittles movement." Although the statements of Origen bear remarkable resemblance to the legend of Akiba on this topic, it is entirely likely that they each stem from differing impetus. In a very famous passage from Origen's commentary to the Psalms, he credits his "Jew" with providing him a key to unlocking his basic theory of scriptural exegesis:

> That great scholar used to say that inspired Scripture taken as a whole was ... like many locked up rooms in one house. Before each room he supposed a key to be placed, but not the one belonging to it; and that the keys were so dispersed all round the rooms.... It would be a troublesome piece of work to discover the keys to suit the rooms they were meant for. It was, he said, just so with the understanding of the Scriptures ... the only way to begin to understand them was, he said, by means of other passages ....

Although this passage is much cited and commented upon, particularly as it relates to Jewish exegesis,[43] the continuation of the passage is rarely even noted. It is very important to Origen's theory of exegesis as a whole, especially when taken in context with the passage just quoted, which immediately precedes it. It happens to also be very apposite to our discussion of jots and tittles, for it provides a clue to the source of Origen's fascination with them. Although the source was a Jew, he was not Origen's Hebrew teacher mentioned above:

> It is just as true that the Holy Spirit has dictated them [the Scriptures], through the ministers of the Word, with the most scrupulous accuracy, lest the parallel meaning which the wisdom of God had constantly in view over the whole range of inspired Scripture, even to the mere letter, should escape us. And perhaps this is why the Saviour says, "One jot or one tittle shall in no wise pass away from the law, till all things be accomplished [Mt. 5: 18]."[44]

---

[43] See above, n. 9.

[44] Philocalia II 3–4, *Comm. in 1 Ps.* N. de Lange would translate (following Harl), "with the most scrupulous accuracy, lest the analogy [to God's attention to the details of creation] in His wisdom in authoring the whole range of Scripture, even to the mere letter, should escape ..."

Origen quite specifically spells out his program. Scriptures are to be interpreted by means of other Scriptures, and exegesis must extend "even to the mere letter." The source for the liberties he takes in broadening the scope of his interpretation to jots and tittles is Jesus himself, speaking in Matthew's Sermon on the Mount. Origen's ingenuity is to be admired, for he has not only biblically justified his allegoric method, he has rendered harmless a troublesome verse of Matthew. It was not the intention of Jesus to give succor to the Jewish-Christians and Judaisers – far from it. The proper exegesis of Matthew 5: 18 is the justification of Origen's radical method of promoting the patristic agenda through allegorical interpretation.

Before anyone jumps to the conclusion that the Sermon on the Mount (or some independent logion later attributed to Jesus) underlies the legend of Akiba's "jots and tittles" too, let us review that tale to see an entirely different verse of Scripture lurking behind it. God says of Akiba to Moses, "He will exegetically infer mound upon mound (*tilin tilin*) of *halakhot* from each and every tittle (*kol qots veqots*)." This is the essence of the Akiban "jots and tittles" tradition, and it derives from a pun on Song 5: 11, "his locks (*qevutsotav*) are wavy (*taltalim*)." *Qevutsotav*, a plural, becomes *kol qots veqots*, each and every tittle. *Taltalim* reduces into its constituent parts, *tilin tilin*, mound upon mound.

This pun is recognized quite explicitly in later rabbinic tradition, in a midrash which opens with a nodding recognition of the Akiba legend and then goes on to actually pay attention to jots and tittles. It does so by considering three sets of letters, each member of a set differentiated from the other by the merest stroke of the scribal quill. The addition or lack of a stroke, then, can change the meaning of the word in which one of these letters is to be found, sometimes with profound consequences.

> "His locks are wavy, black as a raven" (Song 5: 11). What is the meaning of "his locks are wavy" (*qevutsotav taltalin*)?[45] On each and every tittle (*qots veqots*), mound upon mound (*tilin tilin*) of *halakhot*. How so? It is written in the Torah, "And you shall not profane (*tehalelu*) my holy name" (Lev. 22: 32). If you make the letter *het* into a *heh* [so that the text would read *tehalelu* – And you shall not praise ...] you destroy the universe... And so with the verse, "Hear, O Israel: The Lord our God is one (*ehad*) Lord" (Deut. 6: 4) if you make the letter *dalet* into a *resh* [so that the text would read *aher* – our God is a different or an other Lord] you destroy the universe... And so with the verse "They have spoken falsely of

---

[45] This midrash conveniently allegorizes away the erotic element of Song of Songs, a practice regularly employed in both Church and Synagogue. See, e.g., E.E. Urbach, "Homiletical Interpretations of the Sages and the Expositions of Origen on Canticles, and the Jewish-Christian Disputation," *Scripta Hierosolymitana* 22, ed. D. Noy and J. Heinemann (Jerusalem, 1971): 247–75. R. Kimelman, above n.9, and S. Lieberman, "The Rabbinic Song of Songs" [Hebrew] in G. Scholem, *Gnosticism, Merkabah Mysticism and the Talmudic Tradition* (New York, 1965), pp. 118ff.

the Lord (*baYHWH*)" (Jer. 5:12) — if you make the letter *bet* into a *kaf* [so that the text would read *kaYHWH* — spoken falsely as the Lord], you destroy the universe...[46]

In both the Church and Synagogue, the exegesis of Scripture unfolded over the centuries as a kind of dialectic. The ability of the Fathers of the two religions to read the Bible according to a given hermeneutic changed as time went on. Since the sacred text was universally perceived as being, by theological necessity, always profitable, differing means of earning that profit were devised. The means of one generation of exegetes was not always adopted by subsequent generations. Where radical methods once held sway, a certain moderation was later exercised. No longer could one profit from the biblical text at the cost of its obvious meaning, no matter how obscure or difficult that meaning might have been.

The parallel development of this hermeneutic dialectic in both Church and Synagogue was, most probably, an independent phenomenon. It is not necessary to posit borrowing from one another to understand this parallelism or for a synoptic viewing of the two dialectics to prove mutually illuminating. Both sets of Fathers read the same Tanakh, both perceived the same common problems and cruxes. That both, equally trained in the rhetorical, grammatical and exegetical methods then available, should seek similar solutions should not surprise. Nor should it be a shock when earlier solutions are disgarded in a similar fashion.

In the third century, a group of rabbinic exegetes justified their methods by appealing to the authority of the great sage, R. Akiba. They told a legend in which God seemingly approved of a biblical hermeneutic that attended to "jots and tittles" and in so doing left Moses dizzy with incomprehension. Whatever happened to the Torah that Moses received? Was it the same text that these exegetes expounded? That they perceived it to be so offered Moses a modicum of comfort. Any further comfort from the exegesis of jots and tittles was not forthcoming. Those, who like Moses in the story, wondered about the authority for this type of exegesis were rudely told, "Silence! This is according to God's plan."

In the Church, Origen's method was eventually discredited for many, many complex reasons. The champion himself was anathemized on theological grounds. Temporary abandonment of his method, always a handmaiden of theology, was sure to follow.[47] In the Synagogue, where theo-

---

[46] Tanhuma Gen. 1:1, cf. LevR 19:2 and parallels. The letter sets concerned here are ב/כ, ד/ר and ה/ח. This last pair offer a convenient example even in English transcription, where it is convention to write ה as "h" and ח as "ḥ," the only difference being the dot beneath the letter.

[47] Allegoric exegesis as Origen had employed it was too useful a tool to disappear entirely and was soon resurrected by Church Fathers as notable as Augustine, see now, H. Chadwick, "Christian Platonism in Origen and Augustine," in *Origeniana Tertia*, ed. R. Hanson and H. Crouzel (Rome, 1985), pp. 215–30, esp. pp. 218–21.

logy and exegesis were no less wedded, but their import was a pale second to halakhic behavior, the dialectic unfolded less completely. Preservation of the simple meaning of the biblical text did not preclude exegesis of jots and tittles. In fact, once the fate of the *peshat* became somewhat secure, actual exegesis of jots and tittles began in earnest.[48]

---

[48] My thanks to Profs. G. C. Stead and Henry Chadwick for the opportunity to discuss this essay with their Senior Patristics Seminar, University of Cambridge. Particularly, thanks go to Drs. N. R. M. de Lange, Stead, E. Bammel, C. Bammel and M. Hirschman for their helpful comments. The paper was written while I was a Visiting Fellow of Clare Hall, Cambridge, thanks to the generous support of the Jewish Theological Seminary of America.

Mortal Sins

The soul of every wicked man revolves within itself and dwells upon
... this: how it might escape from the memory of its iniquities, drive
out of itself the consciousness of guilt, regain its purity, and begin its
life anew.

Plutarch, Moralia 556a−b

I

Human imagination has, perhaps, been most fully exercised in devising
and committing a seemingly infinite variety of sins. It is as though some
gigantic computer spewed forth all of the permutations of sin that day in
the Garden, and humanity has since then endeavored to tick off each item
with the originality and pristine thoroughness of Adam and Eve. This very
human endeavor was, quite understandably, a matter of grave concern for
the early Church and Synagogue. Each was engaged in the formation of
a community based upon a Hebrew Bible just bursting at the seams with
sins, iniquities, and the appropriate atonements. More often than not, the
atonements prescribed were part of a cultic system which the Rabbis had
happily replaced following the destruction of the Jerusalem Temple and
which the Church had rejected even before that time. The redefinition of
sins and atonements would have impact on the ecclesiology of both bodies.

My concern here is to survey the ideas of sin that replaced the cultic
categories in the century and a half following the destruction in 70 C. E.
The period under consideration is more precisely dated from approximately
100 C. E. to 250 C. E. In rabbinic terms this marks the time from the height
of the Yavnaen era until the redaction of the Tannaitic corpus. For the
Church this surveys the period from the Apostolic Fathers until Origen
and Cyprian. In particular, I am concerned with elements in the rabbinic
literature of this era that are also found in *De pudicitia*, a Montanist tract
of Tertullian. I offer quotes from Plutarch's *De sera numinis vindicta* (ca.
100 C. E.) as a reminder that the exegetes of both Church and Synagogue

lived in a thoroughly hellenized milieu which makes tracing the direct sources of any idea in the period a tortuous task, at best.[1]

Oddly enough, the rabbinic and Christian catalogers of sin during this period, much like later taxonomers of flora and fauna that also originated in the Garden, chose dichotomy as the means for imposing order on the permutations of iniquity. This may merely be a quirk of taxonomy, or it may be a function of the binary logic of the mythic computer that once upon a time generated the manifold varieties of sin.[2] In either case, one is left with a taxonomy of sin that by its dichotomous nature is inadequate to the breadth of human invention. The insufficiency of but two categories to cover the range under consideration is evidenced by the sheer number of dichotomies that have been offered to map the territory of sin.

In fairness to the Fathers who charted these dichotomies, it must be observed that many of them find their source in the Bible. The most basic division of sins was between those directed against God and those directed against a human being. This division first finds expression in the mouth of the priest, Eli, who lectures his sons in 1 Sam 2: 25, "If a person sins

---

[1] Basic bibliography includes standard works on rabbinics: S. Schechter, *Some Aspects of Rabbinic Theology* (London, 1909), esp. 219ff.; E. E. Urbach, *The Sages*, trans. I Abrahams (Jerusalem, 1975), vol. 1, 432ff., 462ff. and notes. More specific to the issue but not much more helpful, A. Büchler, *Studies in Sin and Atonement* (reprint: New York, 1967) 288ff.

For the Church, basic background in J. N. D. Kelly, *Early Christian Doctrines* (London, 1977), esp. 199, 217. More to the issue are G. Esser, *Die Buss-schriften Tertullians de paenitentia und das Indulgenzedikt des Papstes Kallistus* (Bonn, 1905); A. D'Ales, *La theologie de Tertullien* (Paris, 1905); *idem, L'edit de Calliste* (Paris, 1914); *idem, De paenitentia* (Paris, 1926); R. C. Mortimer, *The Origins of Private Penance in the Western Church* (Oxford, 1939); W. Telfer, *The Forgiveness of Sins* (London, 1959); K. Rahner, *Theological Investigations XV Penance in the Early Church*, trans. L. Swain (London, 1983), esp. 127ff. on Tertullian and 252ff. on Origen (and see K. H. Neufeld, "Karl Rahner zu Busse und Beichte," *ZKT* 108 [1986] 55–61); and, most essentially, the seminal works by B. Poschmann, *Paenitentia secunda. Die kirchliche Buße im ältesten Christentum bis Cyprian und Origens* (Bonn, 1940) and *Penance and the Anointing of the Sick*, trans. F. Courtney (London, 1964) with detailed bibliographies at the head of each chapter. A thoroughly annotated English translation of Tertullian's works on penance, *De paenitentia* and *De pudicitia* (the object of my focus here) was published by W. P. Le Saint, *Tertullian, Treatises on Penance* (Ancient Christian Writers [= ACW] no. 28, Maryland, 1959).

None of the works listed above compares or contrasts rabbinic and patristic literatures on sin. The beginnings of recognition of affinities between Tertullian and the Rabbis is expressed in W. H. C. Frend, "A Note on Tertullian and the Jews," *Studia Patristica X* (= *Texte und Untersuchungen* no. 107, Berlin, 1970) 291–96; and Y. Baer, *Scripta Hierosolymitana* 7, 79–149, esp. 85–95.

Plutarch follows the translation of P. H. DeLacy and B. Einarson, "On the Delays on Divine Vengeance," *Moralia* 7 (LCL, Cambridge, MA, 1959) 180–299.

[2] I eschew any further use of the analogy to some pre-lapsarian computer to avoid discussion of original sin, a theological concept completely irrelevant to the present discussion.

against a man, God will mediate for him; but if a man sins against the Lord, who can intercede for him?"

The rabbis take this distinction seriously in a penitential context. While recognizing the biblical source of the dichotomy, they employ other biblical notions to free it of cultic associations,

> "For on this day shall atonement be made for you" (Lev 16: 30) by means of sacrifices. Where [is scriptural proof that] even though there are no sacrifices [since the Temple was destroyed] and there is no scapegoat, the Day [of Atonement nonetheless] itself atones? The text teaches, "For on this day shall atonement be made for you." The Day of Atonement affords forgiveness for sins between man and God. But as for those sins between man and his fellow, the Day of Atonement affords no forgiveness until the person goes and appeases his fellow. For so R. Elazar ben Azariah expounded, "From all your sins you shall be clean before the Lord" (*ibid.*); for things between you and God you are forgiven, but as for things between you and your fellow you are not forgiven until you appease him.[3]

For his part, Tertullian speaks of God's forgiveness even when human means of penance are of no avail. He takes the distinction of sins to refer to the two vehicles for remission of sin, the Church and God. Though in contradiction to his Montanist sternness, he reserves for God the freedom to pardon even when one dies outside of the Church.[4] For the rabbinic Sages, however, the biblical notion is taken more to indicate the direction of the sin, and less so the source of its pardon. This reflects the Sages' hesitance at adopting remission of sins as a function of the synagogue. It also points to the Church's use of communion as a visible symbol of it having embraced this function.[5]

But we are still a long way from atonement and remission of sins; there remain yet many more sins to consider. A prime example of biblical dichotomy is again, cultic,

> But if you err ... if it was done unwittingly ... all the congregation shall offer a young bull ... and the priest shall make atonement for all the congregation ... if one person sins unwittingly you shall have one law for him who does anything unwittingly ... but the person who does anything with a high hand ... his iniquity shall be upon him. (Num 15: 22–31)

---

[3] *Sipra Aḥarei Mot*, chap 8 (ed. Weiss 83a–b), cf. *m. Yoma* 8: 9. R. Elazar fl. ca. 110 C. E.

[4] *De pud.* 3 (ACW 60); see Poschmann, *Penance* 45, "Even a mortal sin is only excluded from ecclesiastical forgiveness; it does not render penance fruitless even in the sight of God." For further discussion, see below.

[5] This is a major difference in ecclesiology and affects any comparison of rabbinic and Patristic thought. To this end I have raised the distinction early so that the reader may continually bear it in mind. The Church's preoccupation with who is "in" and who "out" in contrast to rabbinic ambivalence on the issue is readily apparent in E. P. Sanders, *Paul and Palestinian Judaism* (London, 1977). For more of the effects of this distinction see the discussion on penance below.

Here, high-handedness is contrasted with unwitting error. The two categories of sin are witting and unwitting, or, if you will, malicious and ignorant. Here, too, the Church and Rabbis quibble over precise definition, but both find the witting, malicious sinner to be far worse than the ignorant, unwitting one. Clement, writing about the time of the redaction of the Mishna, wonders, "I know not which of the two is worst, whether the case of a person who sins knowingly, or of one who, after having repented of his sins, transgresses again."[6] Clement has, in essence, equated these two categories of sin. The latter possibly refers to one who sins after the penance of baptism, but could refer to one who sins after the second chance the Church offered sinners, exomologesis.[7] The former, "a person who sins knowingly," is the biblical case, and such a one was generally denied the opportunity for exomologesis if he or she sinned so after baptism.[8]

The Rabbis limited this "unknowing" category to one who had no knowledge that his or her action was a sin, but consciously performed the action. This is well expressed in the Mishna,

> Whosoever, ignorant of the Sabbath law, committed many acts of [prohibited] labor on many Sabbaths, is liable only for one sin-offering. If, however, one was mindful of Sabbath law, but [forgetting it was the Sabbath] committed many acts of work on many Sabbaths, he is liable [to bring a sin-offering] for every Sabbath [thus profaned].[9]

As is clear from the case at hand, the rabbis equally distinguished yet another dichotomy, conscious and unconscious sinning. This latter category is, I suspect, what most modern theologians refer to when they write about "unwitting sin." For the Fathers and the Rabbis, however, unwitting implies a form of epistomological amorality; one simply did not know that such an action was a sin. Had one known so, that person presumably would not have done it. This is very different from the person who knows an action to be a sin but unconsciously commits it, such as a Jew who accidentally eats a piece of pork or makes an apparently innocent statement only to see his or her neighbor hurt by it.

There is yet another dichotomy which has its source in the Bible and is somewhat similar to Tertullian's notion of sins between human beings or a human and God, as discussed above. Throughout the Pentateuch penalties are assigned for given sins. For some, an animal offering suffices to afford atonement, as in the case of the unwitting sinner of Numbers 15 already quoted. More serious sins bear graver consequences, as may also be attested by the end of the same passage, here quoted more fully.

---

[6] *Strom.* 2. 13.
[7] See below.
[8] Poschmann, *Penance* 14.
[9] *Shab.* 7: 1.

But the person who does anything high a high hand ... reviles the Lord, and has broken God's commandment, that person shall be utterly cut off; that person's iniquity shall be upon him. (Num 15: 31)

For the Rabbis, the penalty of being "cut off" (*karet*), was in distinction to another biblical penalty, death. The Bible often notes that a sinner is to be put to death for committing a given sin. The sages reasoned, then, that there were two categories of sin in the Bible which could be deemed mortal, one carried the penalty of death at the hands of a human court. The second, and for the truly pious, more egregious, carried the penalty of death by God's hand. The Sages compiled a list of thirty-six such sins for which the Bible prescribed the punishment of "cutting off."[10] One guilty of such a sin was not executed by a human court, the punishment was left entirely up to God. That such sinners often lived long and apparently fruitful lives was but one more piece to the puzzle of theodicy. The problem and its answer were well put by Plutarch in a manner which, *mutatis mutandis*, would have been equally acceptable to the Fathers of the Church and Synagogue.

The delay and procrastination of the Deity in punishing the wicked ... [made] fresh and new, as it were, my old feeling of exasperation ... God should be indolent in nothing; least of all does it become him to be so in dealing with the wicked ... (*Moralia* 548c–d)
[The response:] Do you not think it better that punishments should take place at a fitting time and in a fitting manner rather than speedily and at once? (*Moralia* 553d)
If the soul survives, we must expect that its due in honor and in punishment is awarded after death rather than before. (*Moralia* 560f).

The assumption of judgment after death allowed both sets of Fathers to retain the biblical dichotomy of sins punishable by death at the hands of a human court or at the hands of God. For the Church in particular, this was to have implications for ecclesiology. The power of the Church was the power of God, but it could not, all the same, limit God's scope of action. As seen above, Tertullian reserved the right for God to reinstate a sinner even after death outside of the Church.[11] Given the interdependent yet separate spheres of action, it was logical for the Church to retain the ideas implicit in the biblical notion of "cutting off." For the Rabbis, who never quite as fully assumed the salvific power of God as their own, "death at the hands of heaven" served theodicy and the exigencies of historic reality equally well.

---

[10] On "cutting off," see *Ker.* 1: 1, which includes transgressions of the sexual prohibitions in Leviticus 18, blasphemy, idolatry, etc. The tractate is generally instructive about rabbinic attitudes toward sin. For death at the hand of a human court see *m. Sanh.*, chaps 7ff. Compare *m. Sanh.* 7: 4 with *m. Ker.* 1: 1, but see *m. Sanh.* 9: 4–6.

[11] Note 4, above. See below.

One last dichotomy of sins in the Hebrew Bible offers a convenient division into do's and don'ts, or positive and negative precepts. Often, as in the Ten Commandments, laws are phrased, "Thou shalt not ..." These are taken to be negative precepts, while the others, such as "Remember the Sabbath day ..." are taken to be positive precepts. Medieval rabbis went so far as to schematize the entire Pentateuch on this basis and counted six hundred and thirteen commandments, two hundred forty-eight positive and three hundred sixty-five negative.[12] Positive and negative precepts are often included in listings of sins, to quote but one example and move on,

> Repentance effects atonement for minor transgressions against both positive and negative commandments; while for major transgressions it suspends punishment until the Day of Atonement comes and effects atonement.[13]

The mechanics of achieving atonement in the rabbinic system will be discussed below, but now we wish to consider the distinction between minor and major sins. This dichotomy is found throughout rabbinic literature and is shared by the Church Fathers. What is troubling is that no exact definition is offered of "minor" and "major," or more precisely many varying definitions are offered. In one instance the rabbis ask point blank, "What constitutes a minor sin?" And the answer there is, "even changing a shoe latch."[14] The Tosefta offers this,

> The sin offering and the certain guilt offering atone for those things [the Bible has] written for them. Death and the Day of Atonement atone with repentance. Repentance atones for *minor* transgressions against positive and negative commandments except for "Thou shalt not take the name of the Lord your God in vain" (Exod 20: 7). These are the *major* transgressions: [Sins for which the penalty is] "cutting off," death at the hands of a human court and Exod 20: 7 is included with them. Rabbi Judah said, "For every transgression from Exod 20: 7 and below (i.e., less serious) repentance atones. For every sin from Exod 20: 7 and above (i.e., more serious), and Exod 20: 7 is included among them, repentance suspends [punishment] and the Day of Atonement atones.[15]

---

[12] So Maimonides, Moses of Coucy, and many others, each of whom have somewhat different listings. See *Midr. Mishle* 31: 29, "248 positive commandments correspond to the 248 members of the human body, 365 negative commandments correspond to the days of the solar year."

[13] *m. Yoma* 8: 8, other examples below.

[14] *b. Sanh.* 74a−b. The question is asked in the context of martyrdom. During times of religious persecution, Jews should be willing to die rather than commit even minor sins forced upon them. "Changing shoe latches" is not technically a sin at all, but in Babylonia, the color of ones shoes was indicative of religion. See. *b. Ta'an.* 22a.

[15] Rabbi Judah fl. ca. 150 C. E. *t. Kipp.* (ed. Lieberman) 4: 5. There is a difficult textual history to this tradition. The other major manuscript of the Tosefta omits a line of Rabbi Judah's statement through homeoteleuton. The parallel in *Mek. Yitro BaḤodesh* chap 7 (ed. Horowitz, 229) reverses the terms "above" and "below." See the commentary of S. Lieberman, *Tosefta ki-Fshutah Kippurim* (New York, 1962) 823ff. for a list of parallels and a thorough explication of the text traditions.

The bewildering ambiguity surrounding the terms "minor" and "major" is instructive. The dichotomy perhaps lacks precision because it is extra-biblical. We will see that this set of terms, as well as other, non-biblical sets, are equally undefined in Church literature. I suspect this may be attributed to the employment of these terms in a non-legal context. For while it is true that there were ecclesiological implications in the distinction between minor and major sins, the rhetorical value of the dichotomy was not lost to preachers.

Tertullian, commenting on 1 John, invokes such rhetoric when he writes,

> It is a fact that there are some sins which beset us every day and to which we are all tempted ... how often we are tempted. So much so that if there were no pardon in such cases, no one would be saved.[16]

Much to the chagrin of the social historian, Tertullian does not inform his readers what sins were part of daily life in late antiquity. Similarly employing the dichotomy between "minor" and "major," Cyprian can write,

> In the case of less serious sins [= minor], sinners do penance for the appropriate period and in accordance with the regular stages in the Church's discipline they come forward to make public confession and through the imposition of hands by the bishop and clergy they receive the right to be admitted to communion.[17]

While Cyprian writes carefully of the procedure through which one is readmitted to communion, being sure not to slight any of the "regular stages in the Church's discipline," he does not bother to define what constitutes a less serious sin.

For the Church Fathers there was yet one more non-biblical dichotomy of sin that served both homiletics and ecclesiology. Though very much like the minor-major distinction shared by the Rabbis, only the Church could distinguish between sins that were remissible as opposed to those that were irremissible. Tertullian makes clear for us the sharpness of the dichotomy,

> We agree that the cases where penance is required are sins. These we divide according to two issues: some will be remissible, others irremissible. ... With reference to this distinction we have already premised certain scriptural antitheses, some retaining, others forgiving sins. But John will also teach us, "... a person sins not unto death" (1 John 5: 16). This will be remissible. "There is a sin unto death..." (*ibid.*). This will be irremissible.[18]

---

[16] *De pud.* 19 (ACW, 114). For a survey of New Testament conceptions of sin, see D. D. Turlington, "Views of the Spirit of God in Mark and 'Q:' A Tradition-Historical Study," Ph. D. dissertation, Columbia University, 1987, 131–183.

[17] *Ep.* 16, 2–3.

[18] *De pud.* 2 (ACW, 59).

Tertullian uses a variety of terms to indicate these two categories: for the remissible sins he uses *modica, mediocra, leviora*; for the irremissible he uses *maiora, graviora et exitosa, quae veniam non capiunt*.[19] The terms *maiora, graviora,* and *leviora* have direct reflection in the rabbinic terminology *kal*, minor (literally, "light") and *ḥamur*, major (literally, "heavy"). Though they are terms frequently used by the Rabbis, they are the only ones that are extra-biblical. In fact, their position is well illustrated in a Mishna which summarizes for us the dichotomies of sin discussed thus far,

> For malicious defilement of the Temple and its sacred objects, atonement is made by [sacrifice of] the goat [whose blood is sprinkled] within the Holy of Holies and by the Day of Atonement. For all other sins in the Torah:
> Minor and Major,
> Malicious or Unwitting,
> Conscious or Unconscious,
> Positive or Negative,
> [Punishable by] cutting off or by Court-ordered death,
> the [Day of Atonement] scapegoat atones.[20]

II

Tertullian includes two more terms in his listing of irremissible sins: *capitalia* and *mortalia*. As we have been above, he draws this terminology from 1 John, but he turns again and again to other parts of Scripture for the notion of "mortal sins." Indeed, the Hebrew Bible is chock full of sins with the penalties of death and cutting off attached to them. But for Tertullian and his fellow Church Fathers, and for the Rabbis as well, the term "mortal sin" took on a different valence. It came to refer not to those sins which the Bible listed as punishable by death (although many of these remained included under the rubric), but rather had an ecclesiological implication. Mortal sins put one outside of the Church. Mortal sins were the stuff of fiery sermons and threats of damnation. Mortal sins became a code phrase for certain groupings of sins that were simply beyond the pale. If Tertullian could speak of "some sins which beset us every day" he also knows that

> there are also sins quite different from these, graver and deadly, which cannot be pardoned: murder, idolatry, injustice, apostasy, blasphemy; yes, and also adultery and fornication and any other violation of the temple of God. For these Christ will not intercede with the Father a second time [viz. after baptism].[21]

---

[19] Poschmann, *Penance* 45.

[20] *m. Ṣeb.* 1:6.

[21] *De pud.* 19 (ACW, 114).

Commission of the sins on this list exile one from the Christian world. Tertullian here recognizes the nuance of *capital* in Roman legal usage. It can refer to crimes which carry the death penalty, but it can also refer to crimes which carry the penalty of exile. He explicitly associates these crimes with the non-Christian world when he writes of "the nations [of the world] ... steeped as they were in the strains of the seven deadly sins: idolatry, blasphemy, murder, adultery, fornication, false witness, and fraud."[22]

Thus far Tertullian has offered extensive listings of mortal sins. More often in his argument he limits himself to but three, and bases his argument in Scripture. "Idolatry, murder, and adultery occupy a primary, but not exclusive place among capital sins," writes Bernhard Poschmann. "Their grouping together as a triad, along with the artificial reasoning by which this is justified by the Decalogue and the Acts of the Apostles are simply to be attributed to the exigencies of Tertullian's polemic."[23]

Tertullian's polemic carries all the scorn and fury of Montanist righteousness. An edict had been issued apparently permitting adulterers to gain readmission to communion through exomologesis.[24] Tertullian wrote *De pudicitia* as a response,

> The Pontifex Maximus, forsooth I mean the "bishop of bishops," issues this pronouncement: "I forgive the sins of adultery and fornication to those who have performed penance." Oh Edict, upon whom one cannot write: "Good deed." And where shall this indulgence be posted? There, I fancy, on the very doors and under the very titles of debauchery. Penitence such as this should be promulgated where the sin itself will be committed.[25]

As should be clear from Tertullian's blistering sarcasm, he will employ every rhetorical device at his disposal to link adultery and fornication with the most heinous of mortal sins. Thus he consistently links together adultery, murder, and idolatry.

Arguing from the Ten Commandments, Tertullian reasons rabbinically, employing the hermeneutic device of *hekesh* to prove his point, by underscoring the textual juxtaposition of murder and idolatry with adultery.

> And so adultery, since it is the next thing to idolatry, for idolatry is often made a matter of reproach to the people under the name of adultery and fornication, will share its fate as it does its rank, and be joined with it in punishment as it is in position. Furthermore it mentions first: "Thou shalt not commit adultery," and then subjoins: "Thou shalt not kill."[26]

---

[22] *Adv. Marc.* 4:9.

[23] *Penance* 47.

[24] For more on the edict and its authorship, see the works by Esser, D'Ales, Rahner, and Poschmann in n. 1, above.

[25] *De pud.* 1 (ACW, 54).

[26] *De pud.* 5 (ACW, 62f.); cf. *Num Rab.* 9:12 where adulterers are homiletically shown to transgress all Ten Commandments.

Tertullian is not without a certain humor about his argument, he charms his readers,

> Adultery, as I see it, has a certain retinue and pomp of its own, with idolatry going on before to lead the way and murder, in attendance, bringing up the rear. Worthily, without a doubt, does she take her place between these two most lofty vertices of vice and, in their midst, with the prestige of equal guilt, she fills, as it were, the vacancy between.[27]

Tertullian cannot rest still with only Ten Commandments for support. He argues that the New Testament is even stricter in its prohibition, citing the stringencies of Matt 5:21ff. as proof texts.[28]

> What is the advantage of today's stricter legislation? Is it, perhaps, that pardon may be granted more easily to your lechery? You may, then, pardon the idolater, also, and every apostate, since we find that as often as the chosen people were guilty of these things, so often were they restored to their former estate. With the murderer, also, you may communicate, because Achab effaced by prayer the blood of Naboth; and David, by confession, purged himself of the slaughter of Uriah and the adultery which caused it. Then you may pardon incests because of Lot; and fornications compounded with incest because of Judah ... It is only right that now the same pardon be granted to everything which was formerly indulged, if pardon for adultery be vindicated by some example or other dug up out of the past.[29]

So much for the argument from the Hebrew Bible. Tertullian instead offers the prohibitions instituted by the so-called council of Jerusalem (Acts 15:20, 29; 21:25), noting as he did for the Ten Commandments, "here, too, adultery and fornication have the place of honor reserved for them between idolatry and murder."[30]

Tertullian consistently links fornication with adultery and explicitly equates them, "usage requires that we speak of fornication also as adultery."[31] Elsewhere he points out that incest is as evil as blasphemy.[32] This lumping together of all sexual crimes into one great mortal sin serves Tertullian's Montanist morality well. It conveniently also connects sexual transgressions to the levitical prohibitions which serve as the catchall for both rabbinic homilies on sexual morality and their own lists of mortal sins.[33]

---

[27] *De pud.* 5 (ACW, 63).
[28] Cf. Tertullian, *De paenitentia* 3 (ACW, 19).
[29] *De pud.* 6 (ACW, 66f.).
[30] *De pud.* 12 (ACW, 84). Acts lists abstention "from the pollutions of idols and from unchastity and from what is strangled and from blood" (RSV). W. Le Saint (ACW, 238, n. 308) notes that this "Apostolic decree" was taken by the Western Church Fathers to refer to the three mortal sins, while the Eastern Fathers understood it to be a "dietary regulation to which was added a prohibition of fornication."
[31] *De pud.* 4 (ACW, 61).
[32] *De pud.* 13 (ACW, 88).
[33] See below.

Tertullian was not alone in the Church in compiling such catalogues. Before him, Hermas counted among his flock a long series of such sinners. Tertullian disdains him for having offered a second penance [viz. exomologesis] even to adulterers,[34] but his listing is instructive all the same.

> Apostates and blasphemers against the Lord, and betrayers of the servants of God, to these repentance is not open, but death lies before them. ... Hypocrites and teachers of wickedness ... are like the former ... [but] they indeed have repentance in their power, if they repent quickly... The rich cleave with difficulty to the servants of God ... but to all these repentance, and that speedy, is open ...[35]

Hermas uses language (repentance is not open ... is in their power) reminiscent of the Rabbis in their lists, as we shall see below. After him, and more in line with Tertullian's exclusion of adultery from penance, we find Origen and Cyprian making their own lists. Origen goes even beyond Tertullian in condemning others who are quick to grant exomologesis, "Certain persons, I know not how ... boast that they are also able to pardon even idolatry and to forgive adultery and fornication."[36] Cyprian, for his part, simply states, "Adultery, fraud, manslaughter are mortal crimes."[37]

The Rabbis are rather consistent throughout the period under consideration and beyond in counting idolatry, murder, and adultery as "mortal sins."[38] It serves as a form of moral shorthand for all that is wrong with sinning humanity. Thus, commenting on the Flood story, the Rabbis can conclude, "'For the earth is filled with violence' (Gen 6: 13). Rabbi Levi said, 'Violence' refers to idolatry, adultery, and murder."[39] Or again, "Why was the First Temple destroyed? Because of three things in it: idolatry, adultery, and murder."[40] The three are associated with other evil generations as well as other evil sins,

> What were the sins which caused the Canaanites to be expelled from the land of Israel? I know only of adultery. By what means may one also include idolatry, murder, and blasphemy among their sins? [By logical inference,] just as adultery was specified as a deed that exiled the Canaanites and removed God's presence [from them], so all of the above mentioned deeds ...[41]

---

[34] *De pud.* 10 (ACW, 82).

[35] *Sim.* 9: 19.

[36] *De orat.* 28. 10; cf. *In lev. hom.* 11. 2 where Origen draws on the Ten Commandments to include adultery with murder as a mortal sin. See too, *In lev. hom.* 15. 2. For the problem of Origen's usage of the term "mortal sin," see M. Borret, *Origene Homilies sur le Levitique* II (Sources Chretiennes, 287: Paris, 1981), note Complementaire 28, 310ff.

[37] *De bono pat.* 14.

[38] For the sake of brevity I employ the term "adultery" to translate the rabbinic term *giluy 'arayot*, with the understanding that it refers to the entire range of sexual transgressions in Leviticus 18, which include adultery but are primarily prohibitions against incest.

[39] *Gen Rab.* 31: 6, Rabbi Levi fl. ca. 300 C. E.

[40] *b. Yoma* 9b.

[41] *Sipre Deut.* #254.

Just as the deeds of the Canaanites were steeped in idolatry, adultery, murder, ho-
mosexual intercourse, and bestiality, so, too, were the deeds of the Egyptians.[42]

Often, the later Sages invoke the three "mortal sins" with a fourth, to give
it extra moral weight,

> See how bad a sin is evil gossip. It is as bad as murder, idolatry and adultery, for
> of each of these three sins Scripture writes *great* [singular], while of evil gossip
> it writes *great* [plural]. Of murder it is written, "My punishment is greater than
> I can bear" (Gen 4:13). Of adultery it is written, "How can I do this great
> wickedness" (Gen 39:9). Of idolatry it is written, "This people have sinned a
> great sin" (Exod 32:31). But of evil gossip it is written [in the plural], "May the
> Lord cut off all flattering lips, the tongue that makes great boasts" (Ps 12:4 [3]).
> [Why is this written in the plural form?] To teach you that evil gossip is worse
> than those three [mortal] sins.[43]

In other instances, the sins are weighed against one another. Murder is
compared to idolatry and idolatry, in turn, to adultery.[44] In the same
source, idolatry is held to be equal to transgression against the entire
Torah.[45] This recalls Tertullian's theory of compensation,

> Why, then, do they remove so heavy a yoke from our necks [viz. the Apostles who
> made all of the commandments remissible except the three mortal sins], except
> that they may lay upon them, in perpetuity, these *compendia* of the Law? ... The
> matter has been settled by compensation; we have gained so much that we may
> give something. Compensation, however, is not revokable, unless, withal, it be
> revoked by the repetition of adultery, murder and idolatry. For the obligation
> of the whole Law is again assumed, if the condition which excuses from its
> observance is violated.[46]

For the Rabbis, the three mortal sins carried a certain moral-legal obligation beyond the homiletic. Ideally, a Jew should rather die than commit
adultery, idolatry, or murder. As is always the case with these lists, theory
was more easily legislated than practice. Nevertheless, the rabbinic maxim,
yehareg v'al ya'avor, "die rather than transgress," lent the three a certain
element of being "mortal sins" even though commission of them did not
exclude a Jew from communion, as it were.

---

[42] *Sipra Aharei Mot*, chap 13 (ed. Weiss, 86a).

[43] *Midr. Pss.* 52:2. For other homiletic invocations of these sins, see e.g., *Midr.
Tannaim* to Deut 21:23 (ed. Hoffman, 132); *ibid.* to Deut 24:4 (p. 156), and *Sipra
Aharei Mot*, chap 4 (ed. Weiss, 81c).

[44] *t. B. Mes.* 6:17.

[45] *t. Bek.* 3:12; cf. *b. Hor.* 8a.

[46] *De pud.* 12 (ACW, 84f.); Tertullian neatly excuses Christians from Old Testament
obligations by his theory of compensation. He adds, however, that violation of the
mortal sins removes the sinner from the system of compensation, i.e., the Church, and so
returns him to the binding obligation of each biblical commandment. Cf. James 2:10ff.

Rabbi Yoḥanan quoted Rabbi Shimeon ben Yehozadak, "They voted in the upper chamber at Bet Netazah in Lydda: Concerning any commandment in the Torah, if a man tells you transgress that you not die, transgress and do not die, except for idolatry, adultery, and murder." Is this so in the case of idolatry? Were we not taught that Rabbi Ishmael said, "Whence do we learn that if a man said to you: Worship this idol in order that you not die, you should worship it and not die? Scripture teaches, '[You shall therefore keep My statutes and My ordinances, by doing which a person] shall live' (Lev 18: 5), and not die by them."[47]

In the case of murder, this moral-legal structure of "die rather than transgress" is later given a utilitarian explanation.

There was a case of one who came before Rava and said to him "My landlord has told me: Go kill so-and-so; if not, I'll kill you."
Rava replied, "Then he must kill you, you may not kill; for who says that your blood is redder than the intended victim's? Perhaps his blood is redder than yours."
Rav Dimi came and quoted Rabbi Yoḥanan, "This ruling [to die rather than transgress] was only taught for times when there was no government persecution, but when there is government persecution one should die rather than transgress even a minor commandment."
Rabbi Abin came and quoted Rabbi Yoḥanan, "This was not taught about times when there was no government persecution, but referred to [threats of death] in private. However, in public one should die rather than transgress even a minor commandment."[48]

The Sages worried about other categories of sin, too. Some instances could be as grave as mortal sins. The foremost among these is the case of one who leads others to sin. The Rabbis offer their opinion of such a one in a balanced formula,

All who bring merit to the many [by leading them to the performance of the commandments] do not have it in their power to transgress a commandment ... while all who lead the many to sin do not have it in their power to repent.[49]

This notion of not having the power to repent is also applied to the repeat offender. So, the Mishna teaches,

One who says, "I will sin and then repent, and sin again and then repent," will not have it in his power to repent. He who says, "I will sin and the Day of Atonement will atone" for such a one the Day of Atonement will not atone.[50]

---

[47] *b. Sanh.* 74a, Rabbi Yoḥanan fl. c. 240 C. E., Rabbi Shimeon fl. c. 230 C. E., Rabbi Ishmael fl. c. 110 C. E. Cf. *j. Sanh.* chap 3 (21b). In any case one is not held culpable in rabbinic law for sin performed under threat of death; the coercion abrogates the legal responsibility.

[48] *b. Sahn.* 74a, the correct reading for the Sage in question is Rava, fl. C. 325.

[49] *t. Kipp.* (ed. Lieberman) 4: 10–11. In the parallel in *m. ʼAbot* 5: 18 the first part reads, "All who bring merit to the many do not sin." Cf Hermas, quoted at n. 35, above.

[50] *m. Yoma* 8: 9.

This recalls the worry of Clement of Alexandria who pondered whether the knowing sinner was worse or "one who, after having repented of his sins, transgresses again."[51] In another formulation, Rabbi Yose guesses at the limits of God's patience for the repeat sinner,

> a person can transgress a commandment once and he is forgiven, twice and he is forgiven, three times and he is forgiven. He will not be forgiven a fourth transgression [of the same commandment], as it is said, "For three sins of Israel [I will forgive], but for four I will not revoke the punishment" (Amos 2: 6).[52]

The Church Fathers shared this concern, especially after working out the opportunity for a sinner to have the opportunity to perform penance even after the cleansing of baptism,

> If anyone is tempted by the devil and sins after that great and holy calling in which the Lord has called His people to everlasting life [i. e., baptism], that person has the opportunity to repent but once [viz. exomologesis]. But if he should sin frequently after this, and then repent, to such a person his repentance will be of no avail.[53]

A rabbinic tractate commenting on Avot's statement that "all who lead the many to sin do not have it in their power to repent," sums up nicely with a tidy listing,

> Five are not forgiven: one who repeatedly repents, one who repeatedly sins, one who sins in an innocent generation, one who sins with the assumption that he will perform penance [and so be forgiven] and one who desecrates God's name.[54]

As Tertullian puts it, "There is a sin which is mortal; I do not say that one is to pray for that' (1 John 5: 16, RSV) ... Where there is no room for prayer there, likewise, neither is there room for remission."[55]

III

Forgiveness of sin requires penance. Just as one may sin against either a human being or against God, so may penance be administered by a human being or by God. Both types of penance take many forms: from prayer, fasting and confession to chastisement, suffering and death. We have seen that between Church and Synagogue, institutional religion can pronounce a variety of penances (sentences) ranging from the rituals of

---

[51] See above, n. 6.
[52] *b. Yoma* 86b. Cf. *t. Kipp.* 4: 13 where additional proof is brought from Exod 34: 7, Job 33: 29, and Prov 25: 17.
[53] Hermas, *Mand.* 4: 3.
[54] *'Abot R. Nat.*, ver. A, chap. 39.
[55] *De pud.* 2 (ACW, 59, but with the RSV of 1 John).

the Day of Atonement (both cultic and post-destruction) to exclusion from communion, from the embarrassment of public confession to death at the hands of a human court.

> Let us reflect that chastisements proceeding from a person do no more than requite pain with pain, and stop in consequence when the suffering has been returned upon the doer, but go no farther, and hence, like curs, bark at the heels of the offender and set out at once in pursuit of the offence; whereas God, we must presume, distinguishes whether the passions of the sick soul to which he administers his justice will in any way yield and make room for repentance, and for those in whose nature vice is not unrelieved or intractable, he fixes a period of grace (Plutarch, *Moralia*, 551c–d).

Bearing in mind Plutarch's words about the efficacy of humanly devised "penances," it is both instructive and satisfying to note that both sets of Fathers afford God an active role in requiting iniquity. God, of course, has the power to bring suffering and death to the sinner. God has the power to reward and punish after death, as well. In fact, for both Church and synagogue, God metes out reward and punishment measure for measure.[56] To some extent, the same is theoretically true of God's representatives on earth. Tertullian, writing of remissible and irremissible sins, is quite explicit about this *lex talionis* relationship.

> According to this distinction of sins the form of penance is also determined. One will be such as is able to win pardon, that is to say in the case of a sin which is remissible. The other will be such as is by no means able to win it, that is to say, in the case of a sin which is irremissible.[57]

In ecclesiological practice, both Church and Synagogue had a variety of means to penance, and not all of them were direct responses to the sins committed. There was a general, if at times, ambiguous, theory of penance and atonement. Rabbi Ishmael is generally credited with enunciating the rabbinic view,[58]

> Rabbi Ishmael spoke[59] of four categories of atonement. If one transgressed a positive commandment and repented, he is forgiven before he even moves from the spot [where he repented], as it is said, "Return, O faithless sons, I will heal

---

[56] Matt 7: 2 and *m. Sota* 1: 7. For other parallels see H. Strack and P. Billerbeck, *Kommentar zum Neuen Testament* (München, 1922), *apud* Matt 7: 2. See also S. Lieberman, "On Sins and Their Punishments," *Texts and Studies* (New York, 1974) 29–56.

[57] *De pud.* 2 (ACW, 60).

[58] *t. Kipp.* (ed. Lieberman) 4: 6–9. Cf. Lieberman's *Tosefta ki-Fshutah* commentary *ad loc.* There are many parallels for this very popular tradition, all listed in Lieberman, *ibid.*, and in the commentary to my Hebrew edition of *Midrash Mishle*, chap 10. Rabbi Ishmael fl. ca. 110 C. E.

[59] The parallel in the *Mek. Yitro BaHodesh*, chap 7 (228) reads, "Rabbi Mattiah ben Heresh went to Rabbi Elazar HaKappar in Lydda to learn the four categories of atonement which Rabbi Ishmael expounded." Other parallels and manuscripts place Rabbi Elazar at Laodicea or Rome.

your faithlessness" (Jer 3: 22). If one transgressed a negative commandment and
repented, penance suspends [punishment] and the Day of Atonement atones, as
it is said, "For on this day shall atonement be made for you" (Lev 16: 30). If
one transgressed [commandments for which the punishment is] cutting off or
death at the hand of a human court and repented, penance and the Day of
Atonement suspend [punishment] and suffering wipes clean [the slate], as it is
said, "Then I will punish their transgression with the rod" (Ps 89: 33 [32]). But
for one who maliciously profaned the name of Heaven and repented, penance
will not suspend, nor will the Day of Atonement atone; but penance and the
Day of Atonement [together] will atone for one third, suffering will atone for one
third and death and its accompanying suffering will atone for a third. Of this
it is said, "Surely this iniquity will not be forgiven you till you die" (Isa 22: 14);
which teaches that the day of death wipes clean [the slate].
The sin offering, the guilt offering, death and the Day of Atonement all require
repentance to atone, as it is said, "On the tenth day of this seventh month is
the day of atonement ... you shall afflict yourselves and present an offering by
fire before the Lord" (Lev 23: 27). If he has repented, the day atones; if he has
not repented, it does not atone for him.[60] Rabbi Lazar says, "He will clear"
(Exod 34: 7) the penitent, but will by no means clear the unpenitent.[61]

I have quoted this lengthy text fully, for it is central to many different
rabbinic compilations of many different eras. Each of the parallel versions
offers a slightly different reading, which may be accounted for not only
by the vicissitudes of oral transmission, but also because of changes in
penitential theology. The gist is clear enough; the many varieties of sin
surveyed above are each offered a corresponding penance. Thus a theory
of atonement is available and scriptural contradictions are harmonized.
One should point out quickly that Rabbi Ishmael's thesis, though popular,
was by no means dogma. Varying opinions were offered, such as that of
Rabbi Judah the Patriarch, redactor of the Mishna,

> Rabbi [Judah the Patriarch] said: The Day of Atonement atones for all of the
> transgressions in the Torah, whether or not one has done penance, except for
> [the following cases]: one who throws off the yoke [of the Law entirely], one who
> [willfully and wrongly] interprets Torah and one who removes circumcision. In
> these cases, if he has repented then the Day of Atonement atones, if not, the
> Day of Atonement does not atone.[62]

Rabbi Judah the Patriarch is unusual in that he suggests that the Day of
Atonement does not require penance to afford atonement. Most of the
parallel versions of Rabbi Ishmael's text above are emphatic about the
necessity of penitence, reading "There are four categories of atonement,

---

[60] There is a pun here. "Penitents" (*shabim*) is paired with "Sabbath of Sabbaths"
(*shabbat shabbaton*) referring to the Day of Atonement in Lev 23: 33.
[61] The Hebrew in Exod 34: 7 uses an intensive construction, *venakeh lo yenakeh*, which
translated literally means, "He will clear, He will not clear."
[62] *b. Yoma* 85b.

which are [actually] three with repentance accompanying each of the others." This tradition calls to mind Plutarch's distinctions about how sin is requited,

> Adrasteia, he said, daughter of Necessity and Zeus, is the supreme requiter; all crimes are under her cognizance, and none of the wicked is so high or low as to escape her either by force or by stealth. There are three others, and each is warden and executioner of a different punishment. (*Moralia* 564e)

Returning to rabbinic accounting, another source contemporary with the Tosefta and Rabbi Judah the Patriarch would also insist upon repentance, "Just as the sin offering and the guilt offering do not atone unless accompanied by repentance, so the Day of Atonement does not atone unless accompanied by repentance."[63] Rabbi Judah the Patriarch also queried the atoning value of death until he could explicitly prove it scripturally, "When the Bible says, 'When I open your graves, and raise you from your graves" (Ezek 37: 13), only then do you learn that the day of death atones."[64]

In addition to the penances just considered and those mentioned in the cataloguing of sins, above, a final category of penance must be given its due. Confession has a place in rabbinic Judaism, and a very important place in the Church. The Hebrew Bible already makes it clear that confession is a part of the ceremony of penance on the Day of Atonement. Lev 16: 21 requires that the High Priest take a scapegoat and "confess over it all the iniquities of the people of Israel, and all their transgressions, all their sins." The necessity of confession even extended to the extremities of penance imposed by the human court. Thus, when a sinner was condemned to death in the time of the Sanhedrin, the Mishna recalls,

> When he was about ten cubits from the place of stoning they used to say to him, "Make thy confession," for such is the way of them that have been condemned to make confession, for everyone that makes his confession has a share in the world to come. For so we have found it with Achan. Joshua said to him, "My son, give glory to the Lord God of Israel, and render praise to Him; and tell me now what you have done; do not hide it from me" (Josh 7: 19). Whence do we learn that his confession made atonement for him? It is written, "Why did you bring trouble on us? The Lord brings trouble on you today" (Josh 7: 25). "Today" thou shall be troubled, but in the world to come thou shall not be troubled.[65]

We may briefly see then by surveying the two extremes of penance, the Day of Atonement and execution, that confession is integral to the rabbinic system. Even Plutarch associated confession with penance and the accompanying torments of the pagan afterlife, as in his vivid description of one punished,

---

[63] *Sipra Emor*, chap 14 (ed. Weiss, 102a).
[64] *Mek. Yitro BaḤodesh*, chap 7 (228 end).
[65] *m. Sanh.* 6: 2.

covered with brands and scars ... and not allowed by those in charge of the punishments to keep silent, but compelled to confess.[66] (*Moralia* 566f)

In the Church, confession was a major stage in public penance. After baptism, which washed away the sins of one before conversion, iniquity could only be remitted through the ceremony of exomologesis. This consisted of public confession, followed by a trial period of "penance" during which one was excluded from communion and had the opportunity to repent of ones sins. What began with public confession was then brought to fruition by laying on of hands by the bishop and restoration to communion.[67] This confession and its accompanying ceremonies were a second chance for sinners in the Church. For the remission of sins, the ritual granted was, like Rabbi Ishmael's four categories of atonement, meant to appease God in a manner similar to that prescribed in the Bible. As Tertullian explains,

> Exomologesis does all this in order to render penitence acceptable and in order to honor God through fear of punishment, so that in passing sentence upon the sinner it may itself be a substitute for the wrath of God and, by temporal punishment, I will not say prevent eternal torments but rather cancel them.[68]

IV

One cannot end so long an essay on mortal sins and their penances without at least alluding, as Tertullian has just done, to the torments of the unrepentant. Both the Church and Synagogue, and for that matter Plutarch as well, assumed that each sinner gains his or her just deserts, if not in the present then in the world to come. But, happy though the solution of an afterlife may be for theodicy, and baroque as the descriptions of torture of the wicked there may be, the pious are denied the satisfaction of seeing sinners punished in the here and now. Plutarch offers a partial palliative, insisting that though ultimate punishment of the wicked is deferred, sinners psychologically pay the penalty of wrongdoing at the very moment of commission.

> Vice frames out of itself each instrument of its own punishment, cunning artisan that it is of a life of wretchedness containing with infamy a host of terrors, regrets, cruel passions and never ending anxieties. Yet some there are no wiser than little children, who see criminals in the amphitheater, clad often in tunics of

---

[66] De Lacy and Einarson (n. 1) note in their translation of Plutarch here that confession is a form of punishment, referring the reader to Norden, *P. Vergilius Maro Aeneis* Buch VI.3, 275.

[67] Ceremonies of exomologesis differed from place to place, but basically followed this format. See n. 1, above.

[68] *De paenitentia* 9 (ACW, 32).

gold cloth and purple mantles ... and struck with awe and wonderment suppose them supremely happy, till the moment when before their eyes the criminals are stabbed and scourged and that gay and sumptuous apparel bursts into flame. (*Moralia* 554b)

This notion was reflected somewhat later in Church and Synagogue. Taking the biblical promise of fiery punishment for the sinner, the Fathers, like Plutarch, wondered as to its source. Origen asks about the meaning of the threat of "eternal fire" (Matt 25:41).

Now we find in the prophet Isaiah that the fire by which each man is punished is described as belonging to himself. For it says, "Walk in the light of your fire and in the flame which you have kindled for yourselves" (Isa 50:11). These words seem to indicate that every sinner kindles for himself the flame of his own fire, and is not plunged into a fire which has been previously kindled by someone else or which exited before him. Of this fire the food and material are our sins, which are called by the apostle Paul [1 Cor 3:12] wood and hay and stubble.[69]

Palestinian Rabbis contemporary with Origen also embrace the notion of fiery torment for sinners, but disagree as to the source of the flames, apparently relying on the more traditional theodicy of punishment in the world to come.

Rabbi Yannai and Resh Laqish said, "There is no Gehenna save a day which will burn up the wicked, as it is said, 'For behold, a day cometh, it burneth as a furnace'" (Mal 3:19). Our rabbis say, "There will be a [locality called] Gehenna, as it is said, 'Whose fire is in Zion, and His furnace in Jerusalem'" (Isa 31:9).

The redactor of the Midrash which offers these two opinions concludes the discussion by bringing the words of another Palestinian Sage, who flourished but half a century after Plutarch,

Rabbi Yehuda bar Ilai said, "Neither a day nor a [locality will exist called] Gehenna; but a fire shall come forth from the bodies of the wicked themselves and burn them up, as it is written, 'Ye conceive chaff, ye shall bring forth stubble, your own spirit shall be a fire to devour you'" (Isa 33:11).[70]

In closing this survey, it must be remarked that though Church and Synagogue lavished attention on sins, penances, and punishments, they were much more concerned with their flock following the Way and so, gaining life eternal. As the Rabbis make clear in the very tractate that discusses administration of the punishments for sin, "All Israel have a share in the world to come."[71] The Church Fathers wished for no less. Though they recognized mortal sins, they sympathized with the words of the prophet,

---

[69] *De princ.* 2, 10, 4, trans. G. W. Butterworth (London, 1936).
[70] *Gen Rab.* 6:6.
[71] *m. Sanh.* 10:1.

"Have I any pleasure in the death of the wicked, says the Lord God, and not rather that he should turn from his way and live?" (Ezek 18: 23).

While each ecclesiastical body charted the territory of sins and offered a map of penances and punishments to set one back on the road to salvation, neither Church nor Synagogue could deny to God the ultimate role as arbiter of both mortal sin and sinful mortality. In regarding the mysterious plan of the Lord, they would have ultimately agreed with Plutarch,

> It is ... presumptuous for mere human beings like ourselves to inquire into the concerns of gods and daemons, where we are like lay people seeking to follow the thoughts of experts by the guesswork of opinion and imputation ... it should [not] be easy or safe for a mortal to say anything else about God but this: that he knows full well the right moment for healing vice, and administers punishment to each patient as a medicine, a punishment neither given in the same amount in every case nor after the same interval for all. For that the cure of the soul, which goes by the name of chastisement and justice, is the greatest of all arts, Pindar has attested with countless others, when he invokes the god who is ruler and sovereign of the world as him "of noblest art," intimating that he is artificer of justice, which has the task of determining for each evil doer the time, the manner, and the measure of his punishment. (*Moralia* 549f–550a).[72]

[72] This paper was prepared thanks to a generous grant from the Abbell Research Fund of the Jewish Theological Seminary of America and was written during my tenure as a Visiting Fellow of Clare Hall, University of Cambridge and as a Visiting Scholar of the Oxford Centre for Post-Graduate Hebrew Studies, Oxford University.

Trinitarian Testimonies

I am a Jew, born at Tarsus in Cilicia, but brought up in this city at the feet of Gamaliel, educated according to the strict manner of the law of our fathers, being zealous for God as you all are this day. (Acts 22: 3)

Circumcised on the eighth day, of the people of Israel, of the tribe of Benjamin, a Hebrew born of Hebrews; as to the law a Pharisee. (Philippians 3: 5)

Brethren, I am a Pharisee, a son of Pharisees. (Acts 23: 6)

I

The self-proclaimed pedigree of the apostle Paul has long tempted scholars into the sin of providing his Gamalielite, Pharisaic background by extensively quoting from Rabbinic literature. Though this phenomenon of "backgrounding" is well known for other parts of the New Testament, it is deemed all the more apt and valid in Pauline studies since the apostle himself, as it were, opened the door to the method by confessing his "yeshiva" training. Raiding Rabbinic literature for Pauline "background" is, at best, a hazardous undertaking – as any careful New Testament scholar is obliged to admit. On one side, there is the temptation to employ the Rabbinic parallels to make the Sages seem very close indeed to Matthew's Pharisees. On the other side, even the best intentioned student of Rabbinic literature will be guilty of some anachronism when citing the Jewish fathers to illustrate Pauline texts composed before the destruction of the Second Temple.

Even if one carefully limits the parallels to the Tannaitic corpus, one is still comparing texts written in the mid-first century with others first redacted (and perhaps only then invented) in the late second and early third centuries. So much the worse when citations are offered from the Talmuds and medieval midrashim. While it is certainly possible that these late Rabbinic texts contain early, even predestruction, traditions, this possibility is at best, difficult to prove. Only very careful exegetes succeed in wending their way through the maze of Rabbinic literature to find appropriate parallels which shed some light on Paul. Even under carefully controlled conditions all that can be offered is background color to the milieu – not the sources of Pauline traditions.

Is it not much more likely that Rabbinic parallels to Paul do not illustrate his Pharasaic background, but rather show some Rabbinic familiarity with Paul? Allow me to carry this logic one step further and suggest that not only do Rabbinic parallels with the New Testament possibly indicate Rabbinic familiarity with the verse in question,[1] but the exegesis of such a Rabbinic passage can be best understood if the NT verse is read within the social context in which the Rabbis heard it. That is to say, proper exegesis of New Testament verses in Rabbinic literature requires an understanding of how that verse was read, interpreted and employed by the church fathers at the time the verse entered the Rabbinic corpus.

In making this argument I do not wish to insist that the study of Rabbinic literature is a fruitless endeavor for students of New Testament. Given careful control of Tannaitic material it can serve a useful purpose of introducing the student to Rabbinic thought a century or more after Paul. To whatever extent current scholarly opinion feels comfortable in making trajectories backward in time, this is a more or less useful tool. My point here is to caution against assuming that a close parallel has given access to Gamalielite, Pharisaic traditions that Paul imbibed while he was yet Saul. Quite the contrary, all those parallels from Rabbinic literature are apt to illuminate is the Rabbinic perception of the patristic interpretation of the Pauline verses. This is particularly the case when the Rabbinic parallels are found in a polemical, probably anti-Christian context. The use of parallels under such circumstances must be considered wholly inadequate as a means of arriving at a critical understanding of a New Testament verse.

II

The temptation to resort to Rabbinic literature to explain Paul rises in direct proportion to the opaqueness of any given passage. Since P. Billerbeck wrote his famous commentary,[2] virtually every difficult Pauline text has had the disadvantage of a "Rabbinic exegesis." I focus here on one particular crux, 1 Corinthians 11:3–12, for it illustrates my point about the uses and abuses of Rabbinics for New Testament exegesis. I intend to demonstrate not only that the Rabbinic parallel in question does not provide Pauline "background," but that the Rabbinic text in fact quotes Paul

---

[1] I limit myself here to the possibility that the Rabbis knew isolated verses of the New Testament. I cannot undertake to prove they were familiar with the entire N. T. canon.

[2] H. Strack, P. Billerbeck, *Kommentar zum Neuen Testament.* (München: Beck, 1926).

as he was cited by the church fathers in the late fourth century Trinitarian controversy.

The text of 1 Corinthians 11: 3–12:[3]

> 3. But I want you to understand that the head of every man is Christ, the head of a woman is her husband, and the head of Christ is God. 4. Any man who prays or prophesies with his head covered dishonors his head, 5. but any woman who prays or prophesies with her head unveiled dishonors her head – it is the same as if her head were shaven. 6. For if a woman will not veil herself, then she should cut off her hair; but if it is disgraceful for a woman to be shorn or shaven, let her wear a veil. 7. For a man ought not to cover his head, since he is the image and glory of God; but woman is the glory of man. 8. For man was not made from woman, but woman from man. 9. Neither was man created for woman, but woman for man. 10. That is why a woman ought to have a veil on her head, because of the angels. 11. Nevertheless, in the Lord woman is not independent of man nor man of woman; 12. for as woman was made from man, so man is now born of woman. And all things are from God.

It is not my concern here to discuss whether Paul is talking about hairstyles or headcoverings, whether he is feminist or chauvinist. It is important to note that this passage contains a blatant contradiction between the vertical hierarchy of men and women in verses 3, 7, 8, 9 and the equality proclaimed in verse 11–12. I am not the first to notice this contradiction, nor am I the first to point out that it mirrors the two creation accounts in Genesis. I may be the first, however, who having pointed out these facts will offer no attempt to harmonize or otherwise resolve them.

I am also not the first to point to a parallel between verses 11–12 and a Rabbinic passage attributed to the mid-third century Sage, R. Simlai,

> In the past, Adam was created from the dust, while Eve was created from Adam. From Adam onward, *In our image, after our likeness* (Genesis 1: 26); it is impossible for there to be man independent of woman, nor is it possible for there to be woman independent of man, neither is it possible for both of them to be independent of the Shekinah.[4]

I think the parallel is beyond quibble; the only difficulty is what to make of the parallel. Billerbeck merely lists the text and its Rabbinic citations without extended discussion. This is the standard technique of his commentary which serves as no more than a source book, leaving the student to decide on the meaning of a text as he or she wishes. G. Delling, who five years later chose to explicate the thorny question, *Paulus' Stellung zur Frau und Ehe*, followed Billerbeck's lead by citing the parallel without discussing it. Close to thirty years passed before another scholar linked

---

[3] RSV, omitting the parentheses employed there. The sense unit runs from 1 Corinthians 11: 2–16, but I quote only the verses relevant to my point.

[4] Gen. Rabbah 8: 9; all translations are mine unless otherwise noted. See below for further discussion of the Rabbinic literature.

the texts together on the printed page. J. Jervell cited the Rabbinic passage as not just a parallel, but as an influence on Paul. The question for the scholar to consider, Jervell noted, is just how Paul understood the Rabbinic saying.[5]

Almost a decade later M. Boucher very kindly offered the Rabbinic parallel to show that the rabbis were theoretically just as fair to women as was Paul.[6] Most recently, and most brilliantly, Mary Rose D'Angelo explicated Paul by using the Rabbinic parallel as background.[7] Dr. D'Angelo excelled for she was careful to study the Rabbinic texts as critically as she did the Pauline verses. Her keen insight connected the two strands of the 1 Corinthians passage with the Genesis accounts. By examining the Rabbinic treatment of Genesis in the parallel, Dr. D'Angelo was able to unravel Paul's convoluted and apparently contradictory rhetoric.

Unfortunately, although Dr. D'Angelo had all the correct instincts in her treatment of the Rabbinic passage, carefully weighed the evidence for the dating of the tradition and cited the fullest version of the parallel to be found in any New Testament commentary, she failed methodologically. Although her method brought her, I suspect, to a correct exegesis of Paul, it did so through inadmissible evidence. Nevertheless, she is a careful New Testament scholar, so we must be grateful to her for her perspicacious reading of Paul.

The failure in invoking the Rabbinic parallel was twofold. First, even the lengthy passage Dr. D'Angelo cited was taken out of context. Within the context it is clearly part of an anti-Trinitarian polemic. This being the case, one must suspect that it is the Rabbis quoting the New Testament and not vice versa. Second, for all her care in considering the dating of the saying, the earliest possible date that might have been offered would have been at the end of the first quarter of the second century, some seventy-five

---

[5] Billerbeck, *Kommentar* on 1 Corinthians 11: 12. G. Delling, *Paulus' Stellung zur Frau und Ehe* (Stuttgart: Kohlhammer, 1931), pp. 109ff. J. Jervell, *Imago Dei: Gen. 1.26f im Spätjudentum, in der Gnosis und in den paulinischen Briefen* (Göttingen: Vandenhoeck, 1960), p. 311 with n. 464 there. See M. Smith's response to Jervell in "On the Shape of God …," *Religions in Antiquity* ed. J. Neusner, (Leiden: Brill, 1968), pp. 315–326.

[6] M. Boucher, "Some Unexplored Parallels to 1 Cor. 11:11–12 and Gal. 3:28: The New Testament and the Role of Women." *Catholic Biblical Quarterly* 31 (1969), pp. 50–58. While the brief on behalf of Judaism's feminism is appreciated, it is not clear that Dr. Boucher explained Paul or the Rabbis correctly within their own social contexts. One other scholar cites Rabbinic parallels to the 1 Corinthians passage, although not the text we are considering: A. Jaubert, *New Testament Studies* 18 (1971–2), pp. 419–430.

[7] Mary Rose D'Angelo, "The Garden: Once and Not Again," *Intrigue in the Garden: Studies in the Exegesis of Genesis 1–3* (New York, forthcoming). I am deeply grateful to Dr. D'Angelo for sharing her article with me before publication. The notes there detail the recent history of exegesis of the Pauline passages.

years after Paul. However, it is even more likely that the text does not antedate the redaction of the Palestinian Talmud, ca. 425 C. E.

III

Let us examine the Rabbinic parallel to 1 Corinthians 11: 11. I am assuming that the polemical context of the Rabbinic text and the general earliness of the Pauline passage must lead one to the consideration that the Sages are quoting Paul. In order to prove this point I first analyze the entire text in order to fix a date and redactive context for the saying in question. Exegesis of a smaller portion of the text will establish that 1 Corinthians 11: 11 is consciously cited in response to patristic usage of the greater Pauline passage in the Trinitarian controversy. When the Sages wish to debunk the Trinitarian argument in all its late fourth century complexity, they do so by following the church father's ground rules – by quoting New Testament texts in support of their argument!

A. The heretics asked R. Simlai, How many gods created the world? He answered them, Me you're asking? Let's ask Adam, as it is said, *For ask now of the days that are past, which were before you, since the day that God created Adam ...* (Deuteronomy 4: 32). It is not written, since gods created (pl.) Adam, but *since the day that God created (sing.) Adam.*

B. They said to him, But it is written, *In the beginning God created* (Genesis 1: 1).[8] He said to them, Is *created* written [as a plural]? What is written here is *created* [in the singular].

C. R. Simlai stated, Every place that the heretics rend [a verse from context to make their point][9] has the appropriate [textual] response right next to it.

D. They returned to ask him, What of this verse, *Let us make man in our image, after our likeness* (Genesis 1: 26).[10] He answered them, It is not written, So God created (pl.) man in his image (pl.), but, *So God created (sing.) man in his own image* (Genesis 1: 27). His disciples said to him, Those you pushed off with but a straw, but what shall you answer us?

He told them, In the past, Adam was created from the dust, while Eve was created from Adam. From Adam onward, *In our image, after our likeness* (Genesis 1: 26); it is impossible for there to be man independent of woman, nor is it possible for there to be woman independent of man, neither is it possible for both of them to be independent of the Shekinah.

E. They returned to ask him, What of this verse, *The Mighty One, God, the Lord! The Mighty One, God, the Lord! He knows* (Joshua 22: 22). He answered them, It is not written, They know (pl.), but rather, *He knows.*

---

[8] The term for God in these verses, *'elohim,* appears to be a masculine plural. If it were, it should take a plural verb. The indication of the singular verb points to the necessity of understanding the noun as a singular too.

[9] The text in the first edition and manuscripts reads *pqr,* to set free of constraints. I translate here accordingly.

[10] The subject, verb and objects appear to be plurals.

His disciples said to him, Rabbi, you pushed those off with but a straw, what will you answer us?

He told them, The three are but one name, like one who says: *Basileus, Kaisar, Augustus.*[11]

F. They returned to ask him, What of this verse, *The Mighty One, God, the Lord, speaks and summons the earth* (Psalm 50: 1)? He asked them, Is speak (pl.) written? Rather *speaks and summons* (both sing.) is written.

His disciples said to him, Rabbi, those you pushed off with but a straw, what shall you answer us?

He answered them, The three are but one name, like one who says: craftsman, builder, architect.

G. They returned to ask him, What of the verse, *He is a holy (pl.) God* (Joshua 24: 19)?

He answered them, It is not written, They are, but *He is a jealous God* (ibid.).

His disciples said to him, Rabbi, those you pushed off with but a straw, what shall you answer us?

R. Yitzhak said, Holy with all types of holiness, as R. Judah said in the name of R. Aha ...

H. They returned to ask him, What of the verse, *For what great nation is there that has a God so near (pl.) to it* (Deuteronomy 4: 7)?

He answered them, It is not written, Whenever we call upon them, but rather, *whenever we call upon him* (ibid.).

His disciples said to him, Rabbi, those you pushed off with but a straw, what shall you answer us?

He told them, Near in all types of nearness as R. Pinhas quoted R. Judah bar Simon. ...[12]

I quote the entire passage in its fullest and earliest form, from the Palestinian Talmud. It is not only the earliest redacted, but the only text to retain all of the parts. Later Midrashim merely record those pieces of the pericope that were relevant to the Biblical text being considered in the given Midrash. Thus, Genesis Rabbah only records those sections relevant to Genesis, Midrash Psalms only the section on Psalms, etc.

---

[11] So transliterated in the Hebrew – the terms translate "Emperor, Caesar, Augustus."

[12] P. Ber 9: 1 (12d–13a). Parallel to A. B. C. D. in Gen. Rabbah 8: 9. Parallel to C. and a much abbreviated version of D. (with only the Hebrew Bible verses) in B. San 38b, in the name of R. Yohanan. In Gen. Rabbah 22: 2, a parallel to D. in a debate between R. Aqiba and R. Yishmael (but cf. Gen. R. 1: 14 and Gen. R. 53: 15 and the discussion below). Parallel to G. (but no students) in Tan. (Buber) Kedoshim 4 and in Tan. (Buber) Genesis 7 (ad Gen. 1: 26!). Parallel to F. at Mid. Ps. 50: 1 with an editorial gloss likening the triplet to Wisdom, Understanding and Knowledge. Parallel to H. (but no students) in Deut. R. 2: 13, also quoting Gen. 1: 1, 1: 26f. See Ex. R. 29: 1 which cites Deuteronomy 4: 33 – perhaps this is parallel to A.; but R. Levi responds in place of Simlai. Yal. Sh. Gen. #14 parallels D, *Pugio Fidei* 293, 484, 485, 552 cites parts of the text, but sections D. E. F. are absent there.

This passage is considered by R. T. Herford, *Christianity in Talmud and Midrash* (London: Williams and Norgate, 1903), pp. 255ff., with no citation of 1 Corinthians 11 in the discussion. Equally unaware of the New Testament verse in this passage is A. Segal, *Two Powers in Heaven* (Leiden: Brill, 1977), pp. 124ff.

The segment which quotes Paul (D.) is generally attributed to R. Simlai, although his name does not appear in that specific section. Simlai is cited immediately preceding (C.), offering a maxim about refuting heretics from the very context out of which they have lifted their apparently damaging proof-text. This same maxim is quoted in the Babylonian Talmud in the name of Simlai's contemporary R. Yohanan. There, the comment is connected to his explication of Genesis 1:26.

The quote from 1 Corinthians 11:11 also appears in a debate between R. Akiba and R. Ishmael in Genesis Rabbah 22:2. The form of the debate, however, follows precisely the debates between them found in Genesis Rabbah 53:15 and in Genesis Rabbah 1:14. Each of these instances revolves around proper use of Nahum of Gimzo's Inclusion/Exclusion methodology for resolution of apparently extraneous particles in Biblical Hebrew. In the instance of the Pauline quote, the debate deviates slightly from the prescribed form in that it does not solve the textual difficulty by explicit mention of the Inclusion/Exclusion method. This leads to the conclusion that the text in Genesis Rabbah 22:2 is an editorial construction based upon the loci in Genesis Rabbah 1:14 and 53:15. The quotation from Paul, then, was lifted out of the Palestinian Talmud to provide dialogue for the invented debate. It cannot be considered as genuinely Akiban or Ishmaelian and must be dated at the redaction of Genesis Rabbah, *circa* fifth to sixth century.[13]

We are left, then, with the earliest form of the entire pericope in a document redacted about 425 C.E. Still the name of R. Simlai (fl. mid-third century) appears rather firmly attached to the text in question, even if not absolutely attached to the segment containing the 1 Corinthians quote. It is, after all, paralleled with little change in Genesis Rabbah. But even this much is not secure, for the fact remains that Simlai's name does not appear in the section under discussion. Further, it should be quite clear that the Pauline passage appears as part of a triplet of exchanges (D. E. F.), each of which has an anonymous Rabbi responding to a Biblical plural with a trinity of his own. Genesis Rabbah only excerpts from this triplet. The sections of the Palestinian Talmud (A. B. C.) preceding this grouping of sayings specifically mention R. Simlai. Since he was well known for his debates with heretics, a redactor could have readily slipped the latter grouping of three sayings into a format which would have them appear under R. Simlai's authority. The sayings (G. H.) that follow mention other Sages entirely. This sandwiching of the anonymous dialogues in between two named segments is the work of the Palestinian Talmudic redactor.

---

[13] This text is discussed by Segal, ibid., 74ff. and D.'Angelo, op. cit. The invention of dialogue between Tannaim and based on a fixed form is found elsewhere. See, e. g., B. Ber 26b–27a and the discussion of R. Goldenberg, "The Deposition of Rabban Gamaliel," *Journal of Jewish Studies* 23 (1972), pp. 167–190.

The era in which he did his work (c. 425 C. E.) is, then, the only secure date which may be offered for the group of three dialogues (D. E. F.) which include the 1 Corinthians parallel.

The Pauline quotation is part of a group of three discussions among an anonymous Rabbi, his students and his heretics. Yet none of the New Testament scholars who cite the passage as "Pauline background" also cited the two connected parts (E. F.) which follow. Only within the full context can the meaning of these dialogues be apprehended.

IV

To facilitate exegesis of the passage, I will consider the three sections of dialogue in the reverse order from that in the Talmudic pericope. Beginning with the last (F.), first:

> F. They returned to ask him, What of this verse, *The Mighty One, God, the Lord, speaks and summons the earth* (Psalm 50: 1)? He asked them, Is speak (pl.) written? Rather *speaks and summons* (both sing.) is written.
> His disciples said to him, Rabbi, those you pushed off with but a straw, what shall you answer us?
> He answered them, The three are but one name, like one who says: craftsman, builder, architect.

Our Rabbi is approached by a group of heretics with an apparent Trinitarian testimony in hand. What could be better proof of the threefold nature of God than an Old Testament verse listing three differing names for God? Our Rabbi rejects the verse as proof, for it carries singular verbs. This apparently satisfies the heretics, who do not bother to argue that one God with three natures could well employ a singular verb.

The disciples are less pleased with this answer, and say so – the Rabbi has pushed them away with but a straw. The disciples expect a better answer, a private one that perhaps could not be made in public, especially to heretics.[14] How may one refute the Trinitarian testimony? By dismissing the import of the proof-text; the three are but one name. If this satisfies the disciples, the Rabbi has had his little joke on them, for his example offers another trinity in its place: craftsman, builder, architect. These are terms used in the Rabbinic academy to refer to God as creator;[15] they surely should satisfy the heretics as terms appropriate to the Trinity. So, the disciples are pacified by an answer which, if offered to the *minim* would

---

[14] See D. Daube, "Public Retort and Private Explanation," *The New Testament and Rabbinic Judaism* (London: Athlone Press, 1956), pp. 141–150. Our text is briefly mentioned on p. 142.

[15] See, e. g., Gen. R. 1: 1.

have been initially seized upon as yet another proof. No teacher appreciates it when his debate with heretics is characterized by his pupils as mere straw. Our Rabbi will have his revenge on his insistent disciples when it dawns on them later that his answer was no answer at all.

The middle dialogue (E.) of the three follows much the same pattern. The heretics ask about a verse with the same triple set of names for God and are dismissed with a singular verb. The students object and are mollified by the explanation that the three names refer but to one God, much like the three names for the one Emperor which regularly appeared together on inscriptions. Again, the students have been satisfied by an explanation that leaves the trinity intact and explicates it by invoking royal formula similar to those invoked by the Sages in their parables about God. As in the case considered above, this explanation should at first blush have been taken as a proof by the *minim* had our Rabbi offered it in their presence. Presumably, as before, the aggressive students who demanded a better explanation will realize only too late that they have been had. The text:

> E. They returned to ask him, What of this verse, *The mighty One, God, the Lord! The Mighty One, God, the Lord! He knows* (Joshua 22: 22). He answered them, It is not written, They know (pl.), but rather, *He knows.*
> His disciples said to him, Rabbi, you pushed those off with but a straw, what will you answer us?
> He told them, The three are but one name, like one who says: *Basileus, Kaisar, Augustus.*

The last segment of this group of three (D.) contains the quotation from 1 Corinthians 11: 11. At its simplest level, the response seems to indicate that when God says *Let us make man in our image, after our likeness* (Genesis 1: 26), he is talking with Adam and Eve. Although their own creation did not follow the established pattern, from then onwards God, man and woman will all be equal partners in the creation of new humans.[16]

> D. They returned to ask him, What of this verse, *Let us make man in our image, after our likeness* (Genesis 1: 26). He answered them, It is not written, So God created (pl.) man in his image (pl.), but, *So God created (sing.) man in his own image* (Genesis 1: 27).
> His disciples said to him, Those you pushed off with but a straw, but what shall you answer us?
> He told them, In the past, Adam was created from the dust, while Eve was created from Adam. From Adam onward, *In our image, after our likeness* (Genesis 1: 26); it is impossible for there to be man independent of woman, nor is it possible for there to be woman independent of man, neither is it possible for both of them to be independent of the Shekinah.

---

[16] So D'Angelo, Segal, Jervell, Daube, Herford, et. al.

The pattern established above is followed here as well, though with certain exceptions. First, the verse invoked has both a plural verb (*let us make*) and plural objects (*our likeness, our image*). Second, though plural, the verse does not explicitly indicate a trinity, merely a plurality. In response to the first problem, our Rabbi does not point to a singular verb, as he has done in the other two cases. Instead, he offers a response which explicates the verse in order to solve the difficulty raised. This approach apparently (but see below) violates the rule suggested by R. Simlai (or R. Yohanan), that the appropriate response to heretics can be found by quoting a verse from the same Scriptural context. As for the second point, about the Trinity, we will see below that Genesis 1:26 had long been a Trinitarian testimony.

Our Rabbi has once more fooled his students. They wanted a better answer – he gave them a trinity (God, Adam, Eve).[17] As an even better joke, he sent them on their way ignorant of the fact that he had satisfied their rigor with a quote from the Apostle Paul.

V

One has to wonder what manner of Rabbi is willing to pull his students' legs by giving aid and comfort to heretics. We must wonder as well, just who these *minim* were, and what was the Trinity they offered testimonies about. A brief excursion into patristic literature will clarify these issues. I say this conscious of the fact that there was very little clarity about the Trinity in the works of the church fathers. Only during the late fourth and early fifth centuries (around the time of the redaction of the Palestinian Talmud) was any type of systematic discussion attempted. There was, therefore, a good deal of confusion, particularly about the status of the third member of the Trinity, the Holy Spirit.[18] Gregory of Nazianzus could thus admit in his Fifth Theological Oration that there were some members of the Church who kept to themselves the opinion that the Holy Spirit was, in fact, to be considered God.[19]

Despite all its confusion, there was a long exegetical tradition linking Genesis 1:26 to the members of the Trinity. As early as the 180's, Irenaeus gave the verse a Trinitarian reading. While he followed the Apostolic

---

[17] Already noted by Herford. A similar argument employing subject-verb agreement (in Greek) is offered from the Gospel of John by Hippolytus (ca. 225) in a debate with a monarchian. See R. Greer in J. Kugel and R. Greer, *Early Biblical Interpretation* (Philadelphia: Westminster, 1986) p. 186.

[18] For a brief summary of this very complex issue see J. N. D. Kelly, *Early Christian Creeds* (London: A. & C. Black, 1960, 2nd ed.), pp. 338–344.

[19] Oration 31, 5, "On the Holy Spirit." See Kelly, *Creeds*, p. 343.

Father, Barnabas, in understanding *Let us make* to be God talking to his Word or Son,[20] he also expanded this theology.

> For with Him were always present the Word and Wisdom, the Son and the Spirit, by whom and in whom, freely and spontaneously, He made all things, to whom also He speaks, saying, "Let us make ..."[21]

Irenaeus makes this point again by reading the plural of Genesis 1:26 as God talking to His hands. He explains,

> Now man is a mixed organization of soul and flesh, who was formed after the likeness of God, and moulded by His hands, that is by the Son and Holy Spirit, to whom also He said, "Let us make man."[22]

Later Christians maintained the assumption that God speaks to the other two members of the Trinity, but at the same time they retreated from explicitly associating the Holy Spirit with the actual creation itself. This seemed to give the Holy Spirit too much power. It was not at all clear that the Spirit should be considered a creator, or for that matter co-equal to the Father and Son as king and royal sovereign. This point was explicitly addressed in the creed of the council of Constantinople in 381 which sought to correct this apprehension about elevating the Spirit. So the creed instructs about the Holy Spirit, "Who with the Father and the Son is together worshipped and together glorified."[23]

I very much doubt that our Rabbi is making an attempt to bring the heretics he debates in line with the creed of Constantinople. Quite the contrary, we see by his taunting answer to his students that if one really wishes to get embroiled in debate about the Trinity, one must attack the heretics at the weak points of their belief. It is not enough merely to trot out Trinitarian testimonies, suggests our Rabbi; if one wishes to accept the divinity of the Trinity, then one must be prepared to accept the Holy Spirit as craftsman, builder and architect of the Universe. One must revere the Spirit as *Basileus, Kaisar, Augustus*. In the privacy of the academy, our Rabbi is not simply having a joke at his students' expense, he is instructing them to engage in *reductio ad absurdum* arguments with the heretics. If you wish to debate heretics, he tells them, then know the details of their beliefs and press them hardest where they are weakest.

---

[20] Barnabus 6:12, in a non-Trinitarian exegesis. Irenaeus, *Adv. haer.* V 15,4. See R. McL. Wilson, "The Early History of the Exegesis of Gen. 1:26," *Studia Patristica* 1 (1957), pp. 420–437. A complete bibliography of Patristic commentary to the verse is found in J. Lebreton, *Histoire du Dogme de la Trinité* (Paris: Gabriel Beauchesne, 1927) I 553, nn. 1–2.

[21] *Adv. haer.* IV 20,1. ET by A. Roberts and W.H. Rambaut (Edinburgh: T & T Clark, 1868).

[22] *Adv. haer.* IV pref. Cf. V 1,3.

[23] See Kelly, *Creeds*, p. 342.

Our Rabbi's active involvement in the anti-Trinitarian debate is even more explicitly revealed by his treatment of Genesis 1:26. He responded to the citation by quoting 1 Corinthians. Let us see how the contemporary church fathers understood these verses. In his work, *On The Trinity*, Augustine writes,

> The apostle says that the man is the image of God, and on that account removes the covering from his head, which he warns the woman to use, speaking thus: "For a man indeed ought not to cover his head, forasmuch as he is the image and glory of God; but the woman is the glory of the man." [1 Corinthians 11:7] What then shall we say to this? If the woman fills up the image of the trinity after the measure of her own person, why is the man still called that image after she has been taken out of his side? ... But we must notice how that which the apostle says, that not the woman but the man is the image of God, is not contrary to that which is written in Genesis, "God created man: in the image of God created He him; male and female created He them: and He blessed them." [Genesis 1:27–28] ... How then did the apostle tell us that the man is the image of God, and therefore he is forbidden to cover his head; but the woman is not so, and therefore is commanded to cover hers? ... The woman together with her own husband is the image of God, so that the whole substance may be one image; but when she is referred separately to her quality of help-meet, which regards the woman herself alone, then she is not the image of God; but as regards the man alone, he is the image of God as fully and completely as when the woman too is joined with him in one.[24]

Leaving Augustine's logic and male chauvinism aside, it should be clear that he specifically makes the connection between the 1 Corinthians passage as a whole and Genesis 1:26–28. If it is not clear from its position in the work, *On the Trinity*, that this juxtaposition of verses has bearing on Augustine's notion of the Trinity, let the following passage make the connection explicit.

> Let him believe in the Father, Son and Holy Spirit, one God, alone, great, omnipotent, good, just, merciful, Creator of all things visible and invisible ... Yet not that the Father Himself is both son and Holy Spirit, or whatever else each is singly called in relation to either of the others; as word, which is not said except of the Son, or gift, which is not said except of the Holy Spirit. On this account also they admit the plural number, as it is written in the Gospel, "I and, my Father are one." [John 10:30] ... Sometimes the meaning is altogether latent, as in Genesis [1:26]: "let us make man after our image and likeness." Both *let us make* and *our* is said in the plural, and ought not to be received except as of relatives ... And God is the Trinity. But because that image of God was not made altogether equal to Him, as being not born of Him, but created by Him ... there are some who draw this distinction, that they will have the Son to be the image, but man not to be the image, but "after the image." But the apostle

---

[24] Augustine, *On the Trinity* XII 7 (9–10), ET A. W. Haddan (Edinburgh: T & T Clark, 1873).

refutes them, saying, "For a man indeed ought not to cover his head, forasmuch as he is the image and glory of God." [1 Corinthians 11: 7][25]

Augustine seems to have linked the hierarchy found in 1 Corinthians 11: 7 (also in 1 Corinthians 11: 3, 8, 9) with Genesis 1: 26–28 in an attempt to define the Trinity. But what has all his talk about Adam and Eve in God's image to do with the Holy Spirit? An Eastern father, Gregory of Nazianzus, shows the importance of this hierarchy for a proper appreciation of the relationships within the Trinity.

> What was Adam? A creature of God. What then was Eve? A fragment of the creature. And what was Seth? The begotten of both. Does it then seem to you that Creature and Fragment and Begotten are the same thing? Of course it does not. But were not these persons consubstantial? Of course they were. Well then, here it is an acknowledged fact that different persons may have the same substance ... did not both Eve and Seth come from the one Adam? And were they both begotten by him? No; but the one was a fragment of him, and other was begotten by him. And yet the two were one and the same thing; both were human beings; no one will deny that. Will you then give up your contention against the Spirit, that He must be altogether begotten, or else cannot be consubstantial, or be God; and admit from human examples the possibility of our position?[26]

Gregory uses the hierarchic relationship of Adam to Eve to make a point about the relationship between God the Father and the Son. He then completes the analogy by likening the Spirit to the begotten of both, Seth. Augustine adapts this model, *mutatis mutandis*, when he cites 1 Corinthians 11: 7. The hierarchy of God, Man, Woman is like the relationship of Father, Son, Spirit. Just as Eve proceeds from God through Adam, so the Holy Spirit proceeds from the Father through the Son.[27]

Our Rabbi manifestly rejects this argument from Scripture. He is clearly aware that Genesis has two accounts: one hierarchic, the other egalitarian. He refers to the former explicitly when he says, "In the past, Adam was created from the dust, while Eve was created from Adam." By stating the proposition in these words he informs his students of his awareness that the account of creation found in Genesis 2 is employed by the church fathers to explicate the Trinity. He knows that there are those, like Augustine, who impose the relationship of Genesis 2 upon Genesis 1: 26. He signals this awareness not by quoting the appropriate Scriptural response from the context in Genesis, but by formulating his explication in language reminiscent of 1 Corinthians 11: 7–8, "[Man] is the image and glory of

---

[25] ibid., VII 6 (12).

[26] Gregory of Nazianzus, Fifth Theological Oration, "On the Holy Spirit," (Or. 31, 11), English translation in *A Select Library of Nicene and Post-Nicene Fathers* Cf. J. N. D. Kelly, *Early Christian Doctrines* (London: A & C. Black, 1968), 268.

[27] For the history of the "filioque" here cited, see Kelly, *Creeds*, pp. 358–367.

God; but woman is the glory of man. For man was not made from woman, but woman from man."

Although the heretics who tangled with our Rabbi may only have known Genesis 1:26 as a Trinitarian testimony, the importance of setting out this series of Scriptural models for the relationship of the three members of the Trinity was clear to the church fathers. The subtle distinctions in the relationships served to define the role of the Holy Spirit as divine, yet proceeding from the Father through the Son. To return to Gregory's model, the Spirit is begotten yet not in the same sense as the Son is begotten.

> If He is Unbegotten, there are two Unoriginates. If He is Begotten, you must make a further subdivision. He is so either by the Father or by the Son. And, if by the Father, there are two sons and they are brothers ... But if by the Son, then such a one will say, we get a glimpse of a Grandson God, than which nothing could be more absurd.[28]

Our Rabbi of the Palestinian Talmud knew just how absurd this would seem. In rejecting the testimony from Genesis 1:26, he was demolishing an intricately assembled Trinitarian theology. He was sensitive to the adaptation of the Genesis 2 hierarchy in 1 Corinthians 11:7-8 and to its use in the Trinitarian argument. When the heretics quoted Genesis to him as a Trinitarian testimony, our Rabbi recognized the unspoken argument from 1 Corinthians 11:7. As in the other two cases, he refuted a Scriptural argument using the maxim attributed to R. Simlai, "Every place that the heretics rend [a verse from context to make their point] has the appropriate [textual] response right next to it." In this instance, however, he did not answer by pointing to a singular verb in the Hebrew text but by quoting 1 Corinthians 11:11, a verse that absolutely contradicts the sense of the earlier verses in that chapter. Just as Genesis has an egalitarian account of creation as well as the hierarchical one from which the Trinitarian argument had been advanced, so does Paul. Just as the egalitarian model from Genesis can be used to undermine Scriptural proof of the relationship between the Holy Spirit and the other members of the Trinity, so too, may the verses of Paul.[29]

> In the Lord woman is not independent of man nor man of woman; for as woman was made from man, so man is now born of woman. And all things are from God. Judge for yourselves.
>
> 1 Corinthians 11:11-13

---

[28] Gregory of Nazianzus, Or. 31, 7.

[29] This essay was written during my tenure as a Visiting Fellow of Clare Hall, University of Cambridge and as a Visiting Scholar at the Oxford Centre for Post-Graduate Hebrew Studies. A generous grant from the Abbell Publication Fund of the Jewish Theological Seminary of America supported the research. Thanks to Prof. Shaye J.D. Cohen for his suggestions.

Overturning the Lamp

I

'And these', he says, 'slander one another with dreadful and unspeakable words of abuse.'[1] Celsus, at least as Origen records him, does not report the insults that the Christian sectarians traded. In the dual interests of dispassionate historigraphy and passionate gossip, however, it is worth our while to dredge through the mud of antiquity to learn just how and why it was slung. Abuse and slander are not unknown in our own day and though there is risk of anachronism one suspects that, as today, the historicity of the accusation is less important than the verisimilitude. Whether innuendo or outright attack is the means, tainting the opponent's reputation is the goal. The truthfulness of the slur is incidental. In fact, as we shall see, the slur itself often follows formulaic patterns, leaving one all the more dubious about the actual events.

Celsus is also to the point when he notes that the vile things that are repeated in whispers are said by Christians about one another. He neglects to mention, of course, that the pagans gleefully repeat and embellish the charges; a subject we shall return to later. In the meanwhile, what did they say about one another that was so shocking? Who said it about whom, and why?

In his First Apology,[2] Justin seems to be offering a defence of Christianity by deflecting a charge:

> We do not know whether they are guilty of those disgraceful and fabulous deeds, the upsetting of the lamp, promiscuous intercourse, and anthropophagy ...

Justin seems to be responding to three accusations by assuming they are aimed at the two groups of 'gnostics' about whom he is writing, the follow-

---

[1] Origen, *Contra Celsum* 5: 63 (ed. H. Chadwick [Cambridge, 1965] 313). Although neither author discusses the rabbinic evidence, for general background see Robert Wilken, *The Christians as the Romans Saw Them* (Yale, 1984), 17–21; Stephen Benko, *Vigilae Christianae* 21 (1967), 103–14; *idem, Aufstieg und Niedergang der Römischen Welt* II 23: 2 (1980), 1081–9; and now *idem, Pagan Rome and the Early Christians* (London, 1985), which was published after this essay was written.

[2] Justin, *1 Apol.* 26: 7.

ers of Simon and Marcion.[3] They are cannibals, they are sexual perverts, and they overturn the lamp. At least as Justin reports it the last charge seems to be independent of the first two, but all three are meant to be-smirch the 'gnostic' heretics. It is a simple matter to denigrate doctrinal deviance by accusations of other, more salacious forms of deviance.

Irenaeus makes the doctrinal distinction more explicit when he reports that certain women admitted to having engaged in promiscuous sex be-fore embracing orthodoxy. He goes further in his charges by linking the promiscuity to the actual practice of the non-orthodox church.[4] Elsewhere Irenaeus is more specific in charging the Nicolaitans with sexual abuses, 'the character of these men is plainly pointed out in the Apocalypse of John, as teaching that it is a matter of indifference to practice adultery.'[5]

Epiphanius runs riot with this report. Tracing these Nicolaitans to 'gnostic' groups of his own day, he offers his own 'first-hand' account:

> First, they have their women in common ... the man leaving his wife says to his own wife: 'Perform the *agape* with the brother. Then the unfortunates unite with each other, and as I am truly ashamed to say the shameful things that are being done by them ... nevertheless I will ... in order that I may cause in every way a horror in those who hear about their shameful practices. After they have had intercourse in the passion of fornication they raise their own blasphemy toward heaven. The woman and the man take the fluid of the emission of the man into their hands, they stand, turn toward heaven ... and they say: 'We offer to thee this gift, the body of Christ.' And then they eat it, their own ugliness ... similarly ... they gather the blood of menstruation of her uncleanness and eat it together and say: 'This is the blood of Christ.' ... and if ... the woman becomes pregnant ... they pull out the embryo ... they all come together, all this company of swine and dogs, and each communicates with the finger from the bruised child. After they have finished this cannibalism ... many other horrible things are done by them.[6]

It is no small thing to be engaged in a controversy about eucharist with Epiphanius. He is not shy about clubbing his opponents with a whole range of abuses, primarily sexual, although the charge of anthropophagy is included. That the disagreement is about eucharist is clear from the way he frames the deviances he reports. Epiphanius is careful to buttress his account with the claim that he personally witnessed this sexual deviance when certain women of the group tried to help him find salvation by the means he describes. Of course, the self-righteous Epiphanius resisted, giving glory to the God who helped him escape by quoting Exodus 14:1.

---

[3] Cf. Hippolytus, *Refut.* 6:14, where Simon's followers are accused of advocating promiscuous intercourse.

[4] Irenaeus, *Adv. Haer.* 1:6:3, cf. 1:13:3.

[5] Irenaeus, *Adv. Haer.* 1:26:3.

[6] Epiphanius, *Panarion 26:4–5 apud* Benko, *ANRW* 1085 and see especially *idem, VC* 109ff.

Similar charges were made in the Gnostic community well before Epiphanius. In the Pistis Sophia, 'Thomas said: "We have heard that there are some on the earth who take the male seed and the female monthly blood and make it into a lentil porridge and eat it ...".'[7] So too, the charge of eating menstrual blood and sperm dates back a few years earlier when it is found in the Second Book of Jeu.[8]

The last example in this parade of vile accusations may be attributed to Clement of Alexandria, who accuses the Carpocratians of sexual licentiousness after they overturn, or put away the lamp (*lumine amoto*).[9] In each of these cases cited, the accusers were Christians attacking others who were (at least as they defined themselves) also Christian. In each instance the accusers point to 'heretical' groups that are engaging in such bizarre behaviour. In some instances the finger-pointing is done to indict the so-called heresies with extra-doctrinal deviances. In other instances, the charges seem to deflect apparent pagan critiques of Christianity on to 'inauthentic' splinter groups.

Although no pagan accusations have survived Church censorship independently, they are represented in abundance in Patristic literature.[10] Athenagoras reports that Christians are charged with Thyestean feasts and Oedipodean intercourse, an accusation repeated by Eusebius who attributed the charges to slaves under torture during the Lyon riots in 177 C. E.[11]

Tertullian three times recalls these charges in his Apology:

> We are said to be the most criminal of men, on the score of our sacramental baby-killing and the baby-eating that goes with it and the incest that follows the banquet, where the dogs are our pimps in the dark, forsooth, and make a sort of decency for guilty lusts by overturning the lamps. That, at all events, is what you always say about us.

Or again, Tertullian quotes the charges levelled: '... add lampstands and lamps, a dog or two, and some sops to set the dogs tumbling the lamps over; above all you must come with your mother and sister ...' It is a charge he cannot ignore, as he fulminates against the injustice of it: 'Meanwhile, as you recline on your couch, reckon the places where your mother, your

---

[7] *Pistis Sophia* Ch. 147, see Benko, *VC* 112f. and *idem, ANRW* 1087.

[8] Ch. 43, see Benko, *ibid.*

[9] Clement, *Strom.* 3: 2: 10–16, cf. Benko, *ANRW* 1083; *idem, VC* 113; Wilken, 19.

[10] Wilken, 21, 'the accusations of promiscuity and ritual murder appear *only* in Christian authors. They are *not* present in the writings of pagan critics of Christianity.' The latter half of this statement is quite true, for the reason I have stated. The former half of the quote must be qualified based on the rabbinic reports cited below.

[11] Athenagoras, *Leg.* 3: 31f.; Eusebius, *HE* 5:1: 14f.; cf. *HE* 5: 1: 52, 5: 1: 26; Wilken, 19ff.; Benko, *ANRW* 1084 and see the sources cited there, n. 104.

sister, may be; make careful note so that, when the darkness of the dogs'
contriving shall fall, you can make no mistake ...'[12]

Tertullian's bitterness at these accusations is readily apparent. He reports only that these are pagan charges against Christianity; nowhere does
he seem aware that his colleagues are levelling the same accusations against
one another. The same is true of Minucius Felix, who states: 'The tall
story of incestuous banqueting is a lying concoction ... [of] ... your own
Fronto.' Minucius Felix places the slur in the mouth of his pagan adver-
sary, Q. Caecilius Natalis:

> Their form of feasting is notorious; it is in everyone's mouth, as testified by the
> speech of our friend of Cirta [viz. Fronto]. On the day appointed they gather
> at a banquet with all their children, sisters and mothers, people of either sex
> and every age. There, after full feasting, when the blood is heated and drink
> has inflamed the passions of incestuous lust, a dog which has been tied to a
> lamp is tempted by a morsel thrown beyond the range of his tether to bound
> forward with a rush. The tale-telling light is upset and extinguished, and in the
> shameless dark lustful embraces are indiscriminately exchanged; and all alike, if
> not in act, yet by complicity, are involved in incest ...[13]

These accounts all embellish the earliest reported accusation, whether by
pagans against Christians, or by Christians against those Christians with
whom they disagreed. In the last instances, Tertullian and Minucius Felix
have their pagan opponents offering detailed charges which, along with
their obvious functions, serve to explicate the obscure charge of overturning the lamp. No longer is it a separate offence, as in Justin, where doctrinal deviance is equated with sexual crimes. Apparently, especially outside
the Christian community, 'overturning the lamp' is understood merely to
abet the process of sexual deviance rather than be another accusation,
worthy of mention alongside cannibalism and incest.

II

Celsus, in the same passage in which he reports that the heretics 'slander
one another with dreadful and unspeakable words of abuse', offers his own
interpretation of the charges. 'They go astray in evil ways,' he explains,
'and wander about in great darkness more iniquitous and impure than
that of the revellers of Antinous in Egypt.'[14] Origen seems to bear this
charge in mind, along with an awareness of the more explicit indictments

---

[12] Tertullian, *Apol.* 7:1, 8:7, 8:3 (Loeb). Cf. the contemporary account of an overturned lamp in Lucian, *Convivium*, 46.

[13] Minucius Felix, *Oct.* 31:1–2, 9:6–7. See Wilken, 18f.; Benko, *VC* 113f.; *idem,
ANRW* 1082f., esp. n. 102, p. 1084.

[14] Origen, *Contra Celsum* 5:63 (Chadwick, 313).

catalogued above. He lays the blame for all the slander at the feet of his Palestinian neighbours, the Jews:

> [Celsus] seems to have behaved in much the same way as the Jews who, when the teaching of Christianity began to be proclaimed, spread abroad a malicious rumor about the gospel, to the effect that Christians sacrifice a child and partake of its flesh, and again that when the followers of the gospel want to do the works of darkness they turn out the light and each man has sexual intercourse with the first woman he meets. This malicious rumour some time ago unreasonably influenced a very large number and persuaded people knowing nothing of the gospel that this was really the character of Christians. And even now it still deceives some ...[15]

It is a startling thought that the origins of the blood-libel are here laid at the feet of the Jews themselves. Origen's charge is all the more disconcerting when we read the words of his Palestinian forerunner, Justin, talking to his Jew, Trypho: 'Have you also believed concerning us that we eat men; and that after the feast, having extinguished the light, we engage in promiscuous concubinage?'[16] Now it is not clear from Justin's words whether he is blaming the Jews for this calumny or merely wondering whether his Trypho has also heard the nasty rumours. In either case it is worth noting that both Justin and Origen, when speaking to or about Jews, recount the three-fold charges: cannibalism, overturning the lamp and promiscuous sex.

There is precious little from the Jewish literature of the period which speaks to these charges. This is partly due to censorship and partly due to a Jewish proclivity for ignoring Christianity in the hope that it would go away. None the less, there are occasional snatches of dialogue, particularly between rabbis and Jewish-Christians (whom the rabbis still considered quasi-Jews after a sort). One particular passage of rabbinic literature stands out for its negative attitude towards Jewish-Christians. It was redacted *en bloc* into the sixth-century midrash, Ecclesiastes Rabbah, beginning with a well known story about R. Eliezer's arrest on charges of being Christian and going on to tell the story of R. Ishmael and his nephew ben Dama. Apposite to our topic, the midrash continues:

> [A.] An incident once took place that a woman came to R. Eliezer to convert. She said to him, 'Rabbi, convert me.' He instructed her to recount her deeds. She reported, 'My younger son is from my older son.' He rebuked her [and dismissed her]. She went to R. Yehoshua who accepted her [for conversion]. His students asked, 'R. Eliezer drives her away and you accept her!?' He explained to them that from the moment she set her mind to convert she could no longer

---

[15] Origen, *ibid.* 6: 27 (Chadwick, 343 and n. 1 there for a full list of parallels to supplement the sampling offered above).

[16] Justin, *Dial. c. Trypho* 10. On whether Celsus knew Justin's work, see most recently G. Burke, *ZNW* 76: 1/2 (1985) 107–16.

be considered alive to the world, as it is said, *None who go to her* [viz. convert] *come back* (Prov. 2: 19); and if they revert [to their former habits], *nor do they regain the paths of life* (ibid.).

[B. In Aramaic] Hanina the nephew of R. Yehoshua went to Caphernaum where the heretics [*minai* – Jewish-Christians?] cast a spell upon him and set him riding upon a donkey on Shabbat. He went to his uncle, Yehoshua, who [uttered the cure for the spell] and placed some oil upon him [to complete the antidote] so he was healed. He told him, 'Since I've gotten mixed up with the [eucharistic?] wine of that evil one, I can no longer remain in the Land of Israel.' He went down to Babylonia and died there in peace.

[C. In Aramaic] One of R. Yonatan's students fled to them [the Jewish-Christians?]. He went and found that he had [indeed] become one of those evil ones. The heretics sent [a message to R. Yonatan], 'Rabbi, come share in deeds of loving-kindness for a bride.' He went and found them occupied [sexually] with a young woman. He exclaimed. 'This is the way Jews behave?!' They replied, 'Is it not written, *Throw in your lot among us, we will have one purse* (Prov. 1: 14)?' He fled and they hurried after him until he got to the door of his house and slammed it in their faces. They taunted him, 'R. Yonatan, R. Yonatan, go boast to your mother that you didn't turn and you didn't look at us. For had you turned and looked at us, you'd be chasing after us more than we have chased after you.'[17]

There is out in the open: charges of incest, magic, and wife-sharing levelled against heretics, probably Jewish-Christians, by the Jews. Story A, about the woman who wishes to convert, is not unlike the report of Irenaeus about the women who admitted to promiscuous sex before their 'conversion' to orthodoxy. Indeed, the account in C where R. Yonatan escaped from his would-be seducers reminds one of the story of poor Epiphanius' narrow escape from the 'salvation' offered to him by his gnostic lady-friends. As for the charge of magic spells and ointments, the following *pas-de-deux* of Origen and Celsus offers instruction.

After this he seems to me to do something like those who, because of their hostility to Christians, assert before those who know nothing whatever of the practices of Christians that they have found *by experience* that Christians eat the flesh of little children and indulge in unrestrained sexual intercourse with the women among them ... Similarly it would be found that Celsus' assertions are also lies when he affirmed that *he has seen among certain elders who were of our opinion books containing barbarian names of demons and magical formulas.*[18]

The charges are pro-forma. The truth of the assertions is incidental to the tarring of the 'heretical' opponents. If Celsus or some other pagan repeats

---

[17] *Eccl. Rabba* 1: 1: 8. The translation is my own, based on the enlightening notes and critical edition of Marc G. Hirschman, 'Midrash Qohelet Rabbah: Chapters 1–4: Commentary (Ch. 1) and Introduction', Ph. D. thesis, Jewish Theological Seminary of America, 1982.

[18] Origen, *Contra Celsum* 6: 40 (Chadwick, 355).

the charges, so much the worse for the Christian community. The essential matter is that in *both* the Jewish and Christian communities heretical groups are routinely accused of the kind of grisly deeds recorded above. However, despite Origen's (and perhaps Justin's) assertions to the contrary, the Jewish literature that does contain anti-Christian calumny nowhere mentions the charge of cannibalism or any type of blood-libel. Nor, at least thus far, are the Christians or Jewish-Christians accused of overturning the lamp.

III

Rabbi Eliezer and R. Joshua, mentioned in the rabbinic legends recounted above, flourished just a little less than a century before Celsus, in the nineties of the Common Era.[19] Stories about these two disciples of Rabban Yohanan ben Zakkai abound. They are, as it were, the saints of the Yavnean era, and their 'lives' are the stuff of which rabbinic hagiography is made. They, their circle of disciples and family, and their opponents are the subjects of dozens of exemplary tales. This story, found in the Babylonian Talmud, is about that circle and bears some relevance to our topic.

> Imma Shalom, the wife of R. Eliezer, was the sister of Rabban Gamaliel [II of Yavneh]. There was a certain [Christian?=] 'philosopher' in the neighbourhood who had the reputation of not taking bribes [when he sat as a magistrate]. They [Gamaliel and Imma Shalom] sought to fool him. She brought a gold lamp to him when she came before him. She said, 'I wish to divide my father's estate [so that I might claim a share for myself].' He said to them, 'Divide.' He [Gamaliel] responded, 'It is written in the Torah, "Where there is a son, a daughter may not inherit."' The 'philosopher' answered, 'From the day that you were exiled from your land, the Torah of Moses was taken away, and the Evangelium [Hebrew: *'awon gilayon*] given in its place. There it is written, "Son and daughter as one shall inherit."'
> The next day Rabban Gamaliel came back and brought him a Lybian donkey. The 'philosopher' then said, 'Let us turn to the end of the Evangelium, for there it is written, "I come not to take away from the Torah of Moses, I come but [other texts read: And I come not] to add." And there it is written, "Where there is a son, a daughter may not inherit."' She reminded him, 'May your light shine forth like a lamp.' But Rabban Gamaliel noted, 'The bushel-carrier has come and overturned the lamp.'[20]

---

[19] For Celsus' date see Chadwick, xxiv–xxviii.

[20] B. Shab. 116a–b. My translation follows the readings in Ms. Munich. For more on this passage see the relevant bibliography listed in E. E. Urbach, *Hazal* (Hebrew-Jerusalem, 1969), 269, n. 50, and more extensively in L. Wallach, *JBL* 60 (1941) 403–15. In the last line of the story I have freely translated the Aramaic term *hamra'* (lit. 'donkey') for the sake of the pun on Mt. 5: 15, explained below. It is necessary here to mention the

Only after reading the many passages above can we appreciate the full force of Rabban Gamaliel's jest. His indictment of the 'philosopher' is not merely for bribery. No, Gamaliel has most cleverly cast aspersions on the Christian's entire character – he overturns the lamp!

Readers familiar with the Gospel of Matthew will appreciate the Talmudic story-teller's acid wit all the more. Let us peruse Matthew 5: 14–17 to appreciate how thoroughly it has been satirized in the tale just recounted:

> (14:) You are the light of the world. A city set on a hill cannot be hid.
> (15:) Nor do men light a lamp and put it under a bushel, but on a stand, and it gives light to all in the house.
> (16:) Let your light so shine before men, that they may see your good works and give glory to your Father who is in heaven.
> (17:) Think not that I have come to abolish the law and the prophets; I have come not to abolish them but to fulfill them.

The extent of the Talmudic parody is awesome. Matthew 5: 17 is quoted with but little change; the Revised Standard Version's 'fulfill' is rather loosely rendered 'to add'. Matthew 5: 16 is offered (again somewhat loosely) by Imma Shalom as a reminder of her bribe. But the *coup de grace* is delivered by Rabban Gamaliel, for the Aramaic and Hebrew term 'donkey' (*ḥamra* in Aramaic, *ḥamor* in Hebrew – translated above as 'bushel-carrier') is very close to the Hebrew term for 'bushel' (*ḥomer*). This ingenious pun turns Matthew 5: 15 on its head – for now the lamp is beneath the bushel![21] And, recalling what we have established above, there is the added insult of the overturned lamp. Alas for Jesus' advice to his follow-

---

recent work of J. Maier, *Jesus in der talmudischen Überlieferung* (Darmstadt, 1978) and especially *Jüdische Auseinandersetzung mit dem Christentum in der Antike* (Darmstadt, 1982), pp. 78–93, 119. In the latter work (p. 93) Maier denies that the Imma Shalom passage relates to Matthew ('von einem NT-Zitat in b Sabb 116a–b keine Rede sein kann'), and in general plays down the anti-Christian polemic (he discusses the Ecclesiastes Rabbah passage on p. 119 where he focuses on the charge of ass-worship). It seems to me this approach completely ignores the manifest evidence. The bibliographies in both books, however, are quite thorough.

[21] The pun on Mt. 5: 15 and the parody on the broader context was recognized over a century ago and has been commented upon ever since, cf. Wallach and Urbach, above. I am little interested here in whether the phrases originate in a pre-Matthean *Sitz-im-Leben*; it is most likely they do, given the redactional history of the Sermon on the Mount. Nor am I interested in locating the logion in the Gospel to the Hebrews or among the Ebionites (see the not very successful attempts documented in Wallach). Most probably by the 90s of the first century the verses were known in more or less the same form as we have them today. I take the attributions to Gamaliel and Imma Shalom to be reasonable, given the other rabbinic material (cited above) which sets its stories in the same era. The Patristic material is somewhat later but, since my concern is not over who borrowed from whom, I would be equally satisfied accepting a later date for the redaction of the Talmudic story.

ers, 'that they may see your good works and give glory to your Father who is in heaven'.

IV

What, then, did it mean in antiquity when one was accused of overturning the lamp? From the evidence it seems it meant many things, but one suspects that they may be sorted into some sensible order. I would conjecture that at the earliest stage the phrase quite simply meant doing wrong, straying from the path. Matthew 5:15 is only one among dozens of verses in the Hebrew Bible and New Testament that invoke the imagery of lamp and light. The Torah is light and the commandments a lamp. Jesus is the light of the world. The Dead Sea sectarians were the children of light, and so on ad infinitum.[22] So, overturning the lamp meant plunging one's immediate world into darkness. It meant heresy. This helps us understand the nature of the threefold charge of cannibalism (preceded by ritual murder), sexual depravity and overturning the lamp. One is tempted to equate this list with the three 'cardinal sins' of rabbinic Judaism, those for which one should rather die than commit: spilling blood (let alone eating it!), incestuous sex and idolatry.

In due time, the phrase 'overturning the lamp' was taken rather literally. When this occurred, one could only conjecture as to its meaning. The simplest guess was to tie the phrase to the sexual activity. One overturned the lamp and then committed wrongful pleasures in the dark. By the time of Tertullian and Minucius Felix, even Christians assumed this to be the proper interpretation, an assumption shared by the pagans who are reported to have listed this among the 'crimes' of Christianity. What began as a charge of doctrinal deviance became an accusation of sexual deviance. In the rabbinic community the phrase had a somewhat different life.[23] On occasion, it could be taken quite literally and then referred to the extinguishing of lamps that was associated with mourning customs in the East.[24] But in the mouth of Rabban Gamaliel it was not only an innuendo about the general morality of his bribe-taking philosopher. 'Overturning the lamp' was an indictment against him for forgetting the words of his Master (Matthew 5:19):

---

[22] See the standard concordances to the Hebrew Bible, New Testament, Dead Sea Scrolls, and the Tannaitic and Patristic literatures. See, too, the rabbinic and Patristic commentaries to those biblical verses.

[23] An apocopated version of the story in b.Shab reported above is preserved in Sifre Numbers #131, j.Yoma 38c, LevRabba 21:9, PesDRK Aḥarei Mot (ed. Buber 177a), and PesDRK Eicha (ed. Buber 122b–123a). It is difficult to know whether the shorter or longer story is original. In either case the same explanation is offered for the phrase.

[24] See S. Lieberman, *Greek in Jewish Palestine* (New York, 1942) 103–6.

Whosoever then relaxes one of the least of these commandments and teaches men so, shall be called least in the kingdom of heaven; but he who does them and teaches them shall be called great in the kingdom of heaven.[25]

[25] My thanks to Drs. Geza Vermes and Sebastian Brock for the opportunity of discussing this paper in their graduate seminar on Problems of Jewish History and Literature at Oxford University. The paper was written during my tenure as a Visiting Fellow, Clare Hall, University of Cambridge and a Visiting Scholar, Oxford Centre for Postgraduate Hebrew Studies. The opportunity to visit these great centres of learning was afforded by a generous grant from the Abbell Publication Fund of the Jewish Theological Seminary of America.

Mary Maudlin Among the Rabbis

When Miriam stood at the banks of the Nile river to see what would become of her baby brother (Exodus 2: 4) she entered the guild of Israelite prophets. She was enshrined there forever when she took up her tambourine and led the Song at the Sea (Exodus 15: 20–21). From that day onward, generation after generation of Jewish parents, and then Christian parents in their turn, named their offspring after the prophet, in the hope that their daughters might take their places as sisters of their holy ancestor. Jewish Miriams and Christian Marys fill the pages of our sacred literatures, attesting to the hold which Miriam exerted in rabbinic Judaism and in nascent Christianity.

The Rabbis of the Babylonian Talmud flourished in the Sassanian Empire from the third through fifth centuries in a country roughly congruent with modern Iraq and ruled by Zoroastrian magi. Except for the gossip and rumors they heard from their colleagues in Palestine, they knew little of Roman or Byzantine Christianity. The local Christianity they might have known was decidedly different, centering in the capital city, Ctesiphon, and built around the Diatessaron and the myth of King Abgar and the apostle Addai.[1] When Babylonian sages spoke of Miriam/Mary it is worth our notice, for they may possibly bear testimony, however confused, to the still little known development of Christian religious thought in the East. Even if we cannot glimpse Mary or Christianity with any clarity, we can, at least better apprehend the Rabbis' own attitudes to Christianity and its saints.

Particular discussion of Mary Magdalene is difficult, since it is unclear whether she is mentioned in Babylonian rabbinic literature at all. This may be a case where the tighter the focus of investigation, the more fuzzy the figure appears, until she vanishes entirely. On the other hand, the sages of Babylonia may know her only too well as a saint of the Church and may

---

[1] W. Bauer, *Rechtgläubigkeit und Ketzerei im Ältesten Christentum* (Tübingen, 1964), ch. 1. And see, J. Neusner, *A History of the Jews in Babylonia* vol I. The Parthian Period (Leiden, 1969), app. 2, pp. 180–183, esp. n. 1. Finally, see my general remarks and notes on the interactions between the Syriac Church and the Rabbis in "Three Syriac Cruxes," *Journal of Jewish Studies* 42 (1991) 167–175.

have turned their male scorn upon her as another means of denigrating the weaker sister religion.

Mary Magdalene is mentioned, maybe, in three passages in the Talmud, the latter two being synoptic parallels of each other. The first passage, found at b. Hag 4b, is a good place to begin, for it avoids, perhaps, the biases of the other two passages which probably refer to Jesus. I translate the passage below, using parentheses to indicate the difficult Hebrew phrases which, not surprisingly, are the crux of this whole article. The brackets are my means of smoothing out the rough spots in the text:

> *Substance is swept away for lack of moderation* (Prov. 13: 23). Rav Yosef used to weep when he came to this verse of Scripture. He would ask, Was there ever a human who went [to death] before the alloted time?"
>
> Yes! [answers the anonymous Talmudic editor], There is the story of Rav Dimi[2] b. Abaye who used to visit with the Angel of Death.
>
> [Rav Dimi once saw] the Angel say to his messenger, Go, bring me Mary Magdalene (*miryam megadla neshaya*). The messenger went and brought him Mary the Nanny (*miryam megadla dardakey*).
>
> The Angel of Death said, I told you Mary Magdalene (*miryam megadla neshaya*)! He said, In that case, I'll return her.
>
> The A. of D. said, Since you've brought her, let her be counted [among the dead]

The entire passage is skewed by translating the hard part, *miryam megadla neshaya*, as Mary Magdalene. It sounds like that name if we jumble the Hebrew vowels a bit (*miryam* = Mary, *megadla* = Magdalene). But, this translation ignores the fact that each of the constituent Hebrew (or more properly, Aramaized) words has meaning, even if that meaning is not entirely certain. Before discussing the meaning and whether it refers to Mary Magdalene, let us examine the textual history of this Talmud passage to have a secure reading as the basis for further discussion.

Editions of the Babylonian Talmud printed in Franco-Germany (Ashkenaz), as well as most modern editions, all have a different text at this point. In place of *miryam megadla neshaya* those printed texts (where not entirely excised by Christian censors) read: *miryam megadla sey'ar neshaya* which means Miriam or Mary the hairdresser. It is also quoted this way in the other two places this Mary is mentioned in the Talmud (b. San. 67b, b. Shab. 104b).

By contrast, the extant fragments of the Sefardic printed text,[3] produced in Spain and Portugal in the years 1492–1497 – during the years of expulsion of the Jews from those countries by their Catholic monarchs – reads as reported above, *sans* the word *sey'ar*. The word for "hair" crept

---

[2] The texts are divided on the name of the Rabbi in question. Others read: Bibi. The latter was, indeed, a son of Abaye. See the *Jewish Encyclopedia* II, 620, s. v. Bebai b. Abaye. Rav Dimi was a colleague of Abaye's, see ibid. IV, 603, s. v. Dimi.

[3] *S'ridei Bavli* ed. H. Z. Dimitrovsky (New York, 1979), 263.

into the Ashkenazic (Franco-German) edition via the text of the commentator par excellence, Rabbi Solomon ben Isaac, a. k. a. Rashi (fl. 11th cent. Troyes). He explains the phrase, *miryam megadla neshaya* to mean: Mary the braider of women's hair (*sey'ar*). The hair went from Rashi's commentary into Ashkenazic texts, forever confusing an already bad pun on Magdalene (if it was ever meant to be one).

Miryam megadla neshaya is also attested in virtually every extant manuscript of the Babylonian Talmud[4] on this passage. The correct reading, then, of the text is: *miryam megadla neshaya*. Now we may turn to its meaning.

Miryam is Mary or Miriam, it is standardly so in Biblical literature, rabbinic literature, Syriac literature – all Semitic texts read Miriam and mean either the Prophetess, sister of Aaron (Ex. 15: 20), or any of the myriad of Marys of New Testament times. Confusions of Marys are not unknown to the Rabbis[5], nor is it beneath them to poke fun at Mary the Theotokos.[6] Their own tendency was exacerbated by a certain confusion of Mary Magdalene with Mary the Theotokos in the Syriac East.[7] This conflation of traditions was seized, perhaps, with some mischievous delight by the Rabbis. If Mary, never mind exactly which one, was so important to those Christians, she's a target for lampoon.

The last word in our phrase, *neshaya*, means women. It stands rather neatly in counterpoint to the other Mary's appelative: *megadla dardakey*, Nanny, or literally, child (*dardakey*) raiser.

Now on to *megadla*. The word can mean many things. As Rashi already informed us, it can mean hair-braider. Indeed, it has biblical Hebrew foundations for the definition: braider (Deut 22: 12 and I Kings 7: 17). Regretably, in every other use of the *GDL* root in the Bible (I'd guess at least 500 times) the verb means to raise up, make big. As in, Mary the child raiser, the Nanny who was meant to die in the Rav Dimi story.

Megadla neshaya means "raiser of women." What could it possibly mean that Mary, who was mistaken by the Angel of Death, was a raiser of women, as opposed to a raiser of children? I confess I have no clear idea. It is less than reassuring that Rashi couldn't even conceive "raiser

---

[4] ed. R. Rabbinovicz, *Variae Lectiones in Mischnam et Talmud Babylonicum* (reprint, New York, 1976), ad loc.; MS. London, Harl. 5508, MS. Göttingen 3; MS. München 095; MS. Vatican Ebr. 171, ad loc.

[5] See, e. g. B. Visotzky, "Most Tender and Fairest of Women: A Study in the Transmission of Aggada," *Harvard Theological Review* 76 (1983) 409, nn. 18–19.

[6] B. Visotzky, "Anti-Christian Polemic in Leviticus Rabbah," *Proceedings of the American Academy for Jewish Research* 56 (1990) 94–100.

[7] So Ephrem in both his commentary to the Diatessaron and his hymns. See R. Murray, *Symbols of Church and Kingdom: A Study in Early Syrian Tradition* (Cambridge, 1975) 146, n. 2. See, too, Raymond E. Brown, *The Gospel According to John XIII–XXI* (Garden City, N. Y., 1970), 904–905, esp. 981.

of women" to be the meaning of the meaning of the phrase and opted to make her a hairdresser.

With all the caution that comes with opposing Rashi's interpretation of any piece of the Babylonian Talmud, it is preferable that she be a raiser of women, because of the symmetrical antinomy set up with raiser of children. If this *was* the meaning of the phrase, given the Rabbis general track record on feminism, it may have had less than positive connotations. Still, it is not necessarily negative. So, one Mary is either a hairdresser or a raiser-of-women, while the other is a raiser-of-children (assuredly positive in rabbinic culture).

It is tempting to suggest that the raiser-of-children is somehow meant to be Mary the Theotokos, while the raiser-of-women is taken as Mary Magdalene (and maybe the Rabbis, too, confused her with the prositiute and the phrase should be rendered: Madame). But this is just idle speculation, particularly since there is another possible reading of the phrase *miryam megadla neshaya*.

In b. Kiddushin 49a the phrase *megodelet* is discussed. There, the Talmud suggests the word means "important," which would fit neatly with our passage. Our Mary would then be "Mary, Important among Women." I am, however, not the first to notice this possibility. Rashi is the one who gives us the meaning "important." His grandchildren, the Tosafists, perhaps noting that the Talmudic context is speaking of a slave-girl or a daughter, reject this definition for b. Kiddushin and quote the eleventh century Sefardic commentator Rabbenu Hannanel ben Hushiel of Kairwan in North Africa, explaining:

> *megadelet sey'ar*, a hair dresser, as in the Talmudic passage, *megadla sey'ar neshaya*.

The citation from Hannanel teaches us that either the Tosafists conflated Rashi's explanatory word *sey'ar* into Hannanel's text or that perhaps his Sefardic Talmudic text already read the way the late Ashkenazic printed texts read.

All of this philological confusion serves to justify, somewhat, translating the difficult phrase as a pun on the name Mary Magdalene rather than as Mary the hairdresser or Mary the raiser of women or Mary important among women. It is true that the inability to decide the meaning of a phrase does not give license to assume it was a pun. On the other hand, punsters are notorious for preferring paranomasia to lexicography. The laugh was as important as the message. The derision the laugh conveyed far more important than the fine points of theology that the passage, in fact, raises.[8]

---

[8] See E. E. Urbach, *HaZaL: Pirqei Emunot VeDe'ot* (Jerusalem, 1975) [Hebrew] 248.

One charming example of the Rabbis ability to use a pun effectively may be found in another passage of the Babylonian Talmud, tractate Shabbat 116a–b. There, the Rabbis are making fun of a local monk who served as a magistrate. While showing him suceptible to bribes and viciously parodying Matthew 5, the Rabbis have the monk quote from the Gospel, using the Greek word Evangelium, transcribed into Hebrew: *'awon gilayon.* Now, the transliteration of Evangelium into Hebrew seems to be dialectically accurate for the Greek of Palestine. But, it is no mere coincidence that the phrase translates as "scroll of sin."[9]

It is precisely this naughty penchant for punning and so, belittling one's opponents, that makes one think Mary Magdalene might be lurking here. Why then, we may ask, Mary M? Why not the other, more famous Mary the Theotokos, whom the Rabbis have elsewhere turned their nasty humor upon? Here, the confusion about Mary in Babylonia helps out. It made no difference which Mary; either was a good stand-in for a parody of Christianity. The possibility that one (Mary the child raiser = Theotokos) has been played off the other (Mary Magdalene) should not be dismissed, either. The Rabbis would have been delighted to add to the confusion of their enemies.

What's the joke, then? Why make the joke in a passage that refers to the Angel of Death making an error of judgment? Perhaps this was the Rabbis' way of insinuating that the Marys whom the Church venerates as saints and mothers-of-god are so unworthy as to be confused by the messenger of the Angel of Death. When the error is noticed, well never mind, leave well enough alone. Let them die before their time! A thought, no doubt, which had occurred to the Rabbis about Christianity itself.

Modern commentators have had their say about this passage of Talmud and it is worth introducing them, however briefly, to record that they are generally in agreement that Mary Magdalene is lampooned here.[10] If anything, they suggest, as I have above, that Mary Magdalene is confused with Mary the Theotokos.[11] One scholar goes so far as to suggest that all Marys were one and the same to the Rabbis. Mary the Theotokos is not only confused with Mary Magdalene, but also with that Mary sister

---

[9] See my discussion of the passage in "Overturning the Lamp," *Journal of Jewish Studies* 38 (1987) 78–79. See, too, H. Strack, *Jesus, die Häretiker und die Christen* (Leipzig, 1910), 19*–20*.

[10] Strack, *Jesus* 34*–37*, R. Travers Herford, *Christianity in Talmud and Midrash* (London, 1903), 40–43, S. Krauss, *Jewish Encyclopedia* VII 170–173, s. v. "Miriam the hairdresser," P. Billerbeck, *Kommentar zum Neuen Testament aus Talmud und Midrasch* (München, 1922) I 39, 147, 1046–47, J. Z. Lauterbach, "Jesus in the Talmud," *Rabbinic Essays* 530–531. The one exception is the apologist J. Maier, *Jesus von Nazareth in der Talmudischen Überlieferung* (Darmstadt, 1978) 240–243.

[11] Even Maier, 240, concurs with this.

of Martha (John 11:2) who, after all, wiped Jesus' feet with her hair – and this is what the text means when it refers to Mary, woman of long hair![12]

This near unanimity of modern scholars is buttressed in large part by the other two passages of Talmud which cite our *miryam megadla neshaya*. Since these passages apparently refer to Jesus, the linkage to Mary seems irrefutable. It is worth noting that every scholar who discusses these passages carries bias writ large. It is hard to enter this slough without some measure of despond.

Twice (b. Shab. 104b = b. San. 67a) the Rabbis see fit to discuss the parentage of a certain [Yeshu (= Jesus)] ben Stada. They open by identifying him as being a. k. a. ben Panthera. Then, as now, confusion about his identity reigns and the sage Rav Hisda opines that ben Panthera's mother had a paramour. Her husband was, in fact, Mr. Stada, but her lover was named Panthera.[13] Another anonymous opinion is cojoined that Stada was his mother rather than his father (from whom he normally would have received the appelative *ben*). His father, then, was Pappos ben Yehuda.[14] Finally, the opinion is offered:

His mother was *miryam megadla neshaya*.

Almost as an afterthought, the anonymous Talmudic editor adds (punning on the name Stada), "It's like we [in the town of] Pumbedita say: That one cuckolded (*satat da*) her husband."

If the "son" of the passage is Jesus, the implications are clear and ugly. They strike directly at the Christian doctrine of Virgin Birth by the Holy Spirit. Elsewhere in the rabbinic corpus the same ben Panthera is given his full name: Yeshu ben Panthera. The Talmud and midrashim are dotted with nasty little tales about ben Panthera or ben Stada, all of them referring to a deceiver, a magician, or a teacher who is quoted by a Jewish-Christian disciple.[15]

---

[12] Lauterbach, ibid.

[13] I. e. Panther, much like someone was Biff or Duke in the 1950's: A tough guy, a ruffian. It is a name associated with the Roman Army, found in graffitio throughout the Empire and cited in many places in Rabbinic literature as a sneer about Jesus' parentage. See D. Rokeah, "Ben Stada is ben Panthera," *Tarbiz* 39 (1969) [Hebrew] 9– 18. To which should be added the recent discussion of M. Hirschman, "Midrash Qohelet Rabbah," Ph. D. Thesis, JTSA, 1982 [Hebrew], p. 55, n. 413 and particularly the reference to S. Lieberman there.

[14] See b. Git 90a and Rashi, ad loc. But, the passage draws on an earlier tradition from T. Sota 5: 9. Lieberman, in his *Tosefta kifshutah* (New York, 1973) commentary, ad loc, emends the text to Yehuda ben Pappos, thus removing this particular gentleman from the current discussion.

[15] See the notes and references in Rokeah, op cit.

With very few exceptions, modern scholars take the b. Shab and the b. San. passages to be anti-Christian.[16] Even the medievals, in their more elliptical fashion (they feared Christian censors), agreed. Indeed, the Narbonnese Tosafists of the twelfth century write, commenting on the passage we examined from b. Hag 4b, above: "*Miryam megadla neshaya* lived in Second Temple times. She was the mother of So-and-So[17] as is explained in tractate Shabbat [viz. the passage we just saw]."

Rashi's grandson Rabbenu Tam (Jacob ben Meir) appears to disagree. But a close look at even his exegesis shows that he, too, allows that our Mary had something to do with Jesus:

> Ben Stada is not Jesus of Nazereth. For ben Stada, we say, lived in the days of Pappos ben Yehuda, who was of the same era as R. Aqiba. ... while Jesus lived in the time of Yehoshua ben Perahya, who lived a long time before R. Aqiba. Now if his mother was *Miryam megadla neshaya* ... it follows that she lived in the time of Rav Bibi [or Dimi, as above]. So, it must be a different *Miryam megadla neshaya*, or equally, the Angel of Death was telling that Rabbi about something that happened a long time ago.

If the A. of D. has a long memory, then Rabbenu Tam also admits of the possibility that our Mary is the mother of Jesus.

Now, if in this passage about parentage of Christ, Mary is identified with *Miryam megadla neshaya*, then the editors of the Talmud most probably assumed that she was the same lady about whom the Angel of Death made his *faux-pas* – Rabbenu Tam's care in the twelfth century to distinguish two such Marys notwithstanding. In other words, the late fifth century editors of the Talmud assumed *miryam megadla neshaya* was intimately connected with the life of Christ. The eleventh and twelfth century Talmudic commentators did the same – however cautious Christian censorship (and other more repressive measures) made them. Most twentieth century scholars share the opinion that this Mary is a Mary who knew Jesus.

Adding the Syriac's Church's confusion of Mary Magdalene with Mary the Theotokos to the confusion of the Rabbis about Mary leaves us with a polemical passage against Christianity. *Miryam megadla neshaya* took the Panther for a lover. The product of her adultery was Jesus. His legal father, maybe, was Stada – but even that name has a derogatory twist to it. It explains why in the story the messenger of the Angel of Death is ready to whisk her from among the living. It explains why the Angel of Death doesn't care about the confusion of Marys – the prevailing attitude seems to be – let them all be damned.

---

[16] See n. 10. The exception, again, is Maier, who consistently refuses to find anti-Christian polemic in rabbinic literature.

[17] It looks like the Christian censor was at work here, substituting So-and-So (*peloni*) for the name Jesus (*Yeshu*).

Among the Rabbis of the Babylonian Talmud, Mary had a certain notoriety. They used her name, even as they confused one Mary with another, to denigrate Christianity's holiest doctrines. Regrettably, this is a passage that exposes the Rabbis as intolerant, misogynistic anti-Christians. It is the hope of this Rabbi, engaging in scholarly discourse on the Miriamic procession, that Jews and Christians both may grow beyond this type of interreligious polemic. Would that the next step in the procession be that we might recognize those things which unite us as sister religions, distinct yet related, and so give honor to our prophetic ancestor who stood at the banks of the River Nile.[18]

---

[18] Thanks to Richard Kalmin, David Kraemer, and the editors of this volume for their helpful comments on earlier drafts of this essay. Thanks to the Abbell Research Fund, for their continued support of my scholarship.

Anti-Christian Polemic in Leviticus Rabbah

By the time Leviticus Rabbah (LR) reached its final literary redaction,[1] the Land of Israel in which it was composed had become a Christian Holy Land.[2] The rabbis of the many synagogues found throughout the Land of Israel[3] could no longer afford to ignore Christianity in the hopes that

[1] The text: *Midrash Wayyikra Rabbah*, ed. M. Margulies (Jerusalem, 1972). A variety of studies have been done on LR, generally dating it to the fifth through sixth centuries. Basic bibliography: M. Margulies, "Introduction, *op. cit.*, H. Albeck, *"Midrash Vayikra Rabbah," Louis Ginzberg Jubilee Volume*, eds. S. Lieberman, et al. (New York, 1946) Hebrew volume 25–43, J. Heinemann, "Profile of a Midrash," *Journal of the American Academy of Religion* 39 (1971) 141–50, idem, "Leviticus Rabbah," *Encyclopaedia Judaica* (Jerusalem, 1972) 11: 147–50, J. Neusner, *Judaism and Scripture* (Chicago, 1986). On the literary quality of LR see R. Sarason, "Toward a New Agendum," *Studies ... in Memory of J. Heinemann* (Jerusalem, 1981) 55–73, N. Cohen, "Leviticus Rabbah Par. 3," *Jewish Quarterly Review* 72 (1981) 18–31, idem, "Structure and Editing," *AJS Review* 6 (1981) 1–20, D. Stern, "Midrash and the Language of Exegesis," in *Midrash and Literature*, eds. G. Hartman and S. Budick (New Haven, 1986) 105–24.
I am much taken with the suggestion of my student, Rabbi Robert Kasman, who sees two redactive stages in LR's literary history, one for the *petihta* materials and a second, later stage, for the final redaction with the *gufa* materials. On *petihta* see: J. Heinemann, "Proem," *Scripta Hierosolymitana* 22 (1971) 100–22, R. Sarason, "The Petihtot in LR," *Journal of Jewish Studies* 33 (1982) 557–67, P. Schäfer, "Die Petichta," *Kairos* 3 (1970) 216–19, A. Shinan, "On the Petihta," *Jerusalem Studies in Hebrew Literature* 1 (1981) 133–43 [Hebrew], M. Jaffee, "The Midrashic Proem," *Approaches to Ancient Judaism*, ed. W. S. Green (Chico, 1983) 4: 95–112, M. Bregman, "Circular Proems," *Studies ... in Memory of J. Heinemann* 34–51 [Hebrew], H. Fox, "Circular Proem," *Proceedings of the American Academy for Jewish Research* 49 (1982) 1–31. On *gufa*, along with the above, see A. Goldberg, "On the term *gufa* in LR," *Leshonenu* 38 (1974) 163–69 [Hebrew].
Following the assumption of two redactors and hints in Shinan and Goldberg I am tempted to see the term *gufa* as meaning something like, 'Now we've finished the *petihta* material on the opening verse of the chapter, let us turn to midrashim relating to verses in the body of the lection (*gufa shel parashah*).
[2] On the "Christianization" of Palestine in the 5th–6th centuries see, most recently, R. Wilken, "Byzantine Palestine: A Christian Holy Land," *Biblical Archeologist* 51 (1988) 214–17, 233–37.
[3] Assuming there is some relationship between these synagogal leaders and the sages of rabbinic literature. See the prudent warnings in S. J. D. Cohen, "Epigraphical Rabbis," *JQR* 72 (1981–82) 1–17. For the wide distribution of synagogues see, e. g., the surveys of Palestinian synagogues in L. I. Levine, *Ancient Synagogues Revealed* (Jerusalem, 1981), H. Shanks, *Judaism in Stone* (New York, 1979), M. Chiat, *Handbook of Synagogue Architecture* (Chico, 1982), idem, "Ancient Synagogues in Erez Yisrael," *Conservative*

the heresy would go away – they had, instead, to confront Christianity as the Imperial religion. The confrontation with such a power was careful, subtle, and often took the form of indirect polemic. Rabbis, cautious of delators and fearful of both legal and mob reprisals,[4] used homily and sermon as their means of combating Christian pretensions to exclusivity of religion in the Empire.[5]

A number of rabbinic texts preserve either fragments of actual sermons or, more securely, literary redactions of rabbinic homilies which polemi-cize against Christianity. Among the encyclopediac chains of materials collected in Midrash Ecclesiastes Rabbah[6] is an entire entry, if you will, under the heading of *minut*.[7] The Yerushalmi Berakhot 9:1 collects anti-Christian materials beginning with an extended anti-Trinitarian polemic[8] and ending with a series of *patron* texts each of which includes a form of death (crucifixion, drowning, burning and exposure to wild animals [in the arena]) associated with Christian martyrdom. In a more scattered form there are anti-Christian polemics dotted throughout Genesis Rabbah and other Palestinian Midrashim.[9]

Turning to LR, a coherently edited, literarily redacted, selfconscious midrash qua book, one might possibly expect to find anti-Christian polemic in some format of note – either an entire chapter devoted to the theme or a structural component (viz. a given *petihta* or a section of *gufa* in each chapter) devoted to the topic. There is a motif which compares Israel to the gentiles and there are other scattered texts which might, if stretched, be construed as relating to Christianity or even as anti-Christian in character.[10] Nevertheless, only five segments of LR discernably qual-

---

[4] See J. Parkes, *The Conflict of the Church and the Synagogue* (New York, reprint 1969), M. Simon, *Verus Israel* (Paris, 1964), chapter 8, esp. 264–74.

[5] The subtlety of these responses is not sufficiently appreciated even now, for sermons and literary homilies require social historical exegesis to illuminate the varied veiled allusions, winks and nods. See, e. g., my "Hillel, Hieronymus and Praetextatus," *Journal of the Ancient Near East Society* 16–17 (1984–85) 217–24.

[6] Ed. M. Hirschman, Ph. D. dissertation, JTSA, 1982. The characterization of Ec-clesiastes Rabbah as encyclopediac chains of materials is suggested by Hirschman, "The Greek Fathers and the Aggada on Ecclesiastes: Formats of Exegesis in Late Antiquity," *HUCA* 59 (1988) 155.

[7] See my treatment of this segment in "Overturning the Lamp," *JJS* 38 (1987) 72–80, esp. 76–77.

[8] J. Ber 9:1 (12d–13a). See my "Trinitarian Testimonies," *Union Seminary Quarterly Review* 42 (1988) 73–85. The *patron* texts merit separate treatment.

[9] See R. Travers Herford, *Christianity in Talmud and Midrash* (London, 1903) *passim*, which remains a useful collection. One can point to clusters of texts in the Babylonian Talmud, as well, but its provenance puts it beyond the boundaries of this essay. See, H. Strack, *Jesus, die Häretiker und die Christen* (Leipzig, 1910).

[10] Israel compared with gentiles: LR 1:12, 1:13, 1:14 (?), 5:7, 13:2. LR 1:5 carries a phrase with a parallel in Lk 14:7–11, but is more likely a text about Hellenistic etiquette

ify as anti-Christian polemic. Even these are not without methodological problems.

I

The first of these texts I will discuss exemplifies the methodological difficulties in treating a rabbinic text as necessarily anti-Christian.[11] LR 6: 6 contends that Be'erah[12] prophesied two verses which, insufficient for separate publication, were included among the prophesies of Isaiah (8: 19–20): *Now should people say to you, "Inquire of the ghosts and familiar spirits that chirp and moan; for a people may inquire of its divine beings – of the dead on behalf of the living – for instruction and message," surely, for one who speaks thus there shall be no dawn.*
LR comments:

Of the dead on behalf of the living, R. Levi said: [This is like the case of] one who lost his child and went to inquire about him among the graves [by means of necromancy]. A wiseacre who was there asked him, 'Your son whom you lost, is he dead or alive?'
He said, 'Alive.'
The other said, 'You cosmic fool! It is the way of the dead that one makes inquiry about them among the living – do the quick have need, then, of the dead?'
Thus our God lives and endures for all eternity ... while the god[s] of the gentiles is [are?] dead. Thus is it written, *They have mouths, but cannot speak, eyes, but cannot see; they have ears, but cannot hear* ... (Ps. 115: 5–6) – they are dead! Shall we abandon the Eternal One and bow to the dead? ...

---

than one related to Christianity. LR 6: 5 offers an angel appearing in the guise of Moses to bring salvation, raising the possibility of parody on Church debate about docetism; but given the large number of angelic appearances in worldly guise, the anti-docetistic angle is remote. LR 23: 5 contains a geography enumerating Jewish towns and their nearby rival centers, many of which are Christian. It is offered in a context of coming redemption (the rival towns will perish in fire), but carries no further barb than the remark that the Jews are "like a lily among thorns" (Song 2: 2). LR 13: 3 carries the news of a new Torah in messianic times – of interest not only for the permission to eat behemoth and leviathan, but for its use in anti-*Jewish* polemic by medieval disputants such as Raymundo Martini. LR 29: 1 offers one of the many rabbinic versions of the twelve hours of Adam and Eve, a text which seems to be in dialogue with Christian versions of the same, see L. Ginzberg, *Legends of the Jews* 5: 106, n. 97. LR's version, however, is not particularly apposite to anti-Christian dialogue. Finally, LR 3: 2 and 5: 3 refer to the Ten Tribes, probably Jewish-Christians. See my "Prolegomenon to the Study of Jewish-Christianities in Rabbinic Literature," *AJS Review* 14 (1989), 47–70.
[11] These pitfalls are commonly violated, e. g. by Herford with his assumption that any *minut* text must be considered anti-Christian.
[12] See Margulies' comments, *ad loc* on the reading of this name, apparently to be identified with the Reubenite chieftain of 1 Chron. 5: 6.

R. Shimon b. Laqish said, 'If this [dead god] cannot shed any light upon himself, how shall he shed light upon others?'

R. Abba b. Kahana said, 'Darkness and gloom pervade this world, but not chaos and emptiness. Where will they pervade [the world in the messianic future]? In the great city of Rome ...

One is tempted to see anti-Christian polemic here for a variety of reasons. First there is the confusion whether the "son" is dead or alive – an apt way for a Jew to view the paradox of crucifixion and resurrection. Second is the sneering question about the value of looking to the dead (i. e. a crucified god who could not even help himself) for assistance. Third, there may be an allusion to the Christian custom of congregating in cemeteries at the graves of martyrs, seeking their intercession.[13] Fourth, Resh Laqish seems to be poking fun at Jesus' statement in Mt. 5:14, "You are the light of the world," and repeated statements in the gospels that Jesus, himself, is the Light.[14] Finally, there is Abba bar Kahana's hope that chaos and emptiness will befall (new?) Rome – capital city of Christianity.

This reading is particularly tempting given the fifth to sixth century redaction date of LR. Treating the document as a redacted whole pushes one to interpret Rome as Christian and religious polemics as anti-Christian rather than anti-pagan.[15] But redactive date is a necessary but not sufficient cause for the interpretation of anti-Christian polemic. In the instance above Rome could easily be pagan, dead gods be pagan gods, the cemeteries pagan cemeteries. In fact, this latter reading would have LR offering a reasonably accurate exegesis of the two verses of Isaiah – for surely neither Isaiah nor Be'erah was speaking of Christianity. In fact, it need not even be the case that Rabbi Levi or Rabbi Abba bar Kahana were speaking of Christianity; both rabbis flourished before the Empire became Christian, ca. 300 C. E. And paganism, while no longer flourishing, persisted probably as late as the first redaction of LR, say late fourth to early fifth century C. E.[16]

When reading between the lines of a midrash looking for anti-Christian polemic, more specific evidences should be brought to bear than redactive date alone. The rabbis often may be responding to a hot issue in the

---

[13] See Peter Brown, *The Cult of the Saints* (Chicago, 1981) *passim*.

[14] E. g. John 1: 4–9, 3: 19–20, and esp. 9: 5.

[15] These are the assumptions which inform J. Neusner's readings of the polemic materials in Genesis Rabbah and Leviticus Rabbah conveniently summarized in his *What is Midrash?* (Philadelphia, 1987) 45–67.

[16] For the possibility of two redactors see above, n. 1. For the persistence of paganism, see S. Dill, *Roman Society in the Last Century of the Western Empire* (reprint, 1958[2]), H. Bloch, "The Pagan Revival in the West at the End of the Fourth Century," in *Paganism and Christianity in the Fourth Century*, ed. A. Momigliano (Oxford, 1963). For more detail and bibliography on the era, see my notes in "Hillel, Hieronymus and Praetextatus" (n. 5, above).

Church. Where the rabbis perceive a weakness in Christian dogma, it is there they will attack. When the rabbis find an issue of the Church to be patently absurd in their eyes, it is then they will engage in parody and *reductio ad absurdum* argument. When the rabbis feel the weakness of a Christian position, it is then that they will thrust and parry in an attempt to drive their opponents off the mark. Thus do they seek to convince their synagogue audience (or readership) of the foolishness of Imperial Christianity and to reinforce their sense of the basic rightness of rabbinic religion.[17] Only careful study of contemporary Christianity can adequately illuminate the targets of otherwise obscure rabbinic polemic.

II

In some cases, the rabbis take up the gauntlet of Christian argument and respond to exegeses of Hebrew Scripture which attempt to justify Church practice or dogma. A case in point is LR 25:6, where the sages relate a series of texts about circumcision and priesthood to the meeting between Abraham and Melchizedek recounted in Genesis 14. Now the Melchizedek narrative of Genesis and mention of Melchizedek in Psalm 110 had already been put to use in Christian argument as early as the Epistle to the Hebrews. There, however, the argument pertained to Christ as high priest who serves to replace the Aaronides and the Law. In the Talmudic/Patristic period both the Hebrew Bible text and the Hebrews verses were offered as proof of the validity of a gentile Christian priesthood meant to replace the Jewish community (which annoyingly persisted even after destruction of the priestly cult) in service to God.

The rabbis respond quite simply, Melchizedek is not proof of the validity of gentile Christian priesthood. *Au contraire*, the Genesis and Psalms mentions of Melchizedek prove that a priesthood once vested among all the nations now resides solely among the properly circumcised offspring of Abraham.[18]

III

There is another instance in LR where the rabbis seem to be responding to Christian polemic against the Jews. Before offering exegesis of the passage

[17] I attempt to demonstrate this tendency in "Trinitarian Testimonies" and "Overturning the Lamp."

[18] R. Travers Herford already recognized the polemical nature of the text in *Christianity in Talmud and Midrash* 338−40. He, however, assumes the polemic to be directed against either gnostics or the community of the Epistle to the Hebrews. The patristic side of the argument is admirably detailed in M. Simon, *Verus Israel*, 110−111, nn. 3−5, 1−4. Simon's annotation of patristic and secondary bibliography obviates the need for extended discussion here.

one must note, however, that the section of LR in which the text is redacted (LR 27: 8) is among those the Midrash shares with Pesikta deRab Kahana. Since the relationship of these two texts remains unclear,[19] it follows that the polemic may not be viewed with absolute security as the anti-Christian polemic of LR. In any event, it certainly belongs to LR at its final redaction and so, merits inspection here.

> The nations of the world deride Israel and say, 'You made the [Golden] Calf.' So God checked into the matter and found it groundless … rather it was the sojourners (*gerim*) who came out of Egypt with the Jews [who made the Golden Calf], *Moreover a mixed multitude went up with them* (Ex. 12: 38). They made the Calf and then derided Israel saying, *This is your god, O Israel* (Ex. 32: 8).

Here the argument seems to be: those would-be Israelites, those Johnny-come-latelies, they who seek the benefits of redemption without the hardships of enslavement – they are idolaters. Further, they seek to ensnare the Jews: they entice Israel to worship their hand-made and false god.

The apologetic offered here is surprising, for the *peshat* of the biblical text seems to justify the accusation of the nations; the Israelites *did* make the Golden Calf. What is at stake here, however, is not simple blame laying about the Calf, but a rather complex patristic argument by which the making of the Calf is seen to be a crime, the punishment for which is the commandments (beyond the Ten Commandments). This ingenious argument at one blow explains the Church to be True Israel obligated only to perform the Ten Commandments, while false Israel, those idolaters, are disciplined for their sin with six hundred thirteen commandments.

This Christian argument is most fully presented in the Didascalia Apostolorum Syriacae (DA), a Syriac (viz. Aramaic) translation of a Greek ecclesiastical tract (originating in a community with a law-observant Jewish-Christian presence) which enjoyed wide circulation in the Eastern Empire in the late third and early fourth centuries. As it is explained in the DA, Chapter 26:

> The Second Legislation was imposed for the making of the calf and for idolatry. But you [Christians] through baptism have been set free from idolatry, and from the Second Legislation, which was (imposed) on account of idols, you have been released.

Or again, citing the first part of Ex. 32: 8 (the same verse with which LR concludes its response) DA argues:

---

[19] The relationship of these midrashim is explored in Albeck, 36–39, Margulies xiii, J. Neusner, "The Priority of LR over Pesikta Derab Kahana," *PAAJR* 54 (1987) 141–68, J. Heinemann, "Chapters of LR with Dubious Sources." *Tarbiz* 37 (1968) 339–54 [Hebrew], A. Goldberg, responding to Heinemann, *Tarbiz* 38 (1969) 184–5 [Hebrew]. Three basic permutations are found among scholars on the relationship of these texts: 1) LR borrows from PRK, 2) PRK borrows from LR, 3) Both share a common source. My own guess wavers between 1 and 3.

Him they denied and said: We have no god to go before us; *and they made them a molten calf and worshipped it* and sacrificed to a graven image.

Therefore the Lord was angry; and in His hot anger ... He bound them with the Second Legislation, and laid heavy burdens upon them, and a hard yoke upon their neck.

DA concludes its diatribe against Law observance (presumably in its own community, but this was an argument which equally explained the error of the Jews):

Everyone who strives to be under the [second] Legislation becomes guilty of calf-worship; for the Second Legislation was imposed for nothing else but idolatry.[20]

True Israel which is the Church, runs the argument, need only observe the Ten Commandments,

The Law then consists of the Ten Words and the Judgments which God spoke before the people made the calf and served idols ... So then the Law is easy and light ... But when the people denied God ... He bound them with the Second Legislation.[21]

The Jews prove themselves untrue calf-worshippers by virtue of their observance of all the commandments.

It is to this argument from the Church that LR responds. God finds the Jews blameless and the blame, instead, is put upon the would-be-Israelites who serve a false God and seek to entice the Jews into the same error.

IV

The DA offers occasion for another polemic of LR. In the same chapter that links the sin of the Golden Calf to the Second Legislation and posits that the Church need only observe the Ten Commandments, the DA expounds,

For whereas He spoke the Ten Words, He signified Jesus: for Ten represents Yod; but Yod is the beginning of the name of Jesus. Now concerning the Law the Lord testifies in David saying thus: *The law of the Lord is without blemish, and converting souls* (Ps. 18 [19]: 8).

The relationship of Jesus to the Ten Words is explained further,

[Jesus] does not undo the Law, but teaches what is the Law and what the Second Legislation. For He said thus: *I am not come to undo the law, nor the prophets, but to fulfil them* (Mt. 5: 17). The Law therefore is indissoluble; but the Second

---

[20] *Didascalia Apostolorum Syriacae* Ch. 26, trans. R. H. Connolly (Oxford, 1929) 224, 222, 232. Syriac texts in P. de LaGarde, *Didascalia* (Leipzig, 1854) 108ff., and more recently, A. Voöbus, *CSCO* 1979 (with an English translation). For more information on the date, provenance and diffusion of DA, see the introductions to these volumes.

[21] DA 26, Connolly 218–22.

Legislation is temporary, and is dissoluble. Now the Law consists of the Ten Words and the Judgments to which Jesus bore witness and said thus: *One Yod letter shall not pass away from the Law* (Mt. 5: 18). Now it is the Yod which passes not away from the Law, even that which may be known from the Law itself through the Ten Words, which is the name of Jesus.[22]

Here again, an ingenious exegesis is offered to justify Christian observance of only the Ten Commandments while ignoring the remainder of the Torah, at the same time explicating the otherwise mysterious words of Jesus in Mt. 5: 17–18.[23] *Yod* is the Ten Commandments, but concomitantly *gematria* yields *Yod* for Jesus. The latter, as it were, fulfils the former, validating the Ten Commandments while pointing to the passing nature of the other commandments. Thus a New Testament (*kaine diatheke*) may replace the Old, while *Yod*, which is both Jesus and the Ten Commandments, persists.

LR will have none of this argument. Using Solomon as the archtypal son-of-David, the Midrash laces into the exegetic mentality offered by the DA to justify the antinomian tendencies of its community in the name of that other son-of-David.[24]

R. Alexandri b. Agri and R. Alexandri Keroba[25] said, 'If all the nations[26] of the world gathered to whiten the wing of a crow they could not do so. So too, if all the nations of the world gathered to uproot one word from the Torah they could not do so.' From whom do you learn this? From King Solomon who tried to uproot a word from the Torah and a prosecutor arose against him. Who prosecuted him? R. Yehuda ben Levi said, 'The *Yod* of *yarbeh* (Dt. 17: 17) prosecuted him.'
R. Shimon ben Yohai recited: The book of Deuteronomy (lit. Second Legislation) arose and bowed before the Holy, praised be He, and said: Master of the Universe, Solomon would uproot me and so render me fraudulent (Gk. *plaster*)

[22] DA 26, Connolly 216–18.
[23] These verses were continually bothersome to non-Law-observant (viz. Great Church) Christians. See, for instance, Origen's equally ingenious explanation of Mt. 5: 18 to mean that Jesus sanctions allegorical interpretation of Scripture, *Philocalia* II 3–4, *Comm. in 1 Ps.* translated and discussed in my "Jots and Tittles: On Scriptural Interpretation in Rabbinic and Patristic Literatures," *Prooftexts* 8 (1988) 265 and n. 44, p. 269.
[24] See Mt. 1: 1 and the comments of Raymond E. Brown, *Birth of the Messiah* (Garden City, 1979) 57– 95. Jesus is regularly characterized as David's son in Syriac sources, see, e. g. Ephraem Syrus, *Hymns on the Nativity*, Hymn IV, "David's son and Mary's Lord," *Nicene and Post-Nicene Fathers*, Second Series, vol. 13 (New York, 1905) 236. This text is discussed in more detail below.
[25] Keroba is probably a functional title for a liturgical poet, see Margulies' notes *ad loc*, LR 19: 2 (pp. 419ff.). The Midrash has parallels in Song of Songs Rabbah 5: 11 (which is borrowed from LR, see Margulies' note to LR 19: 1, p. 412) and in J. San 2: 6 (20c) (which seems to be an expanded and glossed version of our LR text). Other, later parallels are noted in Margulies, *ad loc*.
[26] Following the readings in the ed. princ. and the 13th century Ms. Paris 149. Parallelism also favors the reading.

– for any testament (Gk. *diatheke*) from which even two or three items have
been nullified is entirely null – behold Solomon is trying to uproot the *Yod* from
me ... The Holy, praised be He said: Go on with you! Solomon and a hundred
like him will be null and void [not even] a *Yod* of yours will ever be nullified.

LR argues, let the son-of-David and all who pretend to be like him try
though they might, not one letter of the law is dissoluble. The gentiles
can try to uproot as many *Yods* as they wish – but the Testament they are
proposing is null and void for it has dissolved too many commandments.
God reassures the Jews: don't mind them, they are null and void, your
Torah is here for keeps and will not be replaced.

V

Not all polemic is over the issue of *Verus Israel* or even competing exegeses
of Scripture for varying dogmatic purposes. There were occasions when the
dogmatic exegesis offered seemed so patently absurd to the sages that rather
than debate they wickedly parodied Church doctrine. This was particularly
so when the rabbis knew that the doctrine did not find universal assent in
the Church. What could be more delightful to a polemicist than to find a
wedge to drive between the otherwise closed ranks of the opposition?

One such issue was the Church doctrine of original sin. As early as
the mid-third century this doctrine found a home in Christianity, particularly in North Africa. Though, for instance, Tertullian defends the
notion of free will against the likes of the heretic Marcion, he nevertheless takes account of the involvement of all mankind in the sin of Adam.[27]
This involvement was articulated clearly by Tertullian's successor, Cyprian,
who writes that the Saviour came to heal the wounds received by Adam.
Baptism, he argues, "cleanses us from the stain of primeval contagion."[28]
Cyprian offers proof that original sin is passed on from Adam to successive
generations through intercourse when he cites testimony from Psalm 50: 5
(LXX): *Behold I was conceived in iniquity, and in sin did my mother bear
me.*[29]

Given the rabbinic propensity for proclaiming human responsibility and
freedom of will, it is all the more surprising to find LR unconsciously
echoing Cyprian's proof of original sin when it declares,

---

[27] *C. Marc.* 1: 22, *de carn. Chr.*, 16. Here and for Cyprian, I depend on J. N. D. Kelly,
Early Christian Doctrines (New York, 1960²) 175–77. For a general overview which also
takes account (though ahistoric) of the rabbinic teachings on the subject, see Fredrick
R. Tennant, *The Sources of the Doctrines of the Fall and Original Sin* (New York, 1903,
rpnt. 1968). More recently, following a similar format, Samuel S. Cohon, "Original Sin,"
HUCA 21 (1948) 275–330.

[28] Cyprian, *De op. et eleem.* 1, *De hab. virg.* 23.

[29] *Test.* 3: 54. For dating this document to the mid-third century, see J. Quasten,
Patrology (Westminster, Md., reprint 1986) 2: 363.

Behold I was conceived in iniquity, and in sin did my mother bear me (Ps. 51:7). R. Aha said, *Iniquity* is written *plene*. [The extra letter *vav* teaches us] even the most pious is not without some sin.[30]

This apparent rabbinic foray into the thickets of original sin must be seen in the broader context of Christian doctrine and resultant anti-Christian polemic. By the fifth century original sin had finally replaced free will in doctrinal discussion. This was fueled by the Pelagian controversy in which the British free will advocate found his views on Adam and Eve attacked by none less than Augustine and Jerome.[31]   Since Pelagius had visited Palestine and Jerome lived there, and since the bishop of Hippo's letters and writings were widely circulated in Palestine, it may be surmised that even Jews had heard of the controversy regarding free will and original sin.[32]   This only serves to make LR's declaration seem more disturbing; one would expect a midrash to support the Pelagian stand for free will and oppose the doctrinal proofs for original sin.

The solution to this apparent conundrum may be found in another aspect of Christian doctrine, beginning in the Syriac and Greek East as early as the fourth century and reaching full flower by the sixth century – Mariology. Mary was increasingly venerated in the Eastern Church, as intercessor, protectress and as Mother-of-God.[33]   This last idea, Mary as Mother-of-God, *Theotokos*, must have been seized upon in equal measure by Jews and Christians. The Christians found it a solace, a source of hope, a miracle; while the Jews found it an absurdity, a theological impossibility, a source of parody.

The Church elevated Mary and particularly expanded the New Testament accounts of her virginity. Not only was Jesus conceived while Mary was yet a virgin, but it became a point of (debated) doctrine that Mary remained a perpetual virgin.[34]   Proklos, bishop of Constantinople, writing in the early fifth century complains that "some persons, Jews in particular, had questioned the virgin birth and the perpetual virginity of Mary."[35] Ephraem Syrus also complains, "For my pure conception of thee wicked

---

[30] LR 14:5. The last word of the LR quote, "sin," is found in the ed. princ. Margulies' text simply reads, "not without some." Ms. Munich (and the 'Aruch) read: "some abomination," while the Oxford Mss. read, "lust."

[31] Augustine, e.g. *Ad marcellinum, Ad Timasium et Jacobum contra Pelagium, De gratia Christi et de peccato originali contra Pelagium et Coelestium*, etc. Jerome, *Dialogus adversus Pelaginos*. See now, Elaine Pagels, *Adam, Eve and the Serpent* (New York, 1988).

[32] I hope on another occasion to consider Judaizing tendencies in Pelagianism.

[33] See, e.g., A. Cameron, "The Theotokos in Sixth-Century Constantinople," *Journal of Theological Studies* 29 (1978) 79–108. For the fullest treatment and bibliography of Mariology, see M. O'Carroll, C.S.Sp., *Theotokos: A Theological Encyclopedia of the Blessed Virgin Mary* (Wilmington, 1983).

[34] See *Theotokos ... Encyclopedia*, s.v. Virginity of Mary, 356–62.

[35] Procl. *Or. II de Incarn.* PG 65:696, cf. *Or. IV* PG 65:713, quoted in T.E. Gregory, "The Remarkable Christmas Homily of Kyros Panopolites," *GRBS* 16 (1975) 322.

men have slandered me."[36] Ephraem is aware of the potential absurdity
of his Mariology, for he writes, "who would not marvel, at Mary, David's
daughter, – bearing an infant and her virginity kept."[37]

Ephraem may have had an even higher conception of Mary than perpetual virgin. He writes, "The young girl that carried Him prophesied saying
... I am without spot for thee." Again, he writes of Jesus, "Certainly you
alone and your Mother are from every aspect completely beautiful, for
there is no blemish in thee, my Lord, and no stain in thy Mother."[38] What
Ephraem may already be hinting at here is not simply perpetual virginity,
but a different aspect of Mariology, immaculate conception. If Mary was
to be Theotokos, how could she bear God while carrying the stain of original sin? On the other hand, if original sin is to be transmitted through
generation to all mankind, how could Mary be free of the stain?

That there be no doubt that Mary's pure status was tied to the doctrine
of original sin is made clear when Augustine addresses Pelagius. Everyone
suffers sin, says Augustine, "except the holy Virgin Mary, about whom,
for the honor of the Lord, I want there to be no question when sin is
mentioned."[39] In Mary rests the paradox of original sin – everyone has it
but for she who was born immaculate. Mother-of-God, perpetual virgin,
protectress and intercessor, Mary was the focus of speculation, debate
and prayer throughout the Eastern Empire from the fourth through sixth
centuries.

One last comment on Mary before we turn to see what all of this has
to do with the anti-Christian polemic of LR. As stated above, Mary was
perceived to be immaculate, without sin, and as a concomitant in Christian
theology, perpetually virginal. This gave rise to a certain amount of speculation on just how the miracle of her begetting Jesus through the Holy
Spirit actually occurred. I cite but one example, from a sermon of the
early fifth century bishop of Constantinople, Proklos, mentioned above.
He refers to Mary as "the only bridge for men to God ... the workshop
of the union of natures." As far as her conception, "the Word entered
in through obedience (lit. through hearing) and took upon himself humanity." More explicitly commenting on Mary's virginity both pre- and
post-partum, Proklos writes,

As God he did not cleave the portal of virginity, but went out from his mother
just as he had come in *through hearing*. Thus he was born as he was conceived.[40]

---

[36] Ephraem, *Hymns on the Nativity* IV (Nicene and Post-Nicene Fathers, 236).

[37] Ibid, *Hymn* XIV (251).

[38] Ibid, *Hymn* VI (239), Nisbene Hymn in *CSCO* 218: 61, 219: 76.

[39] This remains a statement which is debated; see, *Theotokos ... Encyclopedia*, s. v.
Immaculate Conception, 180, n. 4.

[40] Proklos, ed. E. Schwartz, *Acta Conciliorum Oecumenicorum* I 1 pt. 1 (Berlin,
Leipzig, 1927) 103– 107, and in PG 65: 679–92. The quotes here *apud* T. E. Gregory,

Given Proklos' extreme notion of Mary's conception of Jesus in defense of her virginity, it is no wonder he complained, "that some persons ... had questioned ... the perpetual virginity of Mary."[41]

For the rabbis all this brouhaha was just too much. Original sin was offense enough to their anthropology and theology, but notions like the immaculate conception, virgin birth, and impregnation through the Holy Spirit (in various body parts!) begged for their response. They answered in an attempt to argue *reductio ad absurdum*. In order to attack a Mariology which had even within the Church engendered debate, the rabbis, for but a brief rhetorical moment, took up the banner of universal sin.

> *Behold I was conceived in iniquity, and in sin did my mother bear me* (Ps. 51: 7). R. Aha said, *Iniquity* is written *plene* [the extra letter *vav* teaches us] even the most pious is not without some sin. For so[42] David said to the Holy, praised by He, 'Master of all worlds, it wasn't father Jesse's intention to have me, he was only interested in his own [sexual] needs. Know that this is so for when they were having sex one turned one way while the other turned in the opposite direction [so achieving coitus interruptus]. It was You who inserted each and every drop [of semen and inseminated my mother].' This is [the meaning of] what David said, *Though my father and mother abandon me, the Lord will gather me in* (Ps. 27: 10).

As we saw above, David and the Davidic family stand in both rabbinic and Christian literature for the would-be-Davidide, Christ. Here, LR 14: 5 puts the anti-Mary parody into Jesus' own mouth. First it is established that no one is immaculate, everyone (even Mary) is besmirched with sin. Then we are told that the Davidic mother and father − presumably Joseph and Mary − had sex for pleasure and performed coitus interruptus to avoid conception. Whether or not the rabbis considered this a sin the point is clear, Mary was no virgin. And as far as the Holy Spirit was concerned, the only role played in begetting Jesus was that of artificial inseminator, carefully gathering up father's sperm from one side of the bed and delivering it safely to mother on the other side. No worse, at least, a conception than Proklos' notion.[43]

---

op. cit. The ambiguous "through hearing" could be translated "through obedience" or "through the ear." The latter, more literal translation, gained favor in Marian circles as time went on.

[41] Quoted in full above, n. 35.

[42] Following the readings of the Oxford and Munich Mss. See above, n. 30, for more textual information. See also n. 27, above for more bibliography on the rabbis' attitudes toward original sin.

[43] I acknowledge the tenuous nature of this translation and interpretation. Some texts (Ms. Oxford, ed. princ.) read "After they had sex," which presumes a less efficient form of contraception. Yet even this reading demands that Jesse and his wife were having sex for pleasure rather than for procreation. One could understand this Midrash as a reaction to the rabbinic opinion that *Jesse* was without sin, see B. Shab 55b = B. BB 17a (and cf. Targ. Isa. 14: 29). One must also note that the rabbis have otherwise parodied

This vulgar parody at once savages many elements of doctrinal debate in the Church in the fifth and sixth centuries. Original sin, immaculate conception, virgin birth and begetting by the Holy Spirit are ribaldly reduced to the crudest possible plot. There is no room for theology here, only scorn.

VI

A variety of anti-Christian polemics scattered through LR has been explicated: 1) the futility of what Christians would call theology of the cross (LR 6: 6); 2) the baselessness of the gentile claim to priesthood (LR 25: 6); 3) the false accusations about idolatry centering around the Golden Calf and the consequences of these charges for the binding power of the Law (LR 27: 8); 4) the concomitant futility of anyone − even a Davidide − to obviate the Law or turn the Torah into an Old Testament (*diatheke*) (LR 19: 2), and 5) the absurdity of Mariology as it developed within the doctrinal context of original sin (LR 14: 5).

Each of these polemics betrays a sophisticated knowledge of the currents of Christian theology and doctrinal debate in Palestine of the fifth and sixth centuries. Christianity was not a mere straw man for the rabbinic apologist-darshan; it was a contemporary challenge met by powerful rhetoric aimed at the weakest points of nascent Christian doctrine. The futility of Imperial Christianity was exposed in the typically unsystematic fashion of the sages; only when occasion demanded did the midrashist respond. On the whole, however, the redactor of LR felt more constrained to get on with the work of his positive program of imagining Judaism for the coming centuries.

In conclusion it must be emphasized that the positive program took the vast majority of the redactor's interest. Relatively little securely identifiable anti-Christian polemic can be found in LR. For our darshan, Jews and Judaism continued to hold center stage in the unfolding of history in the Land of Israel.

Jesus' birth with their stock of Pandera legends, see Eccles. Rabba 1: 1: 8 (ed. Hirschman [n. 6 above] commentary to chapter 1, line 413, with a full bibliography on the name and legends). However, only the full background of the development of Mariology and the doctrines of original sin offered in this reconstruction afford a context for necessarily viewing the LR text as an anti-Christian polemic.

My thanks to Ms. Susan Lazev for research assistance on this essay.

Text, Translation, Targum*

When the English translator of Flaubert's *Madame Bovary* rendered for the
sake of her audience "bumblebees" in place of the French for "bright green
beetles," Vladimir Nabokov told his undergraduates, "Oh those ignoble,
treacherous, and philistine translators!" Such pedantry may be forgiven a
man who was equally comfortable in English, French and Russian from
his earliest childhood, for even Nabokov's frustrations with translation
are instructive. When the master himself tried translation he left a version
of Pushkin's *Eugene Onegin* that is positively ponderous in its cleverness
and shines primarily through Nabokov's epic commentary. It is worth
comparing Nabokov's technique with that of another English speaking
Russian translator.

When D. M. Thomas set his hand to Pushkin, the result was less literal,
far less clever, and delightfully Pushkin. In his novels, homages to Pushkin
and his Russian compatriots, Thomas went even further. The intensity of
The White Hotel and the shimmering brilliance of *Ararat* render a Pushkin
who never existed, but by alternating prose and poetry Thomas brings to
life the Russian culture that produced Pushkin, who in his turn, gave us
Eugene Onegin. D. M. Thomas cannot be said in these instances to be a
translator, treacherous or otherwise. What he has been in some sense is a
targumist.

Targum was produced in a trilingual society which knew its canonical
text very well, much like Nabokov's emigré Russia. The targumists of
the local synagogues of Palestine faced a decision of whether to follow
the school, as it were, of Nabokov or Thomas every Shabbat. Some were

---

* Review of: Michael Klein, *Geniza Manuscripts of Palestinian Targum to the Pentateuch*, 2 volumes. Hebrew Union College Press: Cincinnati, 1986, vol. 1: li + 363 pp.
vol. 2: 131 pp. + 182 plates. Daniel J. Harrington. S. J. and Anthony J. Saldarini, trans.,
Targum Jonathan of the Former Prophets (The Aramaic Bible vol. 10) [Project director: Martin McNamara, M. S. C., editors: Kevin Cathcart, Michael Maher, M.S.C., M.
McNamara, M. S. C., editorial consultants: D. J. Harrington, S. J., Bernard Grossfeld].
Michael Glazier, Inc.: Wilmington, Del., 1987, x + 320 pp. Bruce D. Chilton. *The Isa-
iah Targum* (The Aramaic Bible, vol. 11). Michael Glazier, 1987, lvii + 130 pp. Robert
Hayward. *The Targum of Jeremiah* (The Aramaic Bible, vol. 12). Michael Glazier, 1987,
xviii + 206 pp. Samson H. Levey. *The Targum of Ezekiel* (The Aramaic Bible, vol. 13).
Michael Glazier, 1987, xii + 145 pp.

pedantically literal, clever and wholly uninspired. Some heard the echoes of Sinai in the Text and translated with an artistry which was revelatory. Targum was spontaneous, live performance. Targum was offered in part as prayer and occasionally as acrostic poetry. Targum was a weekly interaction with a congregation, with the Torah, and with God. It was an artistry inspired by the God of all muses. And, as with most great literature written under the muse, much of Targum is lost to us.

We are fortunate that a substantial corpus of the Targum literature survives. Indeed, an explosion of text, translations and studies in Targum during the last half-decade prompts this review article. The five volumes considered here represent the most recent efforts in editions and translations of targumic materials while recent studies will be noted below.

The Targums, as Avigdor Shinan has repeatedly pointed out, are a mother lode of folk-religion, theology and rhetorical style, serving as the nexus of the rabbinic academy with *hoi polloi* of the Palestinian synagogues. These interests dovetail with the plethora of studies already in place on the philology, lexicography and linguistics of the Targums. The availability of so much new material by way of new editions and translations opens a window to students of literature for persual and analysis.

Why such a sudden interest in Targum? Above and beyond the expansion of Jewish studies in recent decades, Targum study seems to have come out of the necessary obscurity of its Aramaic closet. Jewish scholars are taking advantage of the ever increasing availability of Geniza manuscripts to publish, translate and analyze targumic texts. But it must be pointed out that four of the five texts listed above, viz. the translations of the Targums, are being published by a Catholic publishing house.

Interest in Targums by Christian, and especially Catholic scholars is a natural part of the long process of the search for the historical Jesus. The reasoning is remarkably simple. Jesus lived in the Galilee and Jerusalem in the first century. People spoke Aramaic there. It is assumed by these scholars that Jesus spoke Aramaic, the language of the Targums. Hence, targumic study leads one to recover the language, thoughts and general *Weltanschauung* of Jesus.

There are certain difficulties with this theory: all extant ancient gospels are Greek and it is perhaps as likely that Jesus spoke Greek (even Hebrew) as Aramaic. Further, the Targums translated in the Glazier series represent a range of Aramaic dialects from Babylonia to Palestine, and carry a probable dating at least a century if not as much as eight centuries after the crucifixion. Finally, it must be remembered that the world of ideas found in the Targums are a watered down version of rabbinic (and therefore late) theology held captive to the necessity of translating the biblical text (even loosely) in a synagogal-lectionary and live setting.

The possibility of recapturing some shred of the language of Jesus remains great enough, however, for a Catholic publishing house to print twenty volumes of Targum at a total cost of approximately one thousand dollars to readers in their quest for this Aramaic grail. The seductiveness of finding Jesus alive in the Targum may be observed by reading the titles of the scholarly works of Glazier's project director, Martin McNamara, *The New Testament and the Palestinian Targum to the Pentatuech* (1966) and a more recent version, *Targum and Testament* (1972). Despite the terribly careful scholarship which marks these works as worthy of study, Tertullian's question, "What has Athens to do with Jerusalem?" echoes hollowly in this admixture of disciplines.

Translator Robert Hayward introduces the text on Jeremiah with the admission that the text is known to belong in a setting of school and synagogue from the fourth century and afterward. Nonetheless he concludes that "the origins of Targum Jeremiah [are] in ... Israel [sic] during, or slightly before, the first century A.D. [sic]" (p. 38). Bruce Chilton writes in his Isaiah volume (p. xi) "I had been working with the document for some time, in connection with my study of Jesus' preaching ..." This fact is attested to by his book, *A Galilean Rabbi and His Bible. Jesus' Use of the Interpreted Scripture of His Time: Good News Studies 8* (Michael Glazier, 1984), also published in England with the subtitle, *Jesus' Own Interpretation of Isaiah* (London, Society for the Promotion of Christian Knowledge, 1984). Chilton makes his case for the inspired nature of Jesus' interpretations even in this Targum volume when he misreads the status of the targumist as follows, "when the meturgeman speaks in the name of the prophet, his innovations show he does so with almost prophetic authority" (p. xiii). This may be interpreted so in order to show "the importance of the Targum for the study of Early Judaism and the NT" (p. xxv), but I am at a loss to see how Chilton's characterization of the inspired meturgeman has anything to do with the artist-translator, clever though he may have been, mentioned so often in rabbinic literature.

Despite his disagreement with the methodological flaws that led to the publication of The Aramaic Bible, the translations themselves are always reliable and at best, first-rate. The translators are extremely careful and, on the whole, pretty good Aramaists. The only flaws are in subtleties which even the best versed translator might gloss over, but which one might expect to find mentioned in the otherwise useful apparatus and notes in each volume.

One piquant example will suffice. Harrington and Saldarini confront the Targum to Judges 16:1 (MT reads: *isha zona*) *itta pundakeyta,* rendering correctly, "a prostitute." But this misses the subtlety of a word borrowed from the Greek, which even Marcus Jastrow caught in his dictionary (s. v.), "keeper of a public house, harlot." Elsewhere in rabbinic literature a form

of this Greek term more loosely means "delicatessen" or better, "pub."
There is real humor here if one recalls that the Targum's phrase describes
the biblical heroine Rahab, whom the rabbis tell us can cause ejaculation by
mere mention of her name (b. Taanit 5b). But, when one compares this jest
with the late first-century Church document (1 Clement 12) which teaches,
"for her ... *hospitality* Rahab the harlot was saved," we see that we are on to
something in this targumic tradition. Though the Church text concludes
"that all who believe and hope on God shall have redemption through
the blood of the Lord," it's a fair bet we're dealing with a very early
midrashic tradition. The Targum here is either reproducing it innocently
or reacting to the Church's adaptation of the legend. No doubt, the
current translators will see this as evidence of an early layer of Targum
text, dating back at least to First Clement, and perhaps they would be
correct. In any case, one might expect this kind of discussion in the notes
to the translation.

It must be emphasized, especially to the non-Aramaist, that these are
scrupulous translations. Readers will be assisted by the provision of an
English translation of the Masoretic text in the notes to the translation and
by the setting of targumic additions to that text in Italic typeface. Those
looking for the radical departures from the Masoretic text often associated
with Targum will be disappointed with the selections discussed thus far.
The Targums to the Prophets tend to be reasonably straightforward translations of the biblical text with only minor or subtle variations. This will
no doubt also be the case for the four volumes of Onkelos translations of
the Pentateuch by Bernard Grossfeld, announced by Glazier.

The Targum of Ezekiel is less literal, particularly because of the long-
standing associations of the opening chapter of Ezekiel with rabbinic mysticism. The opening of Ezekiel poses special problems for any translator,
Aramaic or otherwise. Here, the Glazier series is well served by the copi-
ous annotation and careful translation of Samson Levey. His familiarity
with rabbinic sources and his wariness of losing his readers to the confusion of the Merkaba lead him to write notes which are full of references.
These enable the reader to get behind the Targum by learning the expanded midrashic traditions it alludes to. The keen renderings of Aramaic
are aided by Levey's clever emendations of often obscure Aramaic texts,
a lovely example being his treatment of Ezek. 1: 14 in translation, apparatus and notes. The Aramaic text reads *ke'anapa' 'eyna' lemiḥeze,* which
Levey, following a manuscript variant, emends *ke'agapa'.* He essentially
keeps both readings in his translation "like the eye seeing a bird on the
wing," rendering an otherwise obscure text reasonably intelligently while
preserving the integrity of the variant manuscript traditions.

Levey, too, falls prey to the temptation of very early dating. Though
he suggests that the final redaction of the Targum to the Prophets belongs

in the time of Saadia Gaon, in the tenth century, he can still write that his Targum to Ezekiel "bears evidence of the redactive hand of Rabban Yohanan ben Zakkai at Yavneh [viz. first century CE]" (Introduction, p. 2). It seems everyone in the Glazier series who knows that the targumic tradition dates back before Christianity concludes that the extant Targums necessarily must in some way reflect that dating. While this insistence surely helped Glazier in its decision to publish the series, one must recall the late Prof. Moses Zucker's rule of thumb that texts must be dated to the *latest* elements in the redaction, otherwise we should have to assign biblical dating to any book that quoted a prooftext. We, however, should be grateful, whatever the date; these translations of "The Aramaic Bible" will serve scholars well for many generations.

These fine translations join the few other extant English versions of the Targum: J. W. Etheridge's *The Targums of Onkelos and Jonathan* (1862) and the appendix to A. Diez-Macho's edition and Spanish translation of *Targum Neophyti* (1970-78). One more translation rounds out the lot, added almost as a bonus to the superb text edition, philological notes, discussions of orthography and phonology, brief bibliography, catalogue of fragments, brief history of the Cairo Geniza and technical introduction which accompany the text transcriptions and plates of Michael Klein's magisterial two-volume *Geniza Manuscripts of Palestinian Targum to the Pentateuch.*

Klein had already established himself as the dean of Targum text editors with his earlier *Fragment Targum of the Pentateuch* (Rome, 1980). Here, he offers in one set of volumes arranged according to the verses of the Pentateuch, the broad variety of targumic traditions available to the "Geniza community" over hundreds of years. It does readers well to see these otherwise disparate targumic materials collected, for it affords a picture of successive generations of Targum-listeners. We can hear, if we listen with them, how targumic traditions evolve, build on one another, undermine previous traditions, and ever expand and contract the surface of the biblical text. When there are many versions of Targum on a given verse or set of verses, Klein does not stint – he lays them out one by one before the reader. Many of the manuscripts have the Masoretic text included, which Klein dutifully transcribes (though omitting the vowel points).

The translations are very literal, which Klein explains in his introduction as an attempt to help the reader get behind the Aramaic shifts away from the biblical text. The reader with acute Aramaic and English will have to judge if Klein has succeeded. But the literary analyst will not be disappointed, since these Pentateuchal Targums are much looser translations than the Targums to the Prophets discussed above. Klein carefully indicates his conjectures and emendations and annotates the midrashic traditions which the Targums parallel. I would have wished for a fuller set of midrashic references, but at least Klein always keys his notes to a midrash which contains the rest of the listings whenever possible.

In short, Michael Klein's two volumes contain something for everyone, even a glossary of the targumic vocabulary. Philologians, literary scholars, neophytes and experts all will find these two volumes useful for a broad range of researches. There are even 182 beautiful plates of facsimiles of the Geniza fragments. Who can resist a book with pictures? This work is worth its very steep price.

All of these volumes prepare scholars for a new journey of discovery in the literature of the Targums. Fortunately, rudimentary maps already exist which will help beginners find their way. In addition to the works already cited, readers will want to consult John Bowker's *The Targum and Rab-binic Literature* (1972). In the same year Bowker published his researches, Bernard Grossfeld published *A Bibliography of Targum Literature*. These two guides, together with the bibliographies found in the volumes under review here will bring any scholar in touch with both major and minor trends in the study of Targum literature.

There are yet three more articles in English which must be called to the attention to the readers of this journal, for they are by one of the leading Israeli scholars of the Targums, and they show a particular sensitivity to the needs of literary scholars. I refer to the scholar with whose name I opened this review article, Avigdor Shinan. The titles of each explain pretty well the content, so I will avoid further comment except to say that each article is a model of careful methodology. Shinan not only maps the territory, he shows the way to conduct further explorations. Most recently he dealt with "The 'Palestinian' Targums –Repetitions, Internal Unity, Contradictions," (*JJS* 36 [1985]: 72-87). On a specific theme in the Targums readers will find useful Shinan's "The Angelology of the Palestinian Targums on the Pentateuch," (*Sefarad* 43 [1983]:181-98). Finally, he offers the rudiments of literary treatment of the Targum in "Live Translation: On the Nature of the Aramaic Targums to the Pentateuch," (*Prooftexts* [where else?] 3 [1983]: 41-49.)

The groundwork has been laid. The text editions are available. Transla-tions are appearing with startling regularity. Various studies map the way. It is time for serious literary study of a great and too long neglected Jew-ish literature. How does Targum translate Scripture? Does the Masoretic text suggest the midrashim incorporated into the translation? What of the poetry in Targum? Can it be evaluated on its own? Why does it crop up on the verses it does and what is its relationship to early liturgical poetry (piyyut)? What constitutes targumic style? Better, we must discern the var-ious styles of the differing Targums and the changing aesthetics reflected in the various versions of a given verse. What was it about Targum that caused it to be the point of departure for translation, midrash and poetry?

Is it literature or liturgy? Can it be literature if it is liturgy? These and many other questions spring to mind in defining the fields of inquiry in the literary study of Targum. The reward for studying this fruitful literature may help redefine the nature of Jewish literary history as a whole.

Lachs' Rabbinic Commentary
on the New Testament*

Since the publication of Paul Billerbeck's *Kommentar zum Neuen Testament aus Talmud und Midrasch* some sixty years ago, New Testament commentaries have repeatedly inflicted the indignity of providing "rabbinic background" upon the texts which they interpreted. More often than not these commentaries drew solely on Billerbeck and so provided a rather skewed view of rabbinic Judaism – a view that was in keeping with Matthew's portrayal of the Pharisees and with Billerbeck's notion of rabbinic Judaism as a works-righteous remnant of *Spätjudentum*. Samuel Lachs has now tried to rectify this situation with his *Rabbinic Commentary*, which is sympathetic in its treatment of both rabbinic literature and the New Testament. Students of both will be grateful for his avoidance of polemics, apologetics, and *Tendenz*.

However, while Lachs has eliminated the bias of the Billerbeck commentary, it is difficult to see how he has advanced our understanding of the New Testament in light of rabbinic literature. Like Billerbeck, Lachs draws his rabbinic parallels from a period of a thousand years, and only briefly raises the question of chronology and method. It is difficult to understand how rabbinic literature can provide a "background" for a canon completed at least a century before the redaction of the earliest rabbinic collections. While it is possible that careful control of tannaitic materials can provide a New Testament reader with some notion of milieu, this hardly produces a commentary. It is no doubt true that a thorough grounding in rabbinics is useful for contextual understanding of New Testament exegesis, but it remains to be proven that a rabbinic commentary is the best method for providing such a context.

Lachs does not address the possibility that the rabbinic parallels to New Testament passages are in fact rabbinic responses to these passages; if so, they can hardly qualify as commentary. Nor does Lachs consider the possibility that the rabbinic understanding of the New Testament was

---

* Review of: Samuel Tobias Lachs. *A Rabbinic Commentary on the New Testament: The Gospels of Matthew, Mark, and Luke.* Hoboken and New York: KTAV and Anti-Defamation League of B'nai B'rith, 1987. Pp. xxx + 468.

filtered through the lenses of the Church Fathers of the "rabbinic era," in which case a patristic commentary on the New Testament would prove far more valuable than a rabbinic commentary. A thoughtful consideration of these issues might have made Lachs' *Commentary* more than an English repetition, minus the bias, of Billerbeck.

There are other methodological problems which beset Lachs' work. The commentary is idiosyncratic – there seems to be no discernible criterion for commenting on one New Testament passage and ignoring another. Nor does Lachs limit himself to rabbinic commentary; he quotes also the Letter to Aristeas, Josephus, and other Jewish writers. Here, too, Lachs' assumptions are not critically examined. What is gained by providing the Jewish background for the Lucan prologue (p. 15)? Does Lachs think Luke was Jewish, or is there an unmentioned Lucan *Vorlage* which stemmed from unnamed Jewish circles? Lachs treats Matthew as a redacted work (he writes of an "editor's hand," p. 6), but never explicitly addresses his theory of Matthean redaction or his assumptions of the community (communities?) which produced that gospel.

When Lachs does address the methodological issues raised above, he does so with sometimes startling naiveté. He informs us that "there has always been an unbroken transmission of rabbinic traditions" (p. xxvi). This is a fine assertion in the midst of tenth century anti-Karaite polemics, but it remains far from a given fact which commands universal scholarly assent today. Again, Lachs tells us that "late compilations of midrashim have preserved early tradition. ... Even late material can often be instructive as an explicit parallel to an early and sometimes difficult and confusing source" (p. xxvi). It may be that late compilations preserve early traditions, but this needs to be proven by way of traditions-criticism in each instance where a parallel is adduced, an exercise which Lachs neglects to undertake. It seems that he has avoided learning the lessons which Jacob Neusner has so painstakingly taught over the past two decades.

There are lacunae in Lachs' bibliography as well. In a commentary centered around Matthew, one wonders why there are no references to the now standard Matthew commentaries of John Meier. One also notes only fleeting references to Raymond Brown's seminal *Birth of the Messiah*. Lachs' bibliographic sins do not stop with Catholic scholars; he omits references to Graham Stanton's collection of important articles on *The Interpretation of Matthew*, and regularly cites Schürer's history in its old edition, without mention of the "New Schürer" being published by Geza Vermes and others at Oxford. Lachs relies on the highly idiosyncratic chronologies of the first century advanced by Solomon Zeitlin (e. g., pp. 11–12), despite the general rejection of his theories during the last two decades. All in all, Lachs' bibliography is at least half a decade out of date, often far more.

One other area of Lachs' method merits specific comment – his retro-version of New Testament Greek into Hebrew and Aramaic. While Lachs blithely retranslates Greek passages into Semitic languages in order to unravel cruxes, he nowhere addresses the meaning of his retranslations. He does not ask what was the original language of the materials behind the gospels. He does not explain why he retranslates sometimes into Hebrew and sometimes into Aramaic. For example, in Luke 1:6 (p. 17), Lachs turns Luke's Greek "before the Lord" into the Hebrew *li-fene 'adonay*. Why not into the Aramaic, *qadam 'elaha'*, as in the Syriac version? Or on Luke 1:11 (p. 18) Lachs turns "and there appeared" into the Aramaic *'ithaze*. Why not into Hebrew? And why not point out that the Ara-maic *'ithaze* is often accompanied by *be-hilma'*, i.e., a dream incubated revelation.

Since the discussion of the methodological difficulties underlying Lachs' work involves details of interpretation, one might raise other issues of de-tail. I limit myself to examples from the section on the Infancy Narra-tives and so-called Six Antitheses, both of which are representative of the general tenor of the book. Lachs comments on the slander about Jesus "illegitimate" lineage (p. 2): "This slander is presumably very old...for it is already refuted in the Gospel of John, 'We were not born of fornication' (8:41)." This is in fact spoken by the Jews when Jesus accuses them of having been fathered by the devil; it is not a refutation for Jesus.

Lachs (p. 3) quotes Louis Finkelstein's interpretation of the significance of the fourteen generations in the Matthean lineage and of the rabbinic chain of tradition in the tractate Abot. It is highly unlikely that Matthew was responding polemically to Abot, if for no other reason than chronol-ogy. Furthermore, Elias Bickermann has long ago pointed out (*RB* 59 [1952]: 44-54) that a fourteen-linked chain of tradition was a common method in the philosophical schools in establishing the legitimacy of the scholarch–an explanation which serves Matthew and the rabbis in equal measure without either dialogue or polemic between them.

Later on Lachs appropriately points out (pp. 16-17) that Luke 1:5 has a reference to the *mishmarot* (watches) of the priests in Jerusalem. He neglects to mention any of the epigraphic evidence which could illumi-nate this verse (see, e.g., J. Naveh, *On Stone and Mosaic* [Jerusalem, 1978] [Hebrew], inscriptions 51, 52, 56, 106, and the secondary litera-ture cited there) or any secondary literature since Schürer. Again Lachs comments (p. 21) that "in the period of the Second Temple, the Jews used substitute names for God ... such as *Hamaqom...Haqadosh barukh hu...Hagevurah*." This is a misleading and indiscriminate treatment of a complex history of rabbinic uses of epithets for God, carefully set forth by E. E. Urbach in a series of chapters of his *Hazal* (Jerusalem, 1969) [Hebrew].

In Lachs' treatment of the Antitheses further errors of fact and lacunae of bibliography may be found. In discussing the canonization of the biblical Writings, he neglects (p. 87) to mention the important work of S. Leiman and relies instead on a work by S. Zeitlin which is half a century out of date. In relating the tale of Imma Shalom, without any exegesis, he overlooks the treatment of it by Urbach (*Ḥazal*, p. 269, n. 50) and Wallach (*JBL* 60 [1941]: 403-15; see now also Visotzky, *JJS* 38 [1987]: 78f.). Lachs refers (p. 88) to the "Nash MS ... the oldest Hebrew document in Aramaic script in Palestine" without any mention of the Dead Sea Scrolls. He speaks (p. 89) of "*kelal* and *peshaṭ*," which surely should read "*kelal u-feraṭ.*" While providing a general rabbinic flavor for the "Antitheses" (pp. 90ff.), Lachs pays no attention to chronological issues nor attempts to establish a relative dating. Nor does he note that in each case Jesus offers a stricter interpretation of the law, a point already noted by Tertullian in the third century. He equates the Greek *synedrion* (p. 92) with a celestial court by reference to Exodus Rabbah, a work composed at least a thousand years after Matthew, and not to any contemporary evidence (there is none). Besides, the philology of *synedrion* can only yield a human council, not a celestial one. One other example of mistranslation, this time from Aramaic: "carob tree" (p. 109) should be rather "rubble-filled lot of real estate (*ḥaroba'*)." Moreover, the note there mistakenly places the story in B. Tam. 32a-b; it is rather in the other parallel cited by Lachs, Lev. Rabbah 27. 1.

Other such petty annoyances are scattered throughout the work; here are two from the Table of Contents: "Luke 3. 1-9, 50" – there is neither a "Luke 3, verse 50" nor a "Luke, chapter 50." The Index is listed as on page 000 (it begins on p. 459); more careful proofreading should have been provided.

To sum up, Lachs' *Rabbinic Commentary* is marred by sloppy editing, errors of fact and interpretation, and outdated scholarship. It is fatally flawed, however, by its uncritical methodology coupled with a lack of serious reflection on the implications of such a commentary for understanding New Testament literary history. While one must admire Lachs for having risen above bias and apologetic, it is necessary to repeat his own introductory warning (p. xxviii), *caveat lector.*"

Segal's Rebecca's Children*

The sociological assumption of the function of myth in society is the frame around which this popular work is built. Each chapter takes a concept of social anthropology as its mode of investigation. Without explicitly discussing this controversial method, Segal addresses myth and covenant, acculturation and assimilation, millenarianism and the like. In successive chapters he surveys Israel between the empires, society in the time of Jesus, Jesus the revolutionary, Paul the convert and apostle, origins of the rabbinic movement, communities in conflict, and the division of the ways. The chapter on Paul is by far the strongest, a polished gem in an otherwise dull setting.

This work is beset by many difficulties which obscure the often brilliant insights Segal brings to the materials he surveys. The very scope of the work all but guarantees a certain lack of expertise which must, one fears, limit the usefulness of the book to high schools, introductory undergraduate courses, and casual readers. This is all the more regrettable since the fertile insights and often penetrating observations in the work may be overlooked by scholars.

Let me begin by underscoring the book's strengths, particularly in the author's treatment of Paul. Segal takes Leon Festinger's theory of cognitive dissonance and applies it to Paul's conversion and apostlehood with extraordinarily fruitful results. The success of Paul's mission is accounted for by this thesis, as is Paul's own reevaluation of Pharisaic Judaism. Having laid the groundwork in earlier chapters about the centrality of the Torah myth to the Jewish people, Segal can also deftly show how Paul replaces the Torah myth with his own, new salvation myth: conversion through baptism in Christ.

Segal astutely points out (114) that Paul perceived his brand of Christianity in a very different light than did gentile converts to Pauline Christianity. He is to the point when he notes (113) that Paul's victory was posthumous and that in his own lifetime Peter and James were more powerful leaders. Paul's dualism is aptly explicated by sociological theory as

---
* Review of: Alan F. Segal,*Rebecca's Children: Judaism and Christianity in the Roman World.* Cambridge: Harvard University Press, 1986, 207 pages.

a means of reducing cognitive dissonance. This observation can well be applied to apocalyptic dualism in general, a point to which Segal hints when he takes care to lay out the importance of apocalyptic for the social setting of first-century Judaism. Unfortunately, for all of the clarity that he brings to Paul, Segal's writing (see 111) is often as confusing about Paul as Paul himself can .be. This may betray the admirable affinity that appears between the author and Paul, but it may simply leave the reader bewildered.

Segal is strong in his treatment of the spread of Christianity and its early success. Social theory serves him well as he explicates the role conversion takes in guaranteeing the cohesiveness of the community. Segal keenly observes that the early Christian community succeeded in preserving the feeling of conversion even for those born into the group, thus guaranteeing its further success.

Sociological observation also illuminates other areas of antiquity when used as tool by Segal. He teaches us that "midrash, pesher, and allegory are at once dissonance-reducing mechanisms and strategies for construct-ing a new social world out of an old one " (100). He informs us that "Paul's genius was to unify the various parts of the Christian community with his new mythological metaphor of the body of believers, which was coupled with the new reality of house churches" (192, n.9). Segal points out that in pre-destruction Judaism, "as long as the sectarian groups tac-itly agreed to the root metaphor of the covenant, their conflict helped the Judean society" (59). He goes on to explain that this is because "the cul-ture encouraged different and opposing concepts of truth. For Judaism to … favor … a single orthodox interpretation would have been futile. Sectarianism was a more practical method for gaining stability."

Segal demonstates (86) that the term 'Messiah' was used by Christians only after the resurrection, that it meant something different to the en-emies of Christ, was not used by Christ himself, and means something entirely different today. He correctly notes (133) that the rabbinic move-ment modified the sectarianism of pre-70 while adopting it into its own social system.

There are other scattered observations which make this a work worth plowing through. But the going will be rough since the work is filled with factual errors, unsubstantiated observations, and a certain credulity toward ancient texts. The argument of the book is laid out in a fashion best called paranetic, a drawback which will dismay those who prefer to see an argument unfold in logical sequence. Through fits and starts Segal makes a statement, contradicts it, and then returns to his original contention. His intuitive sense is keen, so one is left with an impression of an author thinking out loud, arguing with himself on the printed page. His conclusions are mostly sound, but his arguments are tortuous.

The annotation is inappropriate for a work of scholarship: the notes are few and far between. Segal often makes assertions which demand citation, yet there is none. When he does cite his sources, it is by book and without page reference. One would have been better served by a bibliography at the end of the book than by scant references to often outdated literature. A second edition of this book would demand thorough revision of the notes: expansion, pagination, updating. The index of Scripture should be supplemented by an index of all primary sources. Instead, Segal offers a canonical index and a general index, which mixes primary sources, secondary sources, authors, and topics.

While these are serious technical objections, there are problems of substance to be corrected as well. Though he acknowledges Hellenism in Palestine, Segal often distinguishes between Judaism and Hellenism as though Rabbinic Judaism and Christianity were not Hellenistic phenomena. He further points out that those at Qumran regarded Hellenized Jews and Gentiles as "new Canaanites who needed to be wiped out" (50) – language not explicitly employed in Qumranic literature, although the reader is left with that impression.

Segal has difficulty characterizing his ancient sources. He refers to Mishna as a canonical, analytically organized codification (133), which hardly describes the work Rabbi Judah Hanasi orally published. He can state with assurance that the claims of the Sadducean party are the easiest to support in Scripture (46) despite his acknowledgment that we possess no Sadducean literature. Segal asserts that rabbinic Hekhalot traditions belong to the period he studies – a view which he annotates with a literature two decades out of date – despite the lack of actual rabbinic texts from the era in question.

The difficulty of dating the primary literature undermines his use of texts for evidence. Although Segal acknowledges the near impossibility of dating rabbinic materials he asserts that "hidden in some later rabbinic discussion of heresy may be the clue to the first century rabbinic views of Christians." Segal incorrectly refers to a rabbinic story of an insect in Pompey's ear (it was Titus' nose), wrongly asserts that Mishna Sanhedrin 1: 1 speaks of the seventy elders accompanying Moses to receive revelation on Sinai, and quotes Pirke Avot 1: 1 as it appears in prayer books with Sanhedrin 10: 1 attached as an introductory meditation. He cites a story about rabbinic belief in the suffering Messiah following Bar Kokhba by quoting R. Dosa who lived a generation earlier, and quotes a tradition about the Son of Man which is reported in the name of R. Abahu (fl. ca. 300 CE) as an example of contemporary rabbinic opinion. Segal also offers a rationale for accepting the historicity of a debate in Midrash Mishle between R. Joshua and R. Eleazar when Leopold Zunz pointed to the pseudepigraphic nature of precisely these debates a century and a half ago.

I have chosen the above array of errors only from Segal's treatment of rabbinic literature. Dozens of other errors, great and small, are found throughout the pages of this book. A few major misperceptions should yet be listed, such as Segal's assumption that in the third and fourth centuries Jews began to believe they could no longer co-exist with the Roman empire. This assumption is contradicted by both rabbinic literature and archaeological evidence; it is just as well Segal does not cite a source.

Segal asserts "a life of chastity and abstinence was viewed by educated Jew and Gentile alike as the sign of a morally serious religion." (48) If this refers but to some sense of self-restraint it is a reasonable characterization. But if the words "chastity and abstinence" are taken to imply sexual asceticism, then neither first century Judaism nor most of the pagan cults can be considered "morally serious." Segal claims that the Pharisees post-70 migrated to the smaller towns of Galilee. This is only partially true; in order to say so one must ignore the rabbinic communities of Tiberius, Sepphoris, and Caesarea Maritima. Since the Rabbis claim these towns as major loci for their movement, Segal's claim is vitiated.

On the subject of proselytes and semi-proselytes Segal claims that the "audience ... most inclined to proselytism was found in the synagogues of the Diaspora" (98). It seems to be that the New Testament account of Paul's repeated ejection from synagogue after synagogue denies this claim, but surely the demograpics of the Gentile church undermine its veracity. Finally, Segal notes that semi-proselytes "suffered from a double ambiguity in status, since they were no longer pagans but were not yet Jews." It is true they were not yet Jews, but the very nature of paganism allowed them to be considered "pagan" until they themselves rejected non-Jewish cults. The literature does not offer evidence of such exclusivism.

The many flaws in this work make it difficult to recommend to a scholarly audience. One will spend too much time arguing with the author and bemoaning his errors to notice his contribution. This is especially regrettable since the contribution is substantial. Segal's application of social theory brings us all a step closer to understanding both Paul and the success of early Christianity. The author's ability to unravel such mysteries makes him worthy of a renown which this work, alas, may delay.

Two Types of Midrash Study*

In a fragment of a letter from Rome circa 384 CE, Saint Jerome writes of
Origen. "Who has ever managed to read all that he has written?" Here
in America, some sixteen hundred years later, this is the question people ask about the prolific output of Professor Jacob Neusner. Because
of Dr. Neusner's vast *oeuvre*, one is grateful when a volume summarizes
his previous work on a subject, particularly so when the volume is short
and inexpensive. The book here reviewed, written for the Fortress Press
Guides to Biblical Scholarship New Testament Series, summarizes Professor Neusner's various researches into midrashic literature during the last
five years.

Dr. Neusner begins with a definition of midrash as "biblical exegesis by
ancient Judaic authorities," (xi) and continues to narrow his deliberately
broad definition by postulating as follows:

> Three types of Midrash-exegesis, deriving from three distinct Judaisms or Judaic
> religious systems in antiquity, involve the interpretation of Scripture in one of
> three ways: as (1) *prophecy*, characteristic of the Judaism set forth in the Dead
> Sea Scrolls as well as of the Judaism laid out by the school of Matthew, the
> (re)reading of Scripture through (2) systematic *paraphrase*, accomplished by the
> translators of Scripture into Aramaic, the common language of the Jewish world,
> and Greek, and the reconsideration of Scripture as (3) *parable*, inclusive of
> allegorizing tendencies, characteristic of the biblical interpretation of the Judaism
> of the dual Torah. (xi)

Professor Neusner narrows even further when he subdivides Midrash into
three parts, correctly pointing out that the term is used for "Midrash-
exegesis," which is the unit of discourse found in "Midrash-compilation,"
or works of the Sages. Finally, there is "Midrash-process," or the style of
exegesis in which the Midrash engages.

This latter distinction seems to me more cogent than the former which
is superimposed over a vast body of varying literatures. Prophecy, para-
phrase and parable are ill defined and too glibly cast to provide a mean-

---

* This review essay considers the following two books: Jacob Neusner, *What is
Midrash?* Fortress Press, Philadelphia, 1987. 114 + xii pp. Judah Goldin, *Studies
in Midrash and Related Literature*, edited by Barry L. Eichler and Jeffrey H. Tigay,
Jewish Publication Society, Philadelphia, 1988. 419 + xx pp.

ingful net for the understanding of Midrash. The subcategories of exegesis, compilation and process also suffer in their specific applications.
Thus Neusner writes, "we find in certain passages in Matthew, cited below, *Midrash exegeses*, assembled into a *Midrash-compilation*, generated
by a particular process" (9). Or again, "Matthew has taught us ... how
Midrash functions as a work of prophecy" (39). Yet Matthew nowhere
uses the term Midrash, and Neusner nowhere considers the carefully nu-
anced discussion of the problem offered by Raymond E. Brown in *The
Birth of the Messiah*, a work of scholarship which treats the same passages
from Matthew.

The extension of the term Midrash to Matthew (and to certain other
non-Rabbinic texts discussed below), exemplifies a methodological problem in the discussion of *What is Midrash* which Professor Neusner offers.
This booklet, as part of a Fortress Press series in New Testament, addresses questions of primary interest to Christian audiences. Since, however, it treats a Rabbinic phenomenon, it necessarily skews the evidence
under discussion. This is a problem of method which Professor Neusner
repeatedly and correctly has pointed out in reviews of similar works by
other scholars. It is surprising that Dr. Neusner allowed Dan Via, the
editor of the Fortress series, to convince him to commit the same *faux
pas*.

A section on Septuagint, written by Professor Ernest Frerichs, and a
section on Targum by Paul Flesher continue this broad view of Midrash.
Both are competently written, though one might have wished for more attention by Flesher to Pseudo-Jonathan, Onkelos and general comparisons
of the various Targumim rather than the concentration on Neofiti which
dominates the brief treatment.

Flesher is also listed as co-author of the chapter on the Dead Sea Scrolls.
The chapter opens with an oversimplified history of Qumran which treats
the evidence of the scrolls with a credulity that belies Professor Neusner's
cautious use of Rabbinic literature for the same purposes. Further, the
Dead Sea Scrolls discussed do not use the term Midrash for their own enterprise. They call it *pesher*. Flesher and Neusner do write of the "Midrash
of the *pesharim*" without, however, any citation of William Brownlee's extensive discussion of the problem of this nomenclature in his introduction
to *The Midrash Pesher of Habakkuk*.

Before turning to Professor Neusner's treatment of Midrash in Rabbinic
literature, it is worth reviewing, briefly, his notion of Rabbinic historiography in light of Christianity. Neusner contends (46-48) that "Mishnah's
Judaism did not find necessary a doctrine of the authority of Scripture"
because it was "developing a system of Judaism in which Christianity
played no considerable role." After the rise of Christianity in the fourth
century, "There were three specific challenges from Christianity: (1) the

claim that Jesus of Nazareth was the Messiah ... (2) the church's claim to be the successor of Israel as God's people and (3) the appeal to Scripture to demonstrate these two propositions."

This is an enormously appealing construct since it simplifies vastly the complex of reasons which gave rise to Midrash. It also serves as powerful apologetic in an book addressed to a Christian audience. It overemphasizes, however, the role of Christianity as a formative cause of Midrash while at the same time confuses the order of the formation of Midrash and Mishnah.

For Neusner, then, Midrash is first and foremost a Rabbinic reading of history. The Sages "quite naturally appealed to Scripture's account of ancient Israel as the model and paradigm for all of history" (50). "One fact [of midrashic exegesis] is that there are laws of history" (56). "The entire history of Israel ... is unified by a single law. That law ... is the law of history" (59). This presumes that Midrash consistently rereads Biblical history and reads Rabbinic history as a response to Christianity. Yet, as Professor Neusner has pointed out in other contexts, Midrash is patently not history, at least not history as we know it. Further, in his specific analyses of Midrashic passages, the contention that they respond to Christian history is not demonstrated. All in all, Christianity is hardly demonstrated to be the chief context in which to read and understand this vast genre of *Rabbinic* literature.

Professor Neusner begins his survey of Midrash with a trot through the "Tannaitic Midrashim." The Mekilta of either school is notably absent, though with nary a word from the author as to why he omits a work which just about everyone else in Rabbinic scholarship includes under this rubric. One should point out that the Mekilta's banishment is complete; it is not even among the translations of Midrash by Professor Neusner.

These Tannaitic Midrashim are dated to the third and fourth centuries, as responses to Christianity. How *Sifre* Leviticus serves as a response to Christianity, or how it can be construed as "allegorical, in the sense that it compares something to something else, as does a parable" (44) is mercifully unexplained. Professor Neusner does not repeat the detail of his oft advanced arguments for the late dating of the Tannaitic Midrashim, nor does he mention that his theories have brought direct and contradictory response from a broad range of historians and rabbinics scholars. The combination of the erroneous dating with the apologetic to Christianity leaves the book far outside the pale of academic discourse.

When he turns to specific midrashim, these problem persist. Without explanation, he dates Genesis Rabbah to 400-450. Given this periodization, it is not surprising that he claim that "Christian Rome's claim to be Israel precipitated a crisis. The sages of *Genesis Rabbah* dealt with this crisis by conceding that Christian Rome required attention in a way that pagan Rome had not" (53). Yet Neusner's examples in no way compel one to read that the Rome mentioned is Christian and not pagan Rome. He does not adduce one specific instance in which the text can only be understood as referring to Christianity. In a later chapter he does cite a midrash from Genesis Rabbah which interprets Psalm 2:12. Neusner asserts "the particular proof text before us [is] important in Christian exegesis as a proof that Jesus Christ is the son of God" (85). Yet the verse is not cited as a proof in the fourth-century Pseudo-Epiphanius Testimony Book, nor does Professor Neusner offer any evidence of the use of that verse by a specific Church Father.

Leviticus Rabbah is dated "approximately a generation after Genesis Rabbah, in ca. 450 C.E." (60) and again (67) "around 400 C.E." Here, too, Neusner asserts without proof that Rome must be Christian Rome. *Sifre* Numbers, is dated dually to "ca. 300" (69) and "hardly ... before the end of the fourth century" (70). These annoyances are exacerbated by pedestrian translations of texts. Though there are no egregious errors of translation, the addition of paragraphs marked by letters of the alphabet to texts which already existed in English translation hardly justifies the effort or the expense of the many volumes of printed translations from which Dr. Neusner boilerplates. Nor does Dr. Neusner notice that a paragraph of text lifted from his translation of Pesiqta de Rab Kahana (74) parallels his translation of Genesis Rabbah offered but a few pages later (82).

The inattention which the above examples display is exacerbated by an opaque style. Consider:

> When we compare, we first seek perspective on the things compared. Second, we look for the rule that applies to the unfamiliar among the things compared. The unknown thing is like something else, therefore falls under the rule governing the known thing to which it is likened, or it is unlike something else, therefore falls under the opposite rule. (13)

This turgid style persists throughout the book. One more example:

> What we have in Essene Midrash-compilations therefore is an entirely cogent Midrash-exegesis comprising a Midrash-document that expresses a Midrash-process, namely, an approach to the verses of Scriptures in light of an available correlation of concrete events to past words. (35-36)

Unproven assertions, unnecessary translations, erroneous dates and obfuscating writing combine with a Christian academic agenda and Jewish apologetic to make this book a poor choice for rabbis, congregants and scholars, or for Christians who seek to answer the question, What is Midrash. Perhaps all of this could be overlooked had Professor Neusner turned his unusually keen eye to summarizing Rabbinic religion. Yet he can seriously write, "A cogent and uniform world view, one that gener-ated the allegorical reading to begin with, accompanied our sages when they approached the text ..." (81) Or he can summarize, "The ultimate meaning, the point and the payoff of the allegory, insists on the union of Israel's present sanctification and its coming salvation. In all that we have read in the rabbinic Midrash-compilations, the propositions of the Midrash-exegeses repeatedly come down to this one claim" (101). This reductionism reminds one too much of Woody Allen's remark that he had taken a speed reading course and read *War and Peace* in twenty minutes. When asked to comment on the work he replied, "It's about Russia."

I remarked above that Professor Neusner's views of Midrash are outside of the generally accepted notions of the academy. This ability to rely only on his own theses has given rise to a bad book. It is eloquently exemplified by the last section, For Further Reading. There, thirty-four books are cited. Two are by Professor Neusner's students, the remainder by Neusner himself.

I opened with a fragment of a letter composed in 384. I close this portion of the review with a work which dates a decade or so earlier. In it, the rhetor Libanius eulogizes the dead Emperor Julian.

> As though with wings he went through all his business. In a single day he would reply to many ambassadors, send letters to many civil and military rulers and to his inner-circle, whether abroad or at home ... by the speed of his words he reveals the hands of his tachygraphers as laggardly.

Professor Neusner has, paradoxically, outdone even the Emperor Julian – he has become his own tachygrapher.

The essays in Judah Goldin's volume of *Studies* comprise the first of the Jewish Publication Society's Scholar of Distinction Series. At age seventy-five, Goldin has long ago earned that honorific. The volume consists of twenty-five essays of limpid English prose and one study in classically modern Rabbinic Hebrew. These two dozen plus offerings represent the fruits of close to forty-five years of active scholarship, from 1946 to the present.

The volume was collected by Professor Goldin's colleagues at the University of Pennsylvania, Barry Eichler and Jeffrey Tigay. They also have included a bibliography of Goldin's scholarly publications (but see p. 222, n. 31 for a missing item). One only regrets that they did not include among the texts or list in the bibliography any of the lovely poetry Dr. Goldin has been publishing recently.

The studies are divided into two parts which are three. The first part, Textual and Literary Studies, divides into sections of essays on Abot and Abot de Rabbi Natan and a further section on Other Texts which includes,

among others, reflections on Genesis 38, the end of Mishnah Yoma and a
segment of Mekilta. The second part, Thematic Studies, offers articles and
lectures on education, biography (with a keen appreciation of the difference between biography and hagiography, see pp. 299-300), magic and the
conflict between tradition versus majority opinion, among various other
topics.

The editors quite correctly write that "Judah Goldin is known to laymen
and scholars alike for his learned and elegant expositions of classical Jewish
literature and for his graceful translations of early rabbinic texts" (xiii).
These studies will only serve to enhance this reputation. Still, for all the
elegance of style, I have a reviewer's *kvetch* here and there.

On occasion (as in the first two essays) Professor Goldin's style seems
far more suited to the Hebrew of the yeshiva (especially the Hebrew of
pilpul and responsa) than to the English prose of a university professor.
There are simply too many asides and byways. In another essay (the book's
penultimate), Professor Goldin borders on sounding overly simplistic and
perhaps even a touch condescending. But this must be contrasted favorably
with the humility he displays when he elsewhere writes, "I was obviously
tone deaf ... the editor of ARN^A III [Abot de Rabbi Natan, version A,
chapter 3] deserves a public apology" (117).

Allow me two other sets of complaints, one on historiography and the
other on philology. For the first, for all his care Professor Goldin is
sometimes less than rigorous in interpreting his sources. One should not
conclude from "a shift from plural and general to second person singular" (41) that a source is historically accurate. Making the assumption
that *Sh'ma, Tefillah* and *birkat ha-mazon* were recited in pre-destruction
Jerusalem (205) on the basis of hagiographic legends about Rabbi Eliezer
and Rabban Yohanan ben Zakkai is skating on very thin historiographic
ice. So, too, any assumption about Rabban Yoḥanan's behavior during
the siege of Jerusalem based only on the accounts of ARN and Midrash
Mishlei (362 n. 14) must be discounted, as Jacob Neusner taught us in his
various researches on the Yoḥanan legends. Professor Goldin seems to
disagree with Professor Neusner's general lack of faith in the historicity of
Rabbinic sources when he quotes Wolfson: "There is no reason for rejecting a statement which is not inherently impossible nor contradicted by a
more reliable source" (301). This, despite Professor Goldin's recognition
that in rabbinics we more often deal in hagiography than in historiography.

On to philology. It is difficult to complain about a book which is so
admirably and thoroughly grounded in philological method. But on two
occasions Dr. Goldin falters, and they should be noted. In the first, he
translates *beit va'ad as* 'salon' (43). This is exacerbated by his claim (53)
that nothing in Hellenistic literature corresponds to the Rabbinic injunc-
tion in Abot, "let thy home be...." Professor Goldin overlooks all the

household chriae discussed by Henry Fischel in his articles on Hillel, as well as a substantial corpus of archeological remains which indicate the importance of the "house-church" in early Rabbinic Judaism and Christianity. *Beit va'ad* is not a salon, but a house-church.

In writing about allegoric interpretation of the Song of Songs, Professor Goldin mysteriously explains the *beit mishteh* as a "drinking house" (307, n. 40). However, here, as in the Mishnah and practically everywhere else in the Semitic languages, the phrase refers to a wedding party. Recontextualizing the Song of Songs as a wedding song lends it a far different valence than singing it as a bar ditty.

On the side of creative philology one need only to point to Professor Goldin's unique rendering of *seyag la-Torah* (19- 23). I, for one, am always sufficiently stymied by what the Sages meant by this phrase to find refuge in a bad pun. So I tell my students, "Put a fence around the Torah and you'll have a safer Torah."

In a second instance of Goldin's philological panche, I point to his note about the problem of Ḥoni Hameaggel's name. He points out, simply, "whatever else one may say, *'wg*, and *'gl* are not the same root" (332, n. 11). When this is combined with Professor Goldin's interpretation of Ḥoni's circle, "It means simply: *immediately*" (334, his emphasis), one is forced to take a long look at Ḥoni's last name. I doubt it's sound philology, but folk etymology moves me to go to Aramaic for Meaggel: immediately, swiftly, as in *ba'agalah ubizman kariv*. If I may pun once more, I'd follow Professor Goldin's lead and translate the name, Ḥoni the Precipitous.

These are but minor notes in an otherwise magnificent symphony of sound Rabbinic scholarship. The penetrating elegance of Professor Goldin's distinguished scholarship is nowhere better illustrated than toward the middle of the book (222-223) when he answers the question: What is Midrash?

> Midrash, however, is not mere reference to the past: it is the enlistment of the past in the service of the present. Even more specifically, it is a reinsertion into the present of the original divine Word ... that Word is given definition and repeated application by men. Without man, without the scholar, there can be no Midrash ... Since the Word is the word of the Living God, it never ceases to make contact with the human world. The Word does not change, but it fulfills itself through disclosures and interpretations of the scholars. And if the world changes, the Word has been prepared for all contingencies from the outset ... The Word is continuously directed to the world and the world is shaped by the Word through the instrumentality of the Sages. It is therefore not with change and adaptation as such that the Rabbis are preoccupied ... it is with the preservation of that intimate relationship between the inexhaustible Word and human society that they are concerned. Since that relationship cannot be sustained without active human performances, commentary never ceases ...

I cannot think of a better explanation of Midrash in the English language.

I close this review by wishing Professor Goldin forty-five more years of scholarship (*'ad me'ah v'esrim*) to produce yet another volume of such multifaceted Torah learning. He fulfills the charge of our masters, *lehagdil torah ulha'adirah.*

Prolegomenon to the Study of Jewish-Christianities in Rabbinic Literature*

The Christian, Jewish, and Jewish-Christian Communities

They just don't fit very neatly; they never did. Ever since it became clear that the law-free mission to the gentiles would create a church and not a synagogue, Jewish-Christianity has been an uncomfortable reality with which to deal. The "Synagogue" didn't like it. The "Church Catholic" didn't like it. And modern scholarship, far less ready to accept the vagaries of a religion that resembles but cannot be made to fit known varieties of religion, seems to like it even less. Jewish-Christians seemed to want to hang on to an anachronism, a mission that should have failed already in Paul's lifetime.

Yet it is the very fact that Jewish-Christianity occupies a middle ground between Judaism and Christianity (as though there were such "normative" religions in antiquity or today) that makes it the object of fascination to modern scholarship. If one could but define Jewish-Christianity, one could locate the borders of the two "parent" religions – so seems to be the logic of much modern scholarship in dealing with the phenomenon. Hence, a great deal has been written recently, attempting to define Jewish-Christianity so that scholars could get on with the business of placing it somewhere between "real" Judaism and "real" Christianity, neatly.[1]

* This essay was written during my tenure as a Visiting Fellow of Clare Hall, University of Cambridge, and as a Visiting Scholar at the Oxford Centre for Post-Graduate Hebrew Studies. A generous grant from the Abbell Publication Fund of the Jewish Theological Seminary of America supported the research.

[1] For general bibliographies the following works should be consulted: J. Danielou, *The Theology of Jewish Christianity* (London, 1964); *Aspects du Judeo-Christianisme, Colloque de Strasbourg* (Paris, 1965); *Judeo-Christianisme: Recherches historique et théologique offertes en hommage au Cardinal Jean Danielou* (= *Recherches de science religieuse* 60 [1972]); M. Simon, "Reflexions sur le Judeo-Christianisme," in *Christianity, Judaism and other Greco-Roman Sects: Studies for Morton Smith at 60* (Leiden, 1975), 2: 53-76; A. F. J. Klijn, "The Study of Jewish-Christianity," *New Testament Studies* 20: 419-431; B. Malina, "Jewish Christianity: A Select Bibliography," *Australian Journal of Biblical Archeology* 6 (1973): 60-65. Specific mention must be made of the groundbreaking studies of H. J. Schoeps, whose works are listed in the bibliographies above. More specific to the problems of defining Jewish-Christianity, see, e. g., M. Si-

This approach presumes that there are borders which can be drawn when there are virtually none. For the study of Judaism and Christianity in antiquity teaches us that there is not any one normative or real Judaism, nor is there any one true church or Church Catholic. We have learned to speak of ancient Judaisms and ancient Christianities. We must learn not only to speak also of Jewish-Christianities, but to accept that the disparate communities which make up this rather broad rubric will fall along the entire continuum of biblical religions in late antiquity.

The problem has been recognized for some time. Ever since Walter Bauer wrote his *Orthodoxy and Heresy,*[2] scholars have reluctantly recognized that they must abandon the Eusebian notion of a Great Church Catholic towering over antiquity. Instead, studies have had to be limited to a wide variety of Christianities, each different from the One Church over which Constantine would have liked to preside and often identical with the other Christian movements condemned by that church. In other words, a millennium and a half after their existence, scholars were forced to stop viewing certain communities and churches as heretical and to view them instead as authentic expressions of Christian religion in antiquity. It remains a difficult task for a variety of reasons: old views die hard, modern religious beliefs impose certain biases in favor of the monolithic view of the church and, quite simply, scholars are not happy about having to master vast new bodies of literature and a new view of history in order to just get on with their business. But the business has changed; it is no longer the History of Christianity, but the History of Christianities.

A similar reluctance has dogged Jewish studies. Scholars of the period post−70 still prefer to view the history of Judaism in that era as the history of Rabbinic Judaism. When a scholar takes the time (a very long time at that) to master the rabbinic corpus, he or she is loath to turn and ask, what comes next? On the other extreme there are scholars with limited Hebrew skills or with certain prejudices who refrain from mastery of rabbinic literature and rely instead on Apocrypha, Pseudepigrapha, Josephus, Philo, and Qumran for their notion of Judaism in antiquity (these scholars have for the most part ceased using the term *Spätjudenthum*).

Few students at all bother to incorporate the masses of archaeological evidence which point to Judaisms other than rabbinic; to say the least of the even smaller number who try to learn patristic and Greco-Roman

---

mon, "Problemes du Judeo-Christianisme," in *Aspects du Judeo-Christianisme*, pp. 1-17; B. Malina, "Jewish Christianity or Christian Judaism: Toward a Hypothetical Definition," *Journal of Jewish Studies* 7: 46-57; S. Riegel, "Jewish Christianity: Definitions and Terminology," *New Testament Studies* 24: 410-415; and R. Kraft, "In Search of 'Jewish-Christianity' and Its 'Theology': Problems of Definition and Methodology," *Recherches de science religieuse* 60: 81-92.
  [2] W. Bauer, *Rechtgläubigkeit und Ketzerei im Älstesten Christentum* (Tübingen, 1964).

literature for their pictures of Judaism. There is an awesome body of material to master if the job is to be done properly. Unfortunately, many of those who have bothered have tended to treat one literature as primary and the others as buttresses to the view that corpus may present. Even more exasperating are those who attempt to harmonize all of the above into one homogeneous "Judaism in Late Antiquity." Needless to say, the religion of a scholar has a curious effect on the view of Judaism adopted and on the literature he or she chooses to study. We remain yet a long way from the study of Judaism*s* in late antiquity.

Nevertheless, a start has been made in the study of Jewish-Christianities. Two notable articles have contributed a great deal to the idea of multiple communities. The first, for the patristic period, was G. Strecker's appendix to Bauer, which he titled, "On the Problem of Jewish Christianity."[3] Strecker wished to point out an area which Bauer had ignored, but in doing so, described the Jewish-Christian communities of late antiquity as separate entities. He worked from the evidence of two bodies of literature and avoided the temptation to harmonize them into one Jewish-Christianity identifiable with a heresy singled out by the church.

More recently, Raymond Brown has taken this approach for the study of New Testament Jewish-Christianity. He has suggested that at the outset of the Christian mission there were not only a law-free and a law-observant mission, but four different missions, each representing a differing form of early Christianity.[4] The result of Brown's study is to increase the variety of Jewish-Christianities for the New Testament period. His work, combined with Strecker's advances, will force scholars to reexamine the notion of a monolithic Jewish-Christianity, much as must be done for Judaisms and Christianities in late antiquity.

The end result of this new scholarship willing to take account of each small community as an authentic, independent phenomenon will not be visible for at least a generation. By then, scholars will come to be satisfied when they conclude that this painful ambiguity of broad definition is an accurate reflection of late antiquity. Then, and only then, can the study of Jewish-Christianities seriously begin.

My own field, rabbinic literature, is one of the important components in the study of Jewish-Christianity that remains largely ignored.[5] To en-

---

[3] G. Strecker, apud Bauer, op. cit.

[4] R. E. Brown, "Not Jewish Christianity and Gentile Christianity But Types of Jewish/Gentile Christianity," *Catholic Bible Quarterly* 45 (1983): 74-79. Brown credits our colleague, J. Louis Martyn, with the insight that there was a law-observant mission to the gentiles. I might add that Brown and Martyn's theses have but uncovered the tip of the iceberg.

[5] I have not seen the work of A. Schlatter, *Synagogue und Kirche bis zum Bar Kochba-Aufstand. Vier Studien zur Geschichte des Rabbinats und der jüdischen Christenheit in den ersten zwei Jahrhunderten* (Stuttgart, 1966 [written between 1897 and 1915]), which

courage the mingling of the Sea of the Talmud with the murky waters of Jewish-Christianity, I should like to briefly chart some of the territories which must be navigated for such an undertaking.

Christian Literatures as Sources for Jewish-Christianities

There are four major literatures to be surveyed for basic information about Jewish-Christianity: works identified as Jewish-Christian, the works of Christian heresiologists, Gnostic sources, and patristic literature. One must add archaeological data to the above materials, but such data are limited and subject to a great deal of disagreement in interpretation.

Among the Jewish-Christian literatures are the Pseudo-Clementines,[6] the Didascalia Apostolorum,[7] the Apostolic Constitutions,[8] and one must now add the Cologne Mani Codex.[9] None of these texts represents a purely Jewish-Christian literature. In each instance internal evidence has led scholars to identify portions of the text as Jewish-Christian. Each of these identifications has, in turn, led to refutations and refinements of the Jewish-Christian thesis.[10] The list offered above is only representative and not by any means complete. Snippets identified as Jewish-Christian literature abound, and it would be useful to have them collated into one volume. Then the difficult work of categorizing and analyzing could take place within the context of other materials. Even so, the work would remain but a tentative classification pending broader investigations.

The works of the heresiologists are a fruitful, though obviously bi-ased source of information on Jewish-Christianities. The discovery at Nag Hammadi of the library which contained so much Gnostic literature offers scholars a good control for methodologies in using the heresiologists for information about given "heretical" sects.[11] To ease the work in classifying information from the heresiologists, one may turn to the useful anthology

---

I understand makes some contribution to the field. For the limited contribution of scholars of rabbinics, see below.

[6] G. Strecker, *Die Juden-Christentum bei den Pseudo-Klementinen* (Berlin, 1958).

[7] *Didascalia* ed. A. Vööbus, *Corpus scriptorum christianorum orientalium*, 1979, vols. 1-2; his English translation, ibid., see the earlier edition by P. de LaGarde, *Didascalia Apostolorum Syriacae* (Leipzig, 1854) and an earlier English translation with introduction and commentary by R. H. Connolly (Oxford, 1929).

[8] Ed. F. X. Funk, *Didascalia et constitutiones apostolorum* (Paderborn, 1905).

[9] Ed. A. Henrichs, L. Koenen, *Zeitschrift für Papyrologie und Epigraphik* 19, 32, 44, 48, and see my "Rabbinic Randglossen to the Cologne Mani Codex," ibid. 52: 295-300.

[10] E. g., D. Fiensy's thorough study, *Prayers Alleged to Be Jewish: An Examination of the Constitutiones Apostolorum* (Chico, Calif., 1985).

[11] J. M. Robinson, ed., *The Nag Hammadi Library in English* (New York, 1977).

by Drs. A. F. J. Klijn and G. J. Reinink.[12]   In particular one thinks of the reports by Irenaeus, Hippolytus, and Epiphanius which are collected in that volume.

Gnostic literature seems to hold some promise for research in Jewish-Christianity primarily because of the Jewish background evident in the already Christian layers. The assumption here is that such literature represents the product or background of a Jewish-Christian community rather than a Gnostic literature which was first Judaized and then Christianized.[13] Unraveling an already knotty literature is not an enviable task, but it could shed light on certain forms of Jewish-Christianity.

Gnosticism has led me to separate the heresiologists from the rest of the church fathers, a practice otherwise to be avoided. All "orthodox" church fathers are heresiologists in some fashion, as, of course, are the heresiologists the epitome of "orthodox fathers." Thus the Klijn–Reinink volume includes fathers who are not particulary concerned with branding heresies, but do so by the way. Among the patristic evidence that must be weighed is Justin's *Dialogue with the Jew Trypho*, chap. 47, Ignatius of Antioch's letters (Magn. 10: 3, Phil. 6: 1),[14] and those fathers collected by Klijn and Reinink, including Tertullian, Origen, Eusebius, and Jerome. One must also peruse the anti-Jewish sermons of John Chrysostom, particularly 4. 3.[15]

As I suggested above, this material must be viewed in conjunction with archaeological evidence. Unfortunately, such evidence is so difficult to interpret that a find which may be thought by some to be a church may be thought by others to be a specifically Jewish-Christian church. Imagine the debate that ensues when experts are unsure whether a site is a church or a synagogue. Further, the interpretation of funerary monuments with "Christian" motifs but "Jewish" names is a source of debate. Finally, it is not at all clear which motifs are exclusively "Jewish," which exclusively indicative of "Christian," let alone which motifs give evidence of Jewish-Christian artifacts.[16] Thus the application of archaeological findings must

---

[12] A. F. J. Klijn and G. J. Reinink, *Patristic Evidence for Jewish Christian Sects* (Leiden, 1973).

[13] See, e. g., R. M. Grant, "Jewish Christianity at Antioch in the Second Century," *Recherches de science religieuse* 60 (1972): 97-108, and C. K. Barrett, "Jews and Judaisers in the Epistle of Ignatius," in *Jews, Greeks and Christians ... in Honor of W. D. Davies* (Leiden, 1976), pp. 220 ff.

[14] See Barrett, "Jews and Judaisers"; J. Meier in R. E. Brown and J. Meier, *Antioch and Rome* (New York, 1983); E. Schweizer, "Christianity of the Circumcised and Judaism of the Uncircumcised – the Background of Matthew and Colossians," in *Jews, Greeks and Christians*, pp. 245-260.

[15] See R. Wilken, *John Chrysostom and the Jews* (Berkeley, 1983); W. Meeks and R. Wilken, *Jews and Christians in Antioch* (Missoula, 1978).

[16] I offer only a few examples to illustrate the magnitude of the problem. Most notably one must list the works of W. Ramsay and, more recently, B. Bagatti (see below). Then

always refer to the original artifacts themselves and not merely to the conclusions of the archaeologists. This minimal degree of control will at least militate against egregious errors of judgment or "findings" which will soon be overturned.

This segment outlining the church sources necessary for initial consultation in the study of Jewish Christianity is far from comprehensive. It contains but the basic bibliography for those interested in intelligently bringing the resources of their own field to bear on the history of Jewish-Christianities, or vice versa.

Types of Jewish-Christianities in Christian Literatures

The four types of literatures briefly surveyed above offer a significant amount of confusing information about a bewildering variety of Jewish-Christianities. It is not my intention here to order that information into any comprehensive picture of Jewish-Christianities in late antiquity. I should, rather, like to survey the broad categories of information which the literatures present, with some examples from each and some comment on the problems they present. This overview will enable those who are not specialists in Jewish-Christianity to see where they might best apply contributions from their own disciplines.

The Jewish-Christian communities are often identified by name. Thus, we know of Ebionites, Nazorenes, Elchesites, Cerinthians, and Symmachians, among others.[17] There is an almost irresistible desire among scholars to equate these groups, to assume that different heresiologists gave different names to the same group, to take groups described but not named and presume these to be those. While the desire to impose order on this variety of names is an understandable occupation of scholarship, it is dangerous. First, one suspects the idea of monolithic Jewish-Christianity lurking behind the tendency. Second the equation of two groups which have broadly the same outline in no way guarantees the actual existence of but one group in historical reality. Obviously, if groups were Jewish-Christian they had many similarities. Nevertheless, ideology or locale or chronology caused them to be, in fact, disparate communities. Though the

---

there are those who wish that hard-to-classify groups like the Jewish-Christians would just go away, e. g., A. T. Kraabel, "The Disappearance of the God-Fearers," *Numen* 28 (1981): 113-126; this despite the evidence of rabbinic literature and the Sebomenoi inscription. See L. H. Feldman, "The Omnipresence of the God-Fearers," *Biblical Archeology Review* 12 (5, 1986): 58-69, with the response by Kraabel et al., ibid., pp. 44-57, and see J. Gager, "Jews, Gentiles, and Synagogues in the Book of Acts," in G. W. E. Nickelsburg and G. W. MacRae, eds., *Christians Among Jews and Gentiles* (Philadelphia: Fortress Press, 1986) pp. 91-99.

[17] See Klijn and Reinink for full details.

existence of different names does not guarantee the existence of different communities, it is the burden of the scholar to *prove* that only one group existed. Though it is far from tidy, one suspects that the very nature of the Jewish-Christian communities as pariahs from the "Great Church" and "Synagogue" caused considerable fragmentation. When the church gained power and began rooting out "heresies," prudence and safety must have caused the communities to remain small and scattered. The same holds true for the earlier period when Roman or Jewish authorities were the acting powers. Unfortunately for modern scholars, this all but guaranteed a wide variety of theology and praxis. The consequences of this historical necessity were varying locales, theologies, and practices, which will now be surveyed.

A variety of centers are suggested as loci for Jewish-Christianity. Epiphanius (*Pan. haer.* 29.7) alone lists four: Beroea in Coele-Syria, the Decapolis, Pella, and Kokhaba. Of course, most of the locales that supported large Christian communities are suggested as Jewish-Christian centers. So we read reports about the communities of Asia Minor, Palestine (where it all began),[18] Rome (where it all continued),[19] and that most idiosyncratic of all cities in the Levant, Antioch.[20]

The latter two cities have had their histories exhaustively written and rewritten. Rome is so complex that one is almost tempted to exclude it from research simply because it's just too hard to master. But the mastery of Rome has long been a motif in Jewish and Christian literatures, so one must plunge into the Jewish-Christianities of the city. A look at any recent history will provide an adequate point of departure for literary bibliography on both pagan and Christian sources. One should also consider carefully the evidence of the catacombs, both "Christian" and "Jewish," but with the provisos about archaeology mentioned above.[21]

Antioch deserves careful consideration thanks to the evidence of both Ignatius and John Chrysostom regarding Judaizing there. First, one must contend with the problem that when Ignatius writes of Jewish-Christianity, he is writing to communities in Asia Minor and not, at first blush, speaking

---

[18] For Asia Minor the old works of W. Ramsay, *St. Paul the Traveller* (New York, 1896) and *Cities and Bishoprics of Phrygia* (Oxford, 1897), remain useful. See also Barrett, "Jews and Judaisers." For Palestine the most notable, if thoroughly credulous, efforts are by B. Bagatti, *The Church from the Gentiles in Palestine* (Jerusalem, 1971) and *The Church from the Circumcision* (Jerusalem, 1971)

[19] E. g., R. E. Brown in Brown and Meier, *Antioch and Rome*, with the bibliography there.

[20] Meier in ibid.; Grant, "Jewish Christianity at Antioch"; Barrett, "Jews and Judaisers"; Meeks and Wilken, *Jews and Christians in Antioch*.

[21] The material remains require a *critical* reevaluation in light of Jewish-Christianities. The best analysis of the Jewish catacombs remains Harry Leon, *The Jews of Ancient Rome* (Philadelphia, 1960), while the best collection of the art remains E. R. Goodenough, *Jewish Symbols in the Greco-Roman Period*, vol. 3 (New York, 1953).

about Antioch.[22] Second, and more pressing, is whether or not Ignatius speaks of Jewish-Christianity at all. This depends in large part on one's definition of Jewish-Christianity and its relationship to Judaizing. These issues are discussed below.

John Chrysostom speaks clearly about the situation in his own church in Antioch. Again, one must decide whether the Judaizers whom he excoriates are to be counted as Jewish-Christians. Despite the possible lack of evidence from these two main Christian sources on Antioch, most historians of the city write about the Jewish-Christianity there. I suspect that this is a wise course, if for no other reason than the probabilities of demography in antiquity.[23]

Theologies also varied widely among the Jewish-Christian communities. There were those who no doubt merely professed Christ as Messiah. Others were ready to admit of Jesus as Son of God (see the reports in Jerome and Epiphanius). One can be sure that the complexities of Jewish-Christian Christology extended into the higher realms as well, with some communities professing Jesus as God. The last profession necessitated at minimum a kind of dualistic theology, and one presumes that in the theological whirlwind of the forth century there were some forms of Trinitarian communities, too.

Other aspects of the Christology of some Jewish-Christians are known. Jerome reports communities who professed that Jesus was born of the virgin, suffered the passion, and was resurrected. Available evidence does not tell us much about the cosmologies of Jewish-Christians (unless the Gnostic literatures on this subject are considered Jewish-Christian) or other theological considerations. Given the extraordinary range of theological debate in the church from the second through the fifth century, this lack of information is perhaps surprising, but comes as somewhat of a relief. Extra information on theology would provide the temptation of aligning Jewish-Christianities with certain other "theological heresies." The state of Jewish-Christian studies is not ready for such a lure to misadventure.

---

[22] See particularly Barrett, "Jews and Judaisers." On Ignatian problems in general, see the discussions and bibliographies in W. Schoedel, *Ignatius of Antioch* (Philadelphia, 1985), and idem, "Theological Norms and Social Perspectives in Ignatius of Antioch," in E. P. Sanders, ed., *Jewish and Christian Self-Definition*, vol. 1 (Philadelphia, 1980), pp. 34 ff.

[23] See Wilken, *John Chrysostom and the Jews*; Meeks and Wilken, *Jews and Christians in Antioch*; G. Downey, *A History of Antioch in Syria* (Princeton, 1961); J. H. W. G. Leibschuetz, *Antioch: City and Imperial Administration in the Later Roman Empire* (Oxford, 1972); and the older works by C. H. Kraeling, "The Jewish Community at Antioch," *Journal of Biblical Literature* 51 (1932): 130-160; and S. Krauss, "Antioche," *Revue des études juives* 45 (1902): 27-49, and idem, s. v. "Antioch," *Jewish Encyclopedia* 1: 632 f.

More than two decades ago Marcel Simon commented on the importance of observances in defining Jewish-Christianities.[24] Particularly in light of Rabbinic Judaism's emphasis on law observance, this area requires much more attention than Simon's suggestions have attracted. First, one must consider varieties of law observance; the "Jewish" side, if you will, of Jewish-Christianities. Foremost among these observances is circumcision. Since New Testament times this has been the subject of active debate in Christian communities. Since there were even rabbinic Jews prepared to forgo the requirement of circumcision,[25] one must a least speculate on the possibility of Jewish-Christian communities in which circumcision was *not* one of the required observances. Obviously, there were communities which did require circumcision. One wonders, however, how firmly they clung to this requirement in light of Roman (and later Roman-Christian) legislation against the practice.

Another requirement of law-observant Jewish communities was ritual immersion (as distinct from Christian baptism). This demanded a ritual immersion pool (*mikvah*) holding a given amount of "living," that is, flowing, water (for Rabbinic Judaism, 40 *seahs*). The mikvah was probably used for conversion rituals for both men and women. It was also used, in Rabbinic Judaism and at Qumran, for restoring ritual fitness (*taharah*). Literary evidence offers very little about the use of the mikvah in Jewish-Christianity, but archaeological data may yield information. They will only do so, however, when the possibility of mikvah among Jewish-Christians is included in the interpretation of sites (i. e., a mikvah on a site does not automatically make it a Jewish site, nor does an immersion pool in a church automatically have to be a baptismal font).

Eating customs varied widely in antiquity, even among Jewish communities. Thus it is possible that some followed the biblical dietary laws but nevertheless transgressed the rabbinic laws of kashrut. The sectarians of Qumran had their own ways of eating. Acts 15 offers a series of food laws (this belongs more properly below under church custom) which may or may not have been observed. The Cologne Mani Codex evidences vegetarianism. In the rabbinic communities, great care was taken regarding table fellowship, so that ḥaverim would not eat with others. Since table companions formed small communities, Jewish-Christian communities may be distinguished from one another based on their eating customs. Christian literature offers us very little information about the general eating habits of Jewish-Christians.

---

[24] Simon, "Problemes du Judeo-Christianisme" (see n. 1).

[25] See the texts adduced in L. Schiffman, "At the Crossroads: Tannaitic Perspectives on the Jewish-Christian Schism," in *Jewish and Christian Self-Definition* (Philadelphia, 1981), 2: 115-156, and idem, *Who Was a Jew?* (Hoboken, 1985). Schiffman's analyses view the evidence through modern Orthodox Jewry's perspectives.

Jerome and Epiphanius refer to the Sabbath and festival observances of the Jewish-Christian communities they describe. Do they refer only to a Saturday Sabbath rather than Sunday, or are there specific observances attached? Do some Jewish-Christian groups refrain from labor on the Sabbath? If so, do they refrain from the same labors as rabbinic Jews? Qumranites? Pagan authors observed the Jewish custom of Sabbath candle-lighting. [26] Did Jewish-Christians share this practice? It seems the Jewish-Christians frequented the Temple when it stood;[27] did synagogue attendance become the norm following 70?[28]

Both pagan and Christian authors attest to a variety of Jewish fasts, some on the Sabbath. While the latter are usually dismissed as misperceptions, the question is by no means closed. Rabbinic Judaism knows of Sabbath fasting (e. g., b.Taanit 12b, where it is permitted to fast on the Sabbath to avert the effects of a bad dream); why must uninformed pagan minds necessarily err? Like small children, they may well report accurately the mysteries they observe. Were any of the Jewish-Christian communities partners to these fasts?

Jerome also writes of offering sacrifices. Here, too, the literary evidence is dismissed out of hand – after 70 there could not have been sacrifice. Why not? There is rabbinic evidence showing a serious concern about sacrificing after the Temple's destruction.[29] Perhaps the Jewish-Christian communities of whom Jerome speaks took the levitical prescriptions requiring sacrifice seriously enough to ignore or reinterpret the deuteronomic prohibitions against sacrifice outside of Jerusalem Temple. The Qumran community might also offer archaeological evidence for such non-Temple sacrifices.

Last on the list of suggested "Jewish" observances to be considered in the study of Jewish-Christianities is clothing. There is ample evidence that a variety of garments distinguished Jews from non-Jews. First were the biblically enjoined phylacteries and fringes. There is New Testament and archaeological evidence for the former. But there are other dress elements which also distinguished Jews. Art shows us a gamma pattern woven into Jewish clothing. This was later adopted by the Great Church and persists today in the altar cloth. Did Jewish-Christians adorn themselves with gamma cloth? Were they the means by which the pattern came to the church? Finally, the rabbis seem to have carried a wallet and worn a mantle

---

[26] See M. Stern, *Pagan Authors on Jews and Judaism* (Jerusalem, 1974), 1: 422, 436.

[27] See Brown, "Not Jewish Christianity."

[28] John Chrysostom writes about his Judaizers going to the synagogues to hear the shofar blowing, take oaths, and the like. His Judaizers also attended the shrine of Matrona(?).

[29] See, most recently, the discussion and references is B. Bokser, *The Origins of the Seder* (Berkeley, 1984), pp. 101-106.

(see, e. g., m.RH 2: 9), as did members of the philosophic schools. Did any Jewish-Christians consider themselves sufficiently aligned to philosophy (as did the Great Church) that they might have adopted this special garb as well?

After consideration of this dizzying array of practices (which are but a sampling of possible Jewish observances that the Jewish-Christians may have shared), one must also look to their "Christian" rituals. Again, a brief listing of practices which marked distinctions in church communities must suffice. The obvious place to start asking questions about "church" ritual in Jewish-Christianities is at the baptismal font. Was baptism required for "conversion"? Was it accomplished by total immersion, or did aspersion suffice? When were Jewish-Christians baptized – at birth, at the age of reason, or perhaps on the deathbed? Was there but one baptism, or could there be further baptisms for impurities of one sort or another, like mikvah?

If baptism was not like mikvah, one still must ask about the possibility of a second baptism following the custom of exhomologesis. Finally, one may inquire about the role of chrism in Jewish-Christian forms of baptism. Water also raises the issue of types of eucharist, since there is evidence that some communities performed the sacrament with water in place of wine. [30] Water generates many questions and must suffice for the present as a guide to investigating types of "church" ritual in Jewish-Christian communities.

Rituals such as baptism and circumcision lead one to considerations about the demographic makeup of the varying Jewish-Christian communities. I suspect that the simplest way to approach this very complicated issue of prosopography is by inquiring about the parentage of members of these groups. Were they law-observant Jews? Law-observant Christians (I am not clear whether this necessarily means they were Jewish-Christians, it depends upon defining the term)? Perhaps the parents were non-law-observant Jews (there must have been a substantial number in every big city with a Jewish population). Of course, the parents could have been Christians from the law-free church, or pagans.

The Jewish-Christian communities may have required differing levels of observance from those of varying parentage. Thus, a Jewish-Christian coming from a law-observant Jewish family might have been required to remain law-observant, while a Jewish-Christian coming from a pagan background might only have had the requirements of Acts 15 laid upon him – we do not know. That varying degrees of ritual observance may have been enjoined upon members of the same community, depending upon their

---

[30] See e. g., Acts of Thomas 120 (Edgar Hennecke, *New Testament Apocrypha*, edited by W. Schneemelcher [Philadelphia, 1965], 2: 507 and see p. 438), and Irenaeus, *Adv. haer*, V. 1, 3 (see Klijn and Reinink, *Patristic Evidence for Jewish Christian Sects*. p. 72, n. 4).

origins, must be admitted as a possibility. Unfortunately, this possibility exacerbates an already difficult situation if one was intending to sort out varieties of Jewish-Christianity by means of their observances.

One last issue must be considered in this section about types of Jewish-Christianities, and that is the relations of each of these groups with other Christian communities (the Jewish ones are discussed below). Here, chronology surfaces as a vexing problem which has otherwise remained lurking beneath the study of Jewish-Christianities. In the beginning, all Christians were Jewish-Christians. Later, but still during the New Testament era, the Jewish-Christians were generally identified with the Jerusalem community.[31] Still later, Eusebius moved the Jewish-Christian community to Pella, and somewhat later than that, they moved themselves.[32] Of course, this movement of Jewish-Christianity was not simply a linear progression of one community, as R. E. Brown and J. L. Martyn have shown. But their works have only opened the door to understanding the varieties of Jewish-Christianity extant in the first century.

On the other side of the time line, we find Jewish-Christians and Judaizers flourishing in the fourth and fifth centuries (so, e. g., in the reports of Jerome, Epiphanius, and John Chrysostom). While we have more information about these groups, we also remain far from writing the authoritative history of Jewish-Christianities in that period. As for the middle ground – the second and third centuries – not only does it remain obscure for the history of Jewish-Christianities, but it raises the question of continuity between the New Testament Jewish-Christians and those described by the later church fathers.[33]

The question of continuity, of "apostlicity," if you will, affects the relationships of these Jewish-Christian churches with others. If a Jewish-Christian community could claim direct lineage with, say, the community of James, brother of Jesus, another church would be hard-pressed to excommunicate them without first refuting the claim. Even without direct continuity, churches were sensitive enough to varieties of practice and theology to recognize some legitimacy in Jewish-Christian claims. Nevertheless, the theological necessities of the law-free church forced them to take a rigid rather than assimilative stance toward law-observant Christian communities. Hence in attempting to define the parameters of such a community, one must inquire into the relationship of any Jewish-Christian

---

[31] See Brown, "Not Jewish Christianity."

[32] See G. Lüdemann, "The Successors of Pre-70 Jerusalem Christianity: A Critical Evaluation of the Pella-Tradition," in E. P. Sanders, ed., *Jewish and Christian Self-Definition* (Philadelphia, 1980), 1: 161-173; and cf. M. Simon, "La migration à Pella: legende ou realite?" *Recherches de science religieuse* 60 (1972): 37-54.

[33] E. g., J. Munck, "Primitive Jewish Christianity and Later Jewish Christianity: Continuation or Rupture?" in *Aspects du Judeo-Christianisme*, pp. 77-93. Munck favors rupture.

sect with the "Great Church," the Eastern churches (e. g., the Marcionites, those described by Bauer in the first chapter of *Orthodoxy and Heresy*, and those behind the Cologne Mani Codex), and other Christian communities.

Problems of Perception

I have consistently noted that one of the chief problems in the study of Jewish-Christianities is, quite simply, defining the parameters of the discipline. While it is true that such definition is a concern of virtually every scholarly discipline, it is acute in the study of Jewish-Christianities. First, there is no broad consensus of definition about the terminology.[34] Second, the evidence we have is fragmentary. For although the church fathers do write about Jewish-Christianities, and the rabbis seem to as well, the overall corpus of their own literature has been denied to us through the combined efforts of censorship and the ravages of time. Third, the problem is acute because of the need to address the many issues already outlined above.

I wish to address the first issue here, the problem of definition. Aside from the obvious kinds of quibbling that scholars engage in when marking out the borders of their disciplines and attempting to justify encroachment on their colleagues' preserves by claiming a need for intellectual *Lebensraum*, the study of Jewish-Christianities carries with it four other problems in definition. The first relates to the general issues of Jewish and Christian self-definition.[35] As I have indicated by my separation of theology and observance above, there are varying ways of approaching Jewish-Christianity. One must recognize that each of the ways carries with it religious overtones. Approaching Jewish-Christianity as a system or systems of beliefs is to approach the subject from an essentially Great Church Christian point of view. Similarly, approaching Jewish-Christianities by the observances they practice is to approach them from a Jewish *Weltanschauung*.[36] An attempt at synthesizing these two modes of approach may not only well serve the study of Jewish-Christianity, but may also have the happy side effect of mitigating the religious biases of those studying it.[37]

The next aspect of the problem of perception relates to the overall influence of Judaism on Christianity.[38] It cannot be denied that Judaism had an immense formative influence on Christianity and that its influence

---

[34] See above, n. 1.

[35] E. P. Sanders and his colleagues at MacMaster University have edited three notable volumes on the overall subject, called *Jewish and Christian Self-Definition*. None of the chapters deals with this specific aspect of the problem.

[36] Simon, "Problems du Judeo-Christianisme," pp. 1-17.

[37] See below.

[38] See Danielou and Kraft, cited above, n. 1.

continued, though radically curtailed, throughout the patristic period. I speak here of Great Church Christianity (whatever that may be), with full awareness of the profound effects paganism, philosophy, and other aspects of Hellenism had in drawing the church away from the synagogue. This being the case, however, merely identifying Jewish elements, even rabbinic elements, in Christian texts does not prove them Jewish-Christian in origin. A clear definition of Jewish-Christianity must overcome the enormous difficulty this problem poses in sorting out the origins and sources of any given community's (or text's) traditions.

The third issue of definition relates to drawing borders in very difficult territory. When is a Christian a Jewish-Christian and not merely a Judaizer? Need he be circumcised? I have suggested above that this may not be a hard-and-fast requirement for Jewish-Christianity (or Rabbinic Judaism). Need he merely profess Christ? If so, and if he is a law-observer, when does he cease to be a Jew with odd notions about Jesus and become, instead, a Jewish-Christian?[39] Does it depend on his Christology? I have suggested above that there are equally low and high Christologies to be found in the Jewish-Christian communities of antiquity. What, also, of the God-fearers, those semi-proselytes who were fellow travelers of the Jewish communities and were proselytized by the church?[40] In what category of Christianity, Judaism, or Jewish-Christianity will they be classified?

A final issue in the perception and definition of Jewish-Christianities lies in the biases of the observers. Among Christian scholars there are two tendencies which skew analyses. The first, which is very much in line with classical pre-Vatican II church theology, assumes that all Jews must ultimately become Christians. Thus Jewish-Christianity is to be understood as a stepping stone in the "evolution" of Judaism to Christianity. Scholars with this view evince no sympathy for Jewish-Christianity as an authentic religious phenomenon. The second tendency is related, and it presumes Jewish-Christianity to be an aberrant form of "real" Christianity, much as did the heresiologists. Almost all writers before Walter Bauer exhibited this tendency, and many still subscribe to its views. Again, it does not elicit either objective or sympathetic analysis of a religion in late antiquity.

Jewish scholars have a somewhat different set of biases when treating Jewish-Christianity. The first bias presumes it to be merely a Christian heresy, wholly unrelated to Judaism. This attitude causes scholars to overlook the evidence of Jewish-Christianity in rabbinic literature in particular. The second bias also refuses to offer integrity to Jewish-Christianity and

---

[39] These questions particularly affect one's views on Ignatius' and Chrysostom's "Judaizers" in Antioch.

[40] Kraabel, "Disappearance of the God-Fearers," pp. 113 ff., tries very hard to make them disappear. He ignores substantial rabbinic evidence to do this and has been recently confuted by epigraphic evidence; see n. 16 above.

treats it as merely a Jewish heresy. This bias results in an ecumenically more dangerous approach. It assumes that since the Jewish-Christians are really "Jews" and not "Christians," certain rabbinic polemics may be characterized as anti-Jewish-Christian and thus presented as a "family argument" of antiquity.[41] The assertion that such polemics are in no way anti-Christian ignores not only the authenticity of Jewish-Christianity as a religious phenomenon, but the sensitivities of modern Christians as well.

The issues surveyed thus far, and particularly the last set of biases discussed, prepare us to enter a specific discipline and survey its potential for a contribution to the study of Jewish-Christianities. The survey is in no way exhaustive. It is rather, as indicated at the outset of this essay, merely a chart for navigating the confluence of the two bodies of religious literature.

Jewish-Christianity in Rabbinic Literature

Only recently have scholars of rabbinic literature begun actively considering Jewish-Christians as possible targets of rabbinic polemic. Previously, the assumption had been that such passages were directed against Christians without any niceties of distinction.[42] More recently, for the apologetic reasons cited above, the pendulum has swung to the other extreme, citing only Jewish-Christians and virtually eliminating Great Church Christians as the objects of rabbinic polemic. A middle ground must be steered, especially on the polemical materials, since the texts themselves attest to rabbinic awareness of both types of Christianities.[43]

Nonpolemical texts also offer testimonies to both Christianity and Jewish-Christianities. In both sets of rabbinic materials (often hard to distinguish from one another) there are a wide variety of problems for the student to overcome. Primary among these is chronology. Rabbinic material includes more than a millennium of literature produced in many centers. Even the classical talmudic phase of rabbinic literature covers more than four centuries (ca. 70-500) and two major locales (Palestine and Babylonia). Despite repeated warnings, especially on the part of New Testament scholars, problems in rabbinic chronology remain largely ignored. It is not all unusual to see eighth- through eleventh-century documents cited

---

[41] See R. Kimelman, "*Birkat Ha-Minim* and the Lack of Evidence for an Anti-Christian Jewish Prayer in Late Antiquity," in *Jewish and Christian Self-Definition*, vol. 2 (London, 1981), pp. 226-244.

[42] This is betrayed in the titles, if not always the content, of books on the subject, e.g., R. T. Herford, *Christianity in Talmud and Midrash* (London, 1903).

[43] See, e.g., my "Overturning the Lamp," *Journal of Jewish Studies* 38 (1987): 72-80 and "Trinitarian Testimonies," *USQR*, 42 (1988): 73-85.

as sources for second- through fifth-century history. These anachronisms are perpetuated by Jewish and Christian scholars alike.

A concomitant to this problem is the fact that technical terminology does not remain static in the literature. Thus a term may mean one thing in tannaitic times (ca. 70–200) and quite another in amoraic literature (ca. 200–500). Or a term may mean one thing in Babylonia and another in Palestine. Worse, there are variations in technical terms even among the different schools in a given country (e. g., the "schools" of Akiba and Yishmael in second-century Palestine). Again, what may be a very specific term for one sage may mean something else entirely to another. Finally, certain sages seem to purposely embrace ambiguity and obfuscate their meanings (perhaps because of delators) in their choice of multivalent terminology. This is especially true in the polemical literature.

Having offered this pessimistic assessment for the possibilities of making any sense whatsoever out of rabbinic literature, let me list seven terms that are most popularly taken to have some bearing on the study of Jewish-Christianities. Chief among them is *min*, a rabbinic catchall which translates simply as "sectarian." The term abounds in the literature and refers, one suspects, to everything from Christian to Jewish-Christian to Qumranite, Zadokite, and later, even Karaite. Since the time of Jerome (*Ep.* 112. 13), attempts to define this term have been doomed to failure because of its purposely broad lexical range.[44] Nevertheless, one may be sure that among the *minim* one will find some Jewish-Christians.

Another popular rubric is *notsri*, which is variously etymologized as referring to Nazareth, nazirites, or the shoot (*netser*) of the Davidic monarchy who will sprout forth as the messiah. These "heretics" are often identified with the Nazorenes (or Nazarenes) listed in Christian literature and discussed above.[45] They may be Jewish-Christians, they may be Great Church Christians; I, for one, do not know. I suspect we cannot resolve the issue any more definitely here than we may for the *minim* because of the many reasons already suggested.

A third term often found in rabbinic literature is *nokhrim*, which means "strangers." It is euphemistic and so the antecedent is somewhat unclear. Again, as with the previous terms, it seems to refer to both types of Christians. Here the problem is more acute, for it may also suggest Roman pagans. Two other words refer to converts from Judaism to other religions – usually to Christianity or Jewish-Christianity. The first, *mumar*, refers to one who has changed his ideology; the second, *meshumad*, to one who has

---

[44] Thus the simple definitions offered by Schiffman (above, n. 25) and Kimelman (above, n. 41) cannot stand; but see their notes for full bibliography on attempts to limit the scope of the term.

[45] See Kimelman, "*Birkat Ha-Minim.*"

been baptized.[46] Each of these two terms is very suggestive for the study of Jewish-Christianities, since the rabbis were reluctant to admit that one born a Jew could convert away from Judaism. This would be especially true when such a one might still have been law-observant to some degree.

A separate category to be considered in the study of Jewish-Christianity is made up of those who subscribed to the notion of two Powers in heaven. This term implies a dualism which may well have been found in the theologies of some Jewish-Christian sects. I would in no way, however, limit the meaning of this term to Jewish-Christians alone. Rabbinic terminology of this type is far too fluid to be limited to merely one or two specific sects exclusively. [47]

The last item I wish to attend to here is really two separate terms, each of was substituted by censors over the centuries, in place of original terms which referred to Christianity and Jewish-Christianity. Thus passages which contain references to *'akum* (an acronym for *'ovdei kokhavim umazalot*, "constellation worshippers") might refer to idol worship. On the other hand, they may well refer to the Christianities being considered. Reference to manuscripts, particulary Sephardic ones not written in regions dominated by Christianity, usually restores the original reading. The same holds true of the other term often substituted by zealous censors, *ṣaduqim* ("Zadokites" or "Sadducees"). In both instances, context is often the best clue for finding a Christian or Jewish-Christian hiding behind a "new" reading.

Rabbinic literature recognizes the existence of Jews who did not live under rabbinic discipline. There are a large number of references to *'amei 'ares*, hoi polloi who have some affinity for rabbinic halacha, yet are not as strict about it as *ḥaberim*.[48] The rabbis also recognize other groups of law observant Jews, particularly pre-70 sectarians. Hence there are references to Sadducees, Haemerobaptists, and other separatists.[49]

More important to the study of Jewish-Christianities, especially in light of the considerations adduced above, are rabbinic references to semiproselytes, God-fearers, and others of unsure status in the rabbinic community. In addition to the *sebomenoi* and *theobomenoi* of Greek literature, the rabbis speak of *yer'ei shamayim* ("fearers of Heaven"). These fellow-travelers with the Jewish community constituted a class by themselves, frequently discussed in the literature. They are often considered with prose-

---

[46] See Schiffman, *Who Was a Jew?*

[47] Alan Segal, *Two Powers in Heaven* (Leiden, 1977), collects all of the rabbinic passages with this phrase.

[48] See A. Oppenheimer, *The Am Ha-Aretz* (Leiden, 1977).

[49] S. Lieberman, "The Discipline of the So-Called Dead Sea Manual of Discipline," *Texts and Studies* (New York, 1974), pp. 200-207. For other separatists the rabbis used the term *perushim*, otherwise translated Pharisees. See E. Rivkin, *Hebrew Union College Annual*, 1969, pp. 205 ff.

lytes of dubious status, such as the *gerei 'arayot* (usually translated as "lion proselytes").[50] Obviously, they are a fertile ground for Jewish-Christianity, both for the ancient missionizer and the modern scholar.

The Ten Tribes

Investigating evidence of semi-proselytes and the like in rabbinic literature is no simple matter. As Prof. Saul Lieberman points out,

> It is very probable that the people employed different names for the various groups of semi-converts, but in the comparatively scarce material on them, clear evidence of such distinct definitions is not forthcoming. However, it is possible that remnants of these different terms have been preserved in Talmudic literature.[51]

Indeed, among the many terms listed above for "heretics" and other not quite up to par rabbinic Jews, one often finds another slippery, multivalent expression: the Ten Tribes (*'aseret hashevatim*). I wish to suggest here that this term be added to the list of those others which might bear fruit for the study of Jewish-Christianities in rabbinic literature.

The "lost tribes" crop up in talmudic and midrashic texts among many groups, but particularly those with some affinities for Judaism. Of course, the rabbis often refer simply to Ten Tribes of the Bible (1 Kings 11: 31, 35) and their historic disappearance. But sometimes one must wonder if they are entirely assimilated in the sages' eyes. Rav Yehuda quoted the Babylonian Rav Asi, "We worry nowadays about the marriage of a gentile, lest he be from the Ten Tribes."[52] If the good rabbi is worrying about a descendant of the long-lost tribes, one can only marvel at the tenacious way Babylonians hold on to the memory of their ancestors. But perhaps the reference to the Ten Tribes indicates an interest in a much more contemporary phenomenon: Jewish converts to law-observant Jewish-Christianity. This may explain both the rabbis' inability to happily categorize them and the fact that they are often classified with semi-converts and non-Jews.[53]

---

[50] See Kraabel, n. 16 above. The seminal study remains S. Lieberman, "Gentiles and Semi-Proselytes," in his *Greek in Jewish Palestine* (New York, 1942), pp. 64-90.

[51] Lieberman, *Greek in Jewish Palestine*, p. 82. This section on the Ten Tribes is a revised and condensed version of a paper I delivered to the Early Rabbinic Studies Section of the Society for Biblical Literature, Dec. 20, 1982. My thanks to Profs. Shaye J. D. Cohen, J. L. Martyn, and Richard Sarason for their comments on the earlier draft.

[52] See b.Yebam 16a-17a and b. Nidda 56b.

[53] E.g., b.Yebam 17a, where Samuel considers the Ten Tribes to be entirely non-Jewish; the pericope goes on to consider Samaritans, who are deemed either true proselytes (*gerei 'emet*) or dubious ones (*gerei 'arayot*).

Thus, Leviticus Rabbah comments on Psalm 22:24,

Ye that fear God praise Him, All ye the seed of Jacob glorify Him. R. Yehoshua b. Levi said, *Ye that fear God* refers to the fearers of Heaven. R. Samuel b. Nahman said, It refers to full proselytes. R. Abbahu said in the name of R. Eleazar, If [fearers of Heaven are considered as] full proselytes [and] will be admitted in the Future World, Antoninus will come at the head of them. And what is implied by *All ye the seed of Jacob glorify Him?* It refers to the Ten Tribes.[54]

A much later midrash preserves yet another tradition linking the Ten Tribes with partial converts, "*Sheep* (Gen. 32:5) refers to the Ten Tribes ... and *menservants and maidservants* (ibid.) refers to the fearers of Heaven."[55] The Palestinian Talmud, discussing a parallel passage to the midrash extracted above, comments:

R. Lazar and R. Yehuda [disagreed]. One said, They [the Ten Tribes] were not exiled until they became uncircumcised. The other said, They were not exiled until they became *mamzerim.* The one who said uncircumcised [meant that they were so in regard to actual] circumcision [and in regard to observance of] the commandments. The one who said *mamzerim* [meant that they were estranged] from their ancestors. R. Yohanan said, The Israelites were not exiled until they had become twenty-four sects of heretics (*minim*).[56]

The discussion seems to offer intriguing information about the Ten Tribes. There is some disagreement as to their practice of circumcision and observance of commandments. There is the clear opinion that they are not fit to marry rabbinic Jews but are still considered Israelites nevertheless – for that is what it meant to be a *mamzer.*[57] Finally, the editor of the Talmud classifies them with *minim* by juxtaposition of rabbinic opinions. In the rabbinic literature surveyed thus far, the Ten Tribes are associated with God-fearers, and dubious converts. There is a question about their circumcision and observance of Jewish law. They are considered by at least one rabbi to be Jews but unfit to marry within the community.

The locales of these communities of Ten Tribes are often listed in rabbinic texts when tracing the exile of the biblical lost tribes. The same passage of the Palestinian Talmud reports: "Israel [viz., The Ten Tribes] was exiled to three places. First, beyond the River Sanbatyon. Second, to Daphne of Antioch; and third, the Cloud [of Glory] descended and

---

[54] LevR 3:2, following the interpretation of Lieberman, *Greek in Jewish Palestine*, pp. 82f. Cf. j.San 29c.

[55] *Sekhel Tov* to Gen 32:5 (ed. Buber, 181). Lieberman comments: "The Palestinian tradition seems to have compared the fate of the 'fearers of heaven' to that of the Ten Tribes" (*Greek in Jewish Palestine*, p. 83, n. 114)

[56] j. San 29c.

[57] See Schiffman, *Who Was a Jew?*

covered them."[58] Yet another midrash locates the Ten Tribes in Antioch, as Leviticus Rabbah comments on Amos 6:

> *Ah, you who are at ease in Zion* refers to the tribes of Judah and Benjamin. *And confident on the hill of Samaria*, this refers to the Ten Tribes. ... *Cross over to Calneh and see* refers to Ktesiphon. *Go from there to great Hamath* refers to *hamat* of Antioch. *And go down to Gath of the Philistines* – that is the fortresses of Palestine.[59]

Asia Minor is offered as a possible locale in the curious statement of R. Helbo, "The wine of Phrygia and the waters of Emmaus (or: Demosit) did in the Ten Tribes."[60] The juxtaposition of sacramental wine and water is also suggestive of Jewish-Christian or Christian referents for the term, Ten Tribes, used here.

The rabbis puzzled over the ultimate fate of the Ten Tribes. If the term does refer to law-observant Jewish-Christian converts from Judaism, one readily understands the rabbis' reluctance to give up on them entirely. As explained above, such observant Jews could be viewed as within the broad pale of rabbinic Judaism – the rabbis were loath to lose even one Jew of their number, no matter what they thought about Jesus. Yet others (like R. Samuel cited in n. 53) considered them lost to Judaism – they were Christians through and through. This ambiguity might explain a debate found in the chapter of Mishna which begins "All Israel have a place in the world to come," and then goes on to list the twenty exceptions to the rule.

> The Ten Tribes will not return [=repent] in the future, as it is said, *And [God] cast them into another land, as this day* (Deut. 29:27). Just as the day goes and does not return, so they have gone and will not return; this is the opinion of R. Akiba. R. Eliezer says, *As this day,* just as a day begins in darkness and grows light, so too the Ten Tribes who are now in darkness will have light in the future.[61]

If the term Ten Tribes is one of the ambiguous code words used in rabbinic literature, it offers rich possibilities for further research in Jewish-Christianities. I would suggest that the term is a rabbinic response to the Christian claims of being *verus Israel*. The various Jewish-Christian churches claimed to be the true Israel and referred to themselves as the

---

[58] j.San 29c and LamR 2:9, GenR 73:6, PesRabbati 31. Cf. Josephus, *War* VII, 96-99, and Pliny, *Natural History* 31:11, for Sanbatyon.

[59] LevR 5:3 and YalSh Amos #545.

[60] b.Shab 147b; cf. ARN A 14, ARN B 29, and LevR 5:3. For wine as the cause of the destruction of the Ten Tribes, see GenR 36:4, LevR 12:1, EstR 5:1, NumR 9:7 (where they are also accused of wife-swapping), TanB Noah 22-all based on exegesis of Amos 6. For other locales of exile, see b. Yebam 16b-17a, b.Kid 72a, and b.San 94a-b.

[61] m.San 10:3, cf. t.San, chap. 13, b.San 110b, j.San 29c.

Twelve Tribes.[62] The rabbis, whatever they may have thought about the ultimate fate of these Jewish-Christians, denigrated this claim. Only rabbinic Jews were the true Israel, the faithful remnant of Benjamin and Judah. As for the Jewish-Christian pretenders, the rabbis dismissed them as "lost." Some denied them even a share in the world-to-come. Yet by virtue of their Jewish birth and law observance they were accorded the dubious title of the Ten Tribes.

Conclusion

The inclusion of the phrase Ten Tribes with the other rabbinic terms of reference discussed above completes this survey. Rabbinics scholars will, no doubt, have many details to add to my sketch of the field and its potential for the study of Jewish-Christianities. On the other hand, church historians will wish to fill many noticeable lacunae in my overview of nonrabbinic materials. My intention was neither to be comprehensive nor complete – others far more competent than I will spend years completing the task.

The purpose of this prolegomenon has been to offer those in other disciplines a guide to the eddies and swirls one encounters in the study of Jewish-Christianities. This navigational report of my attempts to steer a course is meant to help other students chart their own routes. Jewish-Christianities is a subject which falls outside of the traditionally defined parameters in the study of Judaism and Christianity. Only when scholars in all of the attendant disciplines combine their expertise can the subject be adequately illuminated.

---

[62] Epistle of James 1:1. R. E. Brown (*Antioch and Rome*, p. 131, n. 277) comments that the epistle "is addressed to the twelve tribes (Jewish Christians [*sic*]) in the diaspora."

Three Syriac Cruxes

It is often the case that Syriac and rabbinic literatures prove mutually illu-minative. The linguistic affinities and shared vocabularies of the Aramaic dialects in the two sets of texts offer a starting-point for comparison. The special place of the Syriac Church within the history of Christianity and its propinquity to Babylonian Jewry offers further ground for looking to the common cultural characteristics of the two communities to help unravel knotty textual difficulties. I offer here three instances where the crossing of the literatures helps solve cruxes of interpretation.

I

The Gospel of John reports the aftermath of the death of Jesus:

> Now in the place where Jesus had been crucified there was a garden, and in the garden a new tomb in which no one had ever been buried. And so, because of the Jewish Day of Preparation, they buried Jesus in the nearby tomb. Early on the first day of the week, while it was still dark, Mary Magdalene came to the tomb. She saw that the stone had been moved away from the tomb; so she went running to Simon Peter and to the other disciple (the one whom Jesus loved) and told them, 'They took the Lord from the tomb, and we do not know where they put him!' ... (Remember that as yet they did not understand the Scripture that Jesus had to rise from the dead.)[1]

Matthew 27-28 reports Jesus' prediction, 'after three days I will rise' (27: 63), and its fulfilment on the Sunday after his crucifixion. Mark 15-16 reports the same story, as does Luke 23-24. Paul characterizes it in credal tones in I Cor. 15: 3-4. The rare concurrence of all four gospels with Paul merely serves to underscore the importance of the three days and the difficulty ex-egetes have in explicating how noon Friday to the wee hours of Sunday[2] may be considered the three days of Jesus' prediction. Yet the crux is

---

[1] Raymond E. Brown, *The Gospel According to John* XIII-XXI (Anchor Bible, vol. 29a, Garden City, 1970) 932f., 979 with Brown's notes and commentary ad loc.

[2] Approximately 42 hours, i. e. 30 hours shy of the 72 hours which constitute three complete days.

generally overlooked in Christian exegetical literature in favour of the theological and soteriological significance of the crucifixion and resurrection.[3] The Syriac fathers have turned their attention to the disparate chronology (while not ignoring the theology), and I wish to report on two of them and discuss possible sources for their means of reckoning.

The Didascalia Apostolorum Syriace[4] reports in Chapter 21:

> They crucified Him on the same Friday. He suffered, then, at the sixth hour on Friday. And those hours wherein our Lord was crucified were reckoned a day. And afterwards, again, there was darkness for three hours, and it was reckoned a night. And again, from the ninth hour until evening, three hours, (reckoned) a day. And afterwards again, the night of the Sabbath of the Passover ... And again (there was) the day of the Sabbath and then three hours of the night after the Sabbath, wherein our Lord slept. And that was fulfilled which He said, 'The Son of Man must pass through the heart of the earth three days and three nights' (Matt. 12:40), as it is written in the Gospel. And again, it is written in David: 'Behold, thou hast set up my days in measure' (Ps. 39:6). Now, because those days and nights came short, it was so written.

The DA explicitly recognizes the disparity between the New Testament prediction and the actual resurrection – 'those days and nights came short' – and justifies them with a midrash on Ps. 39:6, which apparently presumes

---

[3] Thus Pheme Perkins, *Resurrection* (Garden City, 1984), index, s. v. 'on the third day', does not attempt to calculate the disparity but dwells on the implications of the event at large. Raymond E. Brown, *The Gospel According to John I-XII* (Anchor Bible, vol. 29, Garden City, 1966), 123, explains '"three days" was an expression that meant a short, but indefinite time'. In a private conversation, Professor Brown alluded to the reckonings discussed below but stated that the Christian viewpoint on the 'three days' was that the resurrection was timeless. This perhaps explains the general lack of interest by the Latin and Greek fathers and modern Catholic exegetes in the exact chronology. For the sake of accuracy it should be noted that Epiphanius, *Haer* LXX: 10-12, paraphrases the Didascalia here (see Connolly, *Didascalia* (below) 181, n. 13, and Funk, *Apostolic Constitutions* II 4-6); Epiphanius probably comes to these traditions through his Palestinian associations and his knowledge of Hebrew and Syriac. Gregory of Nyssa also discusses the chronological crux (Migne, *PG* 46, 612D ff., and 628 D ff., which are Orations I and II of Gregory's *In Christi Resurrectionem*; on the dubious authenticity of Orat. II, see Quasten, *Patrology* III, 227). Gregory might have had access to Semitic traditions, but his reckoning combined with the possible Greek *Vorlage* of Didascalia Apostolorum Syriace as a source for this tradition could point to Hellenistic as well as Syriac traditions on 'the three days'.

[4] Henceforth DA; see Paulus de Lagarde, *Didascalia Apostolorum Syriace* (Wiesbaden, 1854, 1967), 88; A. Vööbus, *CSCO* 407 (Louvain, 1979), 207. English translations in R. H. Connolly, *Didascalia Apostolorum* (Oxford, 1929), 181-2; and the discussion, ibid., 265-7; A. Vööbus, *CSCO* 408 (Louvain, 1979) 190-1. There is no appreciable difference between the Vööbus versions and the earlier text and translations of this passage; I follow Vööbus because it is more recent.

This passage is extant only in the Syriac text and not found in the Verona Latin fragments. It stems, I suspect, from the Syriac recension of DA and not from the hypothetical Greek *Vorlage* (but cf. Apostolic Const., ed. Funk, p. 275 for a late Greek rendering). This explains the affinities with Aphrahat.

God the Father to be speaking to Jesus, 'Behold, thou hast set up my days in measure', that is to say, a lesser measure than the norm. This reading of the verse follows the Peshitta[5] for its text, but the interpretation seems to conform to the targumic rendering, 'You have arranged my days short (or: [too] quickly)'. The NJV seems to take up this reading as well when it translates. 'You have made my life just handbreadths long; [its span is as nothing in your sight]'.

Indeed, for the DA the days run quickly. Day One of the three begins on Friday morning and ends with the 'night' of crucifixion, which fell from the sixth hour (noon) until the ninth hour (3 p.m.). Day Two then begins on Friday mid-afternoon and has its day from the ninth hour until sunset at the twelfth hour. Night Two is Friday night. Day Three starts on Saturday morning and continues into Saturday night for three hours: three full days, as it were, following which the resurrected Jesus appears. Counting morning and then evening, Day One, Two, Three, the DA preserves the prophecy of three full days from death to resurrection with but one small catch: the days are full only to the extent that one may consider nine or fifteen hours a full day.

The Syriac Father, Aphrahat, shares the DA's assumption that part of the day may be counted as a whole day, but reckons his days like the Jews — first evening, then morning — a day. In his Twelfth Homily, on Patscha or Passover,[6] Aphrahat reasons:

> From the time that He gave His Body to be eaten and His Blood to be drunk there were three days and three nights, thus: The hour, it saith, was night when Judas went out from them and they, his eleven disciples, ate our Lord's Body and drank His Blood: behold now one night, that in which the Friday drew on. And until the sixth hour they judged Him: behold one day and one night. And (there were) the three hours wherein there was darkness, from the sixth hour to the ninth, and three hours after the darkness: behold two days and two nights. And (there was) the complete night when the Sabbath drew on and the whole day of the Sabbath. There were fulfilled accordingly to our Lord three days and three nights with the dead; and in the night of the first of the week He rose from the dead.

---

[5] Differing only in the verb *smt* for the Peshitta *yhbt*. Voöbus note, ad loc., is inexplicable.

[6] Syriac text in W. Wright, *The Homilies of Aphraates the Persian Sage* (London, 1869), 221-3; J. Parisot, *Patrologia Syriaca*, I: *Aphraatis Sapientis Persae Demonstrationes* (Paris, 1894), 516-22; Latin translation, ibid., 515-21; English translation in Neusner (below, n. 19), 35-6. I follow here the translation offered by Connolly (above, n. 4), 266-7. Cf. Ephrem, who is also aware of this tradition: *Hymni de Crucifixione* VII in T. J. Lamy (ed.)[=E. Beck (ed.), H. Cruc. VI (*CSCO* 248-9)], *Sancti Ephraem Syri Hymni et Sermones*, vol. I (Mechliniae, 1882), 695-706 (Syriac text and Latin trans.) and see Armenian Hymn 48 in L. Maries and Ch. Mercier (eds.), *Hymnes de Saint Ephrem Conservées en Version Arménienne = Patrologia Orientalis* 30 (Paris, 1967), 222-7 (Armenian and Latin trans.). I omit exegesis of Ephrem for the sake of brevity.

Aphrahat counts his nights and days starting from the Last Supper. Thus his first day runs for a full night and a six-hour day—eighteen hours. Day Two runs from darkness at noon for a three-hour night and for the remainder of Friday before sunset—another three hours – yielding a six-hour long Day Two. Day Three is the twenty-four-hour Sabbath, much as in the Jewish calendar.

Both the DA and Aphrahat explicate the three days and three nights Jesus spent in the grave by implicitly invoking the principle that part of the day may be considered a whole day. For Greek and Latin fathers the principle is unknown and the crux ignored in favour of theological issues. The crux could be addressed only in a milieu where the idea that six or nine or even three hours can be counted as a full day.

The rabbis of the Babylonian Talmud are intimately familiar with this principle and explicitly enunciate it on a variety of occasions. Thus when counting days of menstrual unfitness the sages enquire whether the day on which bleeding ceases may be included among the clean days, for do we not follow the principle that part of the day is considered as the entire day?[7] Or, on the issue of first-born children, the sages require an embryo to have gestated six months before it may have first-born status. What of the last day of month five, the sages enquire. Do we follow the principle that part of the day is considered as the entire day?[8]

Elsewhere in the Talmud the principle is invoked regarding fulfillment of the thirty days of a Nazirite vow.[9] More in keeping with Last Supper chronology, the sages also enquire about the permissibility of labour on the day before Passover. Again, the principle of 'partial days' is invoked to untangle the issue.[10]

The *locus classicus* for the principle of 'partial days' is found regarding a legal matter with even more direct applicability to Jesus' death and resurrection: the rabbinic laws of mourning. How does one count the seven days of bereavement following burial, during which it is forbidden to shave? If the eighth day falls on a Sabbath or festival, could one shave in preparation for the holy day, even though it would still be during the seventh day of mourning? Yes, states the Talmud, for in matters of bereavement following burial the principle is held that a partial day counts as though it were a complete day.[11]

It happens that the Talmud attributes this principle to Abba Sha'ul, an early second-century Palestinian. It is nice to find it reported at such an

---

[7] b.Nidda 33a.

[8] b. Bek 20b and Rashi, ad loc. Cf. b. Bek 21 a.

[9] b. Nazir 5b, 6a and see 15b.

[10] b. Pes 55a and Rashi, ad loc.

[11] b.MK 17b, 19b, 20b and b. Pes 4a. Cf. b. MK 16b, where the principle is invoked for the thirtieth day of a ban.

early era, but for our purpose it is sufficient that it is recognized even two centuries later, in Babylonia.

For members of the Jewish community it was common practice to count partial days as complete ones for a variety of legal situations – as legally serious as menstruation, which carries the penalty of extirpation, or as conservative and superstitious as bereavement and mourning custom. Only with this background could the Syriac Fathers tackle the crux of Jesus' burial and resurrection after the third day.

II

The Syriac Acts of Thomas[12] reports how Judas Thomas was brought as a slave to India, there to preach the gospel. Act two recounts how Thomas agrees to build a palace for King Gundaphar:

> But all the money that is given him for the palace he spends among the poor. When King Gundaphar discovers it he is very angry, and casts Thomas into prison till he shall make up his mind by what death he shall die. Now that very night Gad, the King's brother, dies and is taken by angels to heaven: there he sees a magnificent palace, which is the very palace that has been built for his brother by the Apostle. So Gad begs to be allowed to come back to life that he may buy the palace from the King, as he does not know its value. This is granted; but when the King hears the tale he understands and believes. Thomas is set free, and the King and his brother are both baptised...[13]

This delightful story of building a palace in heaven has all the earmarks of an easily adaptable folk tale.[14] The motif of constructing a palace in the after-life could imaginably be found in any culture that (a) accepted the idea of reward in some other world than this, and (b) found some virtue in almsgiving. I wish to focus here on a celebration of those themes in rabbinic Judaism. As early as the third century we read in the Tosefta:

---

[12] W. Wright, *Apocryphal Acts of the Apostles*, vol. I: *The Syriac Texts* (London, 1871). 172-333, esp. 185-97; ibid., vol. II: *The English Translation* (London, 1871), 146-298, esp. 159-69. The Greek recension in M. Bonnet, *Acta Philippi et Acta Thomae* (Darmstadt, 1959), 99-288, esp. 124-8. More recently A. F. J. Klijn, *The Acts of Thomas: Introduction–Text–Commentary* (Leiden, 1962), passim, esp. 73-9, 200-22. Idem, 'The Influence of Jewish Theology on the Odes of Solomon and the Acts of Thomas', *Aspects du judeo-christianisme: Colloque de Strasbourg, 23-25 Avril 1964* (Paris, 1965). The discussion in F. C. Burkitt, *Early Eastern Christianity*, 199-211, and *Early Christianity Outside the Roman Empire*, 63-86, remains useful.

[13] This summary of Act 2 is from Burkitt, ibid., 66.

[14] Perhaps this motif was suggested by the Ahiqar literature. See now Eli Yassif, 'Traces of Folk Traditions of the Second Temple Period in Rabbinic Literature', *JJS* 39 (1988), 228-9. For more on the importance of folk-motif analysis in rabbinic religious-didactic literature, see my methodological study 'Most Tender and Fairest of Women: A Study in the Transmission of Aggada,' *HTR* 76 (1983), 403-18.

A story of King Monbaz who distributed the entire content of his granaries during the years of famine.

His brothers sent him this message: Your forefathers stored up [their] granaries and added to the stores of their predecessors, while you depleted not only your own granaries, but also those of your predecessors.

He responded to them: My fathers stored below, I stored above, as it is said, *Truth springs up from the earth; justice looks down from heaven. [The Lord also bestows His bounty; our land yields its produce]* (Ps. 85: 12-13).

My fathers stored tangible granaries; I stored intangible granaries, as it is said, *Righteousness and justice are the base of Your throne* (Ps. 89: 15).

My fathers stored granaries which bore no fruit; I stored granaries that do bear fruit, as it is said, *Hail the just man for he shall fare well; he shall eat the fruit of his works* (Isa. 3: 10).

My fathers stored granaries of fiscal value; I stored granaries of lives, as it is said, *The fruit of the righteous is a tree of life* (Prov. 11: 30).

My fathers stored granaries for others; I stored granaries for myself, as it is said, *It will be accounted as your righteousness before the Lord* (Dt. 24: 13).

My fathers stored granaries for this world, I stored granaries for myself in the World to Come, as it is said, *Your righteousness shall march before you* (Isa. 58: 8).[15]

The lengthy justification of his actions attributed to King Monbaz underscores the motif: he builds for the World to Come by giving charity. Here, the Tosefta presumes the building to be the increase of grain in the storehouses rather than an architectural structure. But for the conversion of Gundaphar (though Monbaz came from a family of converts), the lesson remains the same: the king who gives charity builds a palace (or at least a very full silo) in Heaven.

In the Middle Ages, an abbreviated version of the Tosefta's lesson was advanced as part of a general sermon on the value of charity. It is followed by a story which illustrates its theme precisely:

R. Tarfon gave R. Aqiba 180 bars of gold. He told him, Acquire substance [viz. a plot of land] for us [so that we may live on the proceeds]. R. Aqiba went and used the bars to give much charity. Some days passed when he came to R. Tarfon. He asked, What did you do? Did you acquire good property? Aqiba said, Yes its value is out of this world! Where is the receipt? [asked Tarfon]. He said, In the hand of David, [who said]: *He gives freely to the poor, his beneficence lasts forever, his horn is exalted in honour* – in this world – *his righteousness* (sic) *lasts forever* – in the future to come. Thus, *Honour the Lord with your wealth* with what God has given you through His grace – *and your barns will be filled with grain* (Prov. 3: 9-10) – so that your barns will be filled with grain in the future to come.[16]

---

[15] T. Pe'ah 4: 18 (ed. Lieberman, p. 60), cf. j. Pe'ah ch. 1, b. BB 11a and Pes. Rabbati (n. 16, below). The English translations (NJV, but I have modified them for ease in following the midrash) offer *righteousness (sdq)* in each proof-text. The term is used by the rabbis for 'charity'.

[16] Pesikta Rabbati 25 (ed. Friedmann, 126b-127a).

The Pesikta Rabbati illuminates the story of King Monbaz and his storage of grain in the world to come by drawing a parallel with two rabbinic kings, as it were: R. Tarfon and R. Aqiba. They distribute charity by redistributing the good which God has given them. As a result, their barns will be filled with grain in the future to come.

This tale reinforces the common cultural and conceptual heritage which the rabbis and Syriac Fathers shared. The parallel with the Acts of Thomas; is far from exact, however, since one source speaks of palaces, the other of barns and silos. Further, the Acts of Thomas is reported in Syriac while the two rabbinic tales are told not in Aramaic but Hebrew. For a close linguistic affinity, it is worth our while to turn to the Aramaic original which the Pesikta Rabbati reshaped to fit its story of King Monbaz. As the legend is found in Leviticus Rabba, there is no mention of barns or silos: [17]

> R. Tarfon gave R. Aqiba six bars of silver. He told him, Buy us a property so that we may earn a living from it and the two of us can study Torah [undisturbed by the necessity of daily labour]. He took the money and distributed it to teachers of reading and to teachers of Mishna and to those who study Torah. After some days R. Tarfon asked, Did you buy the property as I asked you? Aqiba said, Yes. Is it good? He answered, Yes. He said, will you not show it to me? Aqiba took him and showed him the teachers of reading, the teachers of Mishna, the teachers of Torah and the Torah they had stored up. Tarfon asked, Is there a person who labours free of charge? Where is the receipt? Aqiba answered, With King David, who wrote, *He gives freely to the poor, his beneficence lasts forever* (Ps. 112: 9).

Here our story is not of kings or poor or barns; rather in its original form in Leviticus Rabba it is appropriate to the values of the rabbinical academy. Thus the tale speaks of money to support teachers of Torah, in return for which a store-house of Torah is laid up for the rabbis in the Coming Future.

That the story in Leviticus Rabba is but a variant of the building-castles-in-heaven motif is amply demonstrated by its parallels and by the relatively easy explanation of the permutations it has undergone to be appropriate in the rabbinic academy. Any remaining doubts about the common cultural heritage of the Acts of Thomas and Leviticus Rabba may be dispelled by noting the proem verse which introduces the story in the rabbinic midrash, *Men from your midst shall rebuild your ancient ruins* (Isa 58: 12). Though the rabbis adapted the story to its Torah context, the original motif persisted in the introductory verse: the giving of charity results in building (or here: rebuilding) palaces in heaven.

---

[17] For another linguistic affinity between the Acts of Thomas and rabbinics, see S. Brock 'Jewish Traditions in Syriac Sources' *JJS* 30 (1979), 221, n. 31. Leviticus Rabba 34: 16 from M. Margulies (ed.), 812-13. See the commentary ad loc.

III

It is a commonplace that the rabbis were not celibates but joyfully raised families and satisfied their wives so long as they played by the rules of family purity. This is rather piquantly expressed by citation of the passage in b Nedarim 20b:

> The sages say ... Anything a man so desires to do with his wife he may do. It may be likened to beef from the butcher – if he wishes he may eat it pickled, roasted, baked or boiled ...

This rabbinic attitude is often contrasted with the monastic attitudes of the Church. It offers stark contrast with the emphasis on celibacy as a potential price of admission to baptism in the Syriac Church.[18] The Church took celibacy so seriously that they employed a special term of approbation for one who accepted that yoke: Holy Ones.[19] As Sebastian Brock explains:

> In early Syriac literature the term *qaddisha*, besides meaning 'holy', can have the technical sense of 'continent', and it is used of married couples who abstain from sexual intercourse.[20]

Brock demonstrates that the idea is not wholly unknown in Judaism, even in rabbinic Judaism.[21] Still under the sway, one supposes, of the contrast drawn above, Brock writes: 'There appear to be no clear instances where *qaddisha* has this technical sense in Jewish texts.'[22] This may be technically true, but given the affinities of rabbinic Judaism and Syriac Christianity it is worth examining the term *qdsh* in rabbinic texts to see if it ever bears the sense attached to it in Syriac Church literature.

Leviticus Rabba affords us a glimpse of this sense when it asks:

---

[18] See F. C. Burkitt, *Early Eastern Christianity*, 125-9. For a discussion of Burkitt's general thesis and various details, see e.g. G. Richter, 'Über die älteste Auseinandersetzung der syrischen Christen mit den Juden', ZNW 35 (1936), 101-14; A. Vööbus, *Celibacy a Requirement for Admission to Baptism in the Early Syrian Church* (Stockholm, 1951); and especially Robert Murray, 'The Exhortation to Candidates for Ascetical Vows at Baptism in the Ancient Syriac Church', NTS 21 (1974), 59-80. S. Brock, 'Some Syriac Accounts of the Jewish Sects', in R. H. Fisher (ed.), *Tribute to Arthur Vööbus* (Chicago, 1977), 272; idem, 'Jewish Traditions in Syriac Sources', JJS 30 (1979), 226.

[19] See the secondary literature in n. 18. For primary literature, see especially Aphrahat, Dem. VI (relevant portions translated in Burkitt, *Early Eastern Christianity*, 133-7) and Dem. XVIII (translated in Neusner, *Aphrahat and Judaism: The Christian-Jewish Argument in Fourth-Century Iran* [Leiden, 1971], 76-83, who misses the technical aspect of the term 'holiness' [which he renders 'sanctity'] as meaning 'celibacy'). Murray (n. 18) points to similar usage by Ephrem, *H. Epiph.* 8, 16.5 (p. 65, op. cit.) and in the *Acts of Thomas* (ed. Wright, Syriac p. 301, English p. 267, and Klijn, p. 131).

[20] Brock, 'Jewish Traditions in Syriac Sources', 218, and see n. 16, there.

[21] Ibid., 217-18, 226, esp. n. 53, there.

[22] Ibid., 218.

Why is the section about forbidden sexual unions juxtaposed with the holiness
lection (*parashat qedoshim*)? To teach you that wherever you fence in sexual
impropriety, there you find holiness. This is according to the teaching of R.
Yehuda b. Pazi who said, Whoever guards himself against sexual impropriety is
to be called holy (*qadosh*).[23]

This further calls to mind a story repeated four times in the Palestinian
Talmud about Rabbi Yehuda the Patriarch:

Why was he called Our Holy Rabbi (*Rabbenu HaQadosh*)? For he never looked
at his circumcision in his life.[24]

There is, as it were, commentary to this Palestinian tradition in the Babylonian Talmud:[25]

R. Yose said, All my life I never looked at my circumcision. Is this so? They
said, after all, to Rabbi [Yehuda the Patriarch], What is the reason they call
you Our Holy Rabbi? He said to them, In all my life I never looked at my
circumcision. In the case of Rabbi [Yehuda the Patriarch] there was another
matter [to his credit], for he never even put his hand beneath his tunic. R. Yose
said, In all my life the beams of my house never saw my undershirt!

R. Yose's holier-than-thou attitude illustrates the somewhat exclusive hold
R. Yehuda had on the reason for his nickname, *Rabbenu HaQadosh*. Nevertheless, I think that this story not only establishes the use of the term
qadosh as a term for some form of continence in rabbinic literature but
points to a greater phenomenon as well. Though one could not go so far
as to say that the attitude of the Syriac Church towards celibacy is found
among the rabbinic sages, the term *qadosh* has afforded us a glimpse of a
prudishness beyond the confines of the laws of marital purity.

I conclude not only by pointing to the lexical hint Syriac literature has
given us for understanding a nuance of *qadosh* in rabbinic literature, but by
quoting one last text which illustrates this underlying attitude. The text[26]
does not use the term *qadosh*, but amply demonstrates that R. Yehuda the
Patriarch and R. Yose were not anomalies in the rabbinic community.

R. Shimeon b. Yohai said, There are four things that the Holy, praised be He,
hates, and I am not in love with them either. [They are:(1)] A man who holds
his penis while he urinates, (2) a man who has intercourse naked, (3) a man who
brazenly reports things that take place between himself and his wife and (4) one
who suddenly bursts into his house.

---

[23] LevR 24:6 (ed. Margulies, 559) with parallels noted, ad loc.

[24] jMeg 3:2 (74a), jMeg. 1:11, j'AZ 3:1, jSan 10:5.

[25] bShab 118b.

[26] LevR 21:8 (ed. Margulies, 486) with parallels noted, ad loc. See the corrupted text
in bNidda 16b-17a and the emendation of Tosafot, ad loc., 17a, s. v.*umashtiyn*.

R. Shimeon's second and third dislikes indicate a restraint which sets the
rabbis within the broad lexical range of *qedusha*. It should be noted,
however, that his first item, holy though it may seem, was but a *topos* in
antiquity. Athenaeus, roughly a contemporary of R. Shimeon b. Yohai
and R. Yehuda the Patriarch, reports:[27]

> Aristotle also used to say jokingly of Xenocrates of Chalcedon that when he
> made water he never put his hand to his member, and he would quote [Euripides]:
> 'My hands are pure, it is my mind that has a taint.'

[27] *Deipnosophists* XII 530 (trans. B. Gulick,*LCL*, vol. 5, pp. 392-5). My thanks
to Professors Shaye J. D. Cohen and Sebastian Brock for their comments on an earlier
draft of this paper.

Hillel, Hieronymus and Praetextatus

He was a pagan's pagan.[1] The Vestal Virgins liked him so much they bent the rules a bit and erected a statue in his honor.[2] And the inscription that his wife, Paulina, raised to him after his death read like a *Who's Who* of pagan priesthoods.[3] Vettius Agorius Praetextatus so embodied the greatness of hellenistic culture that when Macrobius wrote his *Saturnalia* some years after the former's death, Praetextatus led the cast of characters. He enshrined the moribund civilization that was crushed under the weight of a Christian exclusivisim legally manifested as intolerance.[4]

Praetextatus' culture took many forms, hinted at in the inscriptions and surviving literature which mention him. He was a senator, praetorian praefect, and at the time of his death, consul designate for the year 385.[5]

---

[1] The specific era which is the focus of this study lies beyond the general scope of the late Prof. Bickerman's research. Still, those who knew him will recognize my debt to his method, which I strive for in this article. Bickerman himself characterized this approach to the literatures of antiquity with the disarming explanation he offered his students, "I teach you to read slow."

[2] *CIL* vi 2145, Symmachus, *Ep.* ii 36, see S. Dill, *Roman Society in the Last Century of the Western Empire* (rpnt. 1958²), 17 and H. Bloch, "A New Document of the Last Pagan Revival in the West 393-394 A.D.,"*HTR* 38 (1945), 216-17 (henceforth: "Document").

[3] *CIL* vi 1778, 1779, 1780. See Dill, 18, 77; Bloch, "Document," 204ff., 242f., and the chart there, nos. 7 and 23; and *idem.*, "The Pagan Revival in the West at the End of the Fourth Century," in *Paganism and Christianity in the Fourth Century*, ed. A. Momigliano (Oxford, 1963), 203f., and figs. 7 and 8 where the monumental inscriptions are shown. In addition, see Otto Seeck, *Monumenta Germaniae Historica Auctorum Antiquissimorum* VI (1883), lxxxiii-xc, and Johanna Nistler, "Vettius Agorius Praetextatus," *Klio* X (1910), 462-75, where much of the primary material on Praetextatus is collected. For a competent overview of the era see F. Homes Dudden, *The Life and Times of St. Abrose* (Oxford, 1935). Two important biographies are P. Brown, *Augustine of Hippo* (California, 1967) and J. N. D. Kelly, *Jerome* (New York, 1975). The primary sources not only include the works of these three Church figures, but also the works of Symmachus, Ammianus Marcellinus and Macrobius. See too, the appropriate entries in *P.-W.* and *PLRE*.

[4] E. g., *C. Th.* xvi 4-11; *Nov. Th.* 3. For Macrobius see A. Cameron, "The Date and Identity of Macrobius," *JRS* 56 (1966), 25-38.

[5] *CIL* vi 102, 1777-1780; *C. Th* viii 14, 1; xiv 4, 4; ix 40, 10; vi 35, 7; xiii 3, 8; i 6, 6. Cf. Seeck, lxxxvii f., n. 403 and Nistler, 465, n. 4.

He translated, edited and held forth at symposia.[6] Praetextatus' pagan credentials dated back to his association with the emperor Julian.[7] But these classical activities were of less import (*sed ista parva*) to this great Roman than his religious life (*omnis me beatam*).[8] Macrobius refers to him as *praesul omnium sacrorum* (I 17, 1) and even (perhaps in opposition to the Christian emperors who, since the advent of Gratian had refused the robes of *pontifex maximus*) *princeps religiosorum* (I 11, 1). Yet for all his knowledge of Roman antiquities and all of his classical priesthoods, Praetextatus was a thoroughgoing syncretist.[9] Now it is true that paganism and syncretism may go hand in hand, but Praetextatus' mixture of Roman and Eastern cults stands in stark contrast to the "pure" Roman religion of his stuffy colleague Symmachus.

Symmachus was liberal enough to declare (albeit in defense of paganism before the bar of Christianity) that "one cannot reach so great a secret by one way alone" (*Rel.* iii 10) and "everyone has his custom, his religion" (*Rel.* iii 8).[10] But Symmachus limited his praxis to the old Roman religion and did not go in for those new-fangled religions of the East, be they pagan or Christian. The limitations of his point of view are well expressed by Arthur Darby Nock, "Symmachus merely asked for toleration of the survivals of a dead faith."[11] His prissiness in this regard led to an extreme conservatism which caused him to oppose the Vestals' statue to Praetextatus, mentioned above, and to advocate the extremities of ancient punishment for a lapsed Vestal in another instance.[12] Nonetheless, Symmachus seemed to possess a self-awareness of the limitations of his chosen avenue of paganism. When the more eclectic Praetextatus died, Symmachus did not feel up to the challenge of carrying on the fight alone. Perhaps he knew that his particular umbrella could not extend widely enough to cover all the factions in the pagan cause. In any case, Symmachus resigned his public office and retired as leader of the pagan revival.[13]

Praetextatus' syncretism bears closer examination since his and his many followers' fascination with Eastern cults set them apart from Symmachus and the many other particularists of the old religion. To explain Praetextatus' religious interest as merely showing that "the accumulation of priesthoods is evidence of the scarcity of people who were willing to shoulder the responsibility of these cults" misses the point somewhat.[14] Though it

---

[6] Macrobius, passim; Bloch, "Pagan Revival" 210; idem., "Document," 205, 240.

[7] Amm. Mar. xxii 7, 6; Bloch, "Document," 204-8.

[8] *CIL* vi 1779d and Brown, *Augustine*, 27.

[9] See Bloch, "Document," 207 and the chart there following, 244.

[10] Translated by Bloch, "Pagan Revival," 196f. Cf. Dill, *Society*, 30 at n. 6.

[11] Nock, *Sallustius* ciii, n. 19 *apud* Bloch, "Document," 209.

[12] See n. 2.

[13] *Rel.* x 2-3; Bloch, "Document", 217-20.

[14] Bloch, "Pagan Revival," 203.

is a truism that economic hardship was the rule of the day and that the wealth necessary to pursue priesthoods and public office was becoming ev-ermore concentrated in the hands of the few, this negative factor is hardly sufficient to explain such a widespread religious phenomenon.

In the first place, the economic picture, though bleak, was not suffi-ciently dire to limit distribution of offices among a wide spectrum. Con-strasting the vast wealth and conspicuous consumption of earlier ages, Macrobius can but point out that peahens' eggs, meat stuffed pig and fatted hares and snails are no longer banquet fare in his day. Still, they managed to dine on oysters and doormice. Folks remained wealthy enough to be pestered by legacy hunters, while pagan and Christian alike sketched an up-per class that knew how to luxuriate and make the most of its advantages.[15]

It is important to note that the high life was not limited to pagans. Jerome (the Hieronymus of the title of this essay) describes a priest who boasts as follows:

> I can tell unerringly on what coast a mussel has been picked. I can distinguish by the flavor the province from which a bird comes. Dainty dishes delight me because their ingredients are scarce and I end by finding pleasure in their ruinous cost.

To another he writes:

> A clergyman who engages in business, and who rises from poverty to wealth, and from obscurity to high position, avoid as you would the plague ... You despise gold; he loves it. You spurn wealth; he eagerly pursues it. You love silence, meekness, privacy; he takes delight in talking and effrontery ...

And of the monks, Jerome is equally bald in his assertions:

> I myself have seen monks ... whose ... property has incrased rather than dimin-ished. They still have the same servants and keep the same table. Out of cheap glasses and common earthenware they swallow gold. With servants about them in swarms they claim for themselves the name of hermit.[16]

Given this charge from a churchman, it is not suprising to find Ammianus Marcellinus write:

> Bearing in mind the ostentation in city life, I do not deny that those who are desirous of such a thing ought to struggle with the exercise of all their strength to gain what they seek; for when they attain it, they will be so free from care that they are enriched from the offerings of matrons, ride seated in carriages, wearing clothing chosen with care, and serve banquets so lavish that their entertainments outdo the table of kings.

---

[15] Macrobius, *Sat.* iii 13 *passim*; Amm. Mar. xiv 6; Hieron. *Epp.* 22, 52, 125. Even Ambrose notes the wealth surrounding him; see Dudden, *Ambrose*, 28-33 and Dill, *Society*, 129-36.
[16] Hieron. *Ep.* 52: 6, 5; *Ep.* 125: 16.

Ammianus is not here describing social-climbing pagans or even priests, he is describing a conflict for the papacy that took place in Rome, ca. 366-67:

> Damasus and Urcinus, burning with a superhuman desire of seizing the bishopric, engaged in a bitter strife because of their opposing interests; and the supporters of both parties went even so far as conflicts ending in bloodshed and death ... In the struggle Damasus was victorious through the efforts of the party which favored him. It is a well-known fact that in the basilica of Sicininus, where the assembly of the Christian sect is held, in a single day a hundred and thirty-seven corpses of the slain were found, and that it was only with difficulty that the long-continued frenzy of the people was afterward quieted.[17]

This last incident sets the background for what is to come, so I have allowed Ammianus to describe it at length. Damasus became Pope through the intervention of the pagan praefect of Rome, Vettius Agorius Praetextatus. Shortly afterward Praetextatus restored the *Porticus Deorum Consentium*, "the last pagan religious monument dedicated by an official of Rome."[18] In 384, Praetextatus would be the Praetorian Praefect of Italy while Jerome was there acting as Damasus' secretary. In the same year, the pagan Symmachus wrote a recommendation for the professorship of rhetoric in Milan. His cousin, the powerful bishop, Ambrose, accepted the recommendation and appointed Augustine to the post.[19]

We see that the world of the upper classes was small and wealthy. In such a world the concentration of power among an "ol' boys" network was not unusual. But to presume that an upper class exclusivism accounts for the "accumulation of priesthoods" underestimates the priesthoods themselves. Surely there was enough power and honor around to keep the most ambitious pagans and Christians busy. And, there were enough ambitious pagans and Christians to keep the positions widely distributed. I would suggest that the answer to the prosopographical dilemma of pagan priesthoods concentrated among the very few lies in the religious satisfaction those priesthoods offered.

Paganism exercised an attraction at many points along its compass. The most common contact with Roman religion came early in one's education, be he pagan, Christian or Jew. [20] The influence of a grammar and rhetoric

---

[17] Amm. Mar. xxvii 3, 14 and 12-13.

[18] *CIL* vi 102; Bloch, "Pagan Revival," 195.

[19] Augustine, *Conf.* v. 13; Dudden, *Ambrose*, 327; Brown, *Augustine*, 66f.

[20] On the thoroughgoing pagan character of grammatical and rhetorical education, see H. Marrou, *A History of Education in Antiquity* (New York, 1956), part 3 and especially chapter 9 there for the Christian educational issues. I hope to demonstrate on another occasion the formal nature of the hellenistic rhetoric taught in the rabbinic academies, but for the general background see the various studies collected in H. Fischel, ed., *Essays in Greco-Roman and Related Talmudic Literature* (New York, 1977) as well as S. Lieberman, *Greek in Jewish Palestine* (New York, 1942), and *Hellenism in Jewish Palestine* (New York, 1962²).

steeped in the blood of pagan sacrifice extended far beyond Julian, Libanius and the literati of Praetextatus' and Symmachus' circles. As mentioned above, Augustine taught rhetoric; he was a convert to philosophy well before his more famous conversion to Christianity. Even following that latter conversion, he was "preoccupied with Cicero and the Neoplatonists ... he was deeply immersed in philosophical and literary labours."[21] Ambrose, that stalwart defender of Christianity, quoted liberally from the classics all the while he was prosecuting paganism. The Arians could even accuse him of the heinous crime of levity because he cited pagan myths to illustrate his points. Ambrose archly replied that if an apostle might quote Aratus, surely a bishop could refer to Homer or Virgil.[22]

Jerome was chief among the Christians of this period who grappled with the theological problem which the study of classics offered. He laid out the dilemma in a letter to Eustochium, written from Rome, ca. 384:

> Many years ago ... when I was on my way to Jerusalem to wage my warfare, I still could not bring myself to forego the library which I had formed for myself at Rome with great care and toil. And so, miserable man that I was, I would fast only that I might afterwards read Cicero. After many nights spent in vigil ... after the recollection of my past sins, I would once more take up Plautus. And when at times I returned to my right mind, and began to read the prophets, their style seemed rude and repellent ... Suddenly, I was caught up in the spirit and dragged before the judgement seat ... Asked who and what I was I replied: "I am a Christian." But He who presided said: "Thou liest, thou art a follower of Cicero and not of Christ" ... Accordingly I made oath and called upon His name, saying: "Lord, if I ever again posess worldly books, or if ever again I read such, I have denied Thee" ... thenceforth I read the books of God with a greater zeal than I had previously given to the books of men.[23]

Of course, Jerome went right on studying and quoting the classics. He claims to have held out against the lure of pagan literature for fifteen years; but recommends rhetoric to Paulinus of Nola a decade after his letter to Eustochium, and avidly defends his citations of the classics in a long apologetic to the Roman orator Magnus in 397.[24]

The lure of literature, however, is not the call of the cult. What separated the encyclopaedic Christian clergy from the pagan priesthood was the difference in their respective altars. One might say that the persistence of paganism, especially following the removal of the altar of Victory by Constantius, indicated that the blood of sacrifice was sometimes thicker than

---

[21] *Confessions, passim.* See P. Brown, *Augustine*, 101 ff. and A. D. Nock, *Conversion* (Oxford, 1933), 259-66. The quote is from Dudden, *Ambrose*, 335, who devotes an entire chapter to Augustine (321-44).

[22] Dudden, *Ambrose*, 8-10; for Aratus see Hieron. *Ep.* 70: 2 and below.

[23] *Ep.* 22: 30. Cf. B. Ned. 8a for a method of release from bans pronounced in a dream.

[24] *Com. in Gal.* iii, praef; *Epp.* 53 and 58 to Paulinus; *Ep.* 70 to Magnus. See Kelly, *Jerome*, 41f.

the water of baptism.[25] The simple fact is that the pagans believed in the efficacy of their sacrifices. When famine struck Rome in 380, Symmachus was quick to place the blame on the Christian emperors' abandonment of the cult.[26] As A. D. Nock so aptly puts it,

> What did the ancients love? They loved ... the worships of the household and of the State ... What did they fear? The possible loss of the benefits thought to be derived by State and individual from these inherited ways ... So long as you did not try to take from these men anything which they had in religion, they could not as a rule object ... So long as the priest and the silent Vestal climbed the Capitol, Balbus might build his Mithraeum, with the feeling that the established order was secured ... But ask of him that he should consent to the ending of the Capitoline cult, and he would be shocked or even frightened: and if you were to win him you had to convince him, to convert him.[27]

The attempt of the emperors to employ the proscriptions previously used against Christianity spurred the pagans to cling more firmly to the old ways. It was just so that individual's priesthoods began to accumulate. Rational explanation or appeal was futile. The pagans had already moved toward monotheism. Praetextatus himself − *pontifex Vestae, augur, quindecimvir, pontifex Solis*, priest of Hercules, Liber and Hecate, initiate of Eleusis, Lerna, Aegina, Serapis, Magna Mater and Mithra − it is he who early in the *Saturnalia* (I 17, 1) explains the answer to Avienus' query:

> What is the reason that we venerate the Sun sometimes as Apollo, sometimes as Liber, sometimes under a variety of other names? Please explain to me the reason of so great variety in the names of one deity?[28]

Praetextatus' answer, which equates a string of some dozen and a half gods with the Sun, shows the ease with which Eastern and Western deities had been syncretized in his theology. It is a theology which explicates his priesthoods − he served them all because all were one. One can imagine him standing before his lararium, arm in arm with Fabia Paulina, sighing, "What can be a greater source of happiness than belief in a household god!" [29]

---

[25] Constantius removed the altar in 356. It became a *cause célèbre* for the pagans and was restored and removed again and bickered over from the time of Julian until 392. See Symmachus, *Rel* iii; J. Wytzes, *Der Streit um den Altar der Viktoria* (Amsterdam, 1936); Bloch, "Document," 213−15; *idem.*, "Pagan Revival,"196; and A. Alföldi, "A Festival of Isis in Rome Under the Christian Emperors of the Fourth Century," *Diss. Pannon.* ser. 2, vii (1937).

[26] Symmachus to Flavianus ii 7; Bloch, "Document," 214.

[27] Nock, *Conversion*, 162f.

[28] *CIL* vi 1779; Bloch, "Document," 205ff., and chart.

[29] Aphorism #65 in Franz Kafka, *The Great Wall of China: Stories and Reflections* (New York, 1970), 175. On the syncretism see F. Cumont, *Oriental Religions in Roman Paganism* (New York, rpnt., 1956), 208 and 211. Cf. R. MacMullen, *Paganism in the Roman Empire* (New Haven, 1981), 83-94.

It was this belief which accounted for the many priesthoods. It was the liberalism of pagan theology which, though monotheistic in tendency, mitigated against Old Testament exclusivism. And, in the end, it was the inability to be exclusive which prevented the conversion of these tenacious pagans, despite the Herculean efforts of Ambrose and his charges. Not only their theology prevented their exclusivism, a certain *laissez faire* attitude contributed as well. Symmachus exemplified it in his statements, quoted above, about many ways to the secret. He also reports that Praetextatus might altogether miss his turn at service in the Sacred Colleges when he was off at his country home or vacationing in Campania.[30]

Serious though they may have been about protecting their cults from the onslaught of Christian legislation, the ease with which these old pagans took to their religion made them somewhat mirthful about the attempts to convert them to Christianity. This very mirth enraged the Christian clergy all the more. Jerome cannot conceal his bile when he writes to Marcella immediately after Praetextatus' death in 384:

> The consul-elect ... is now in Tartarus ... See the consul, not now in his triumphal robe but clothed in mourning ... A few days ago the highest dignitaries of the city walked before him as he ascended the ramparts of the capitol like a general celebrating a triumph; the Roman people leapt up to welcome and applaud him, and at the news of his death the whole city was moved. Now he is desolate and naked, a prisoner in the foulest darkness, and not, as his unhappy wife falsely asserts, set in the royal abode of the Milky Way.[31]

The public acclaim for Praetextatus annoyed Jerome no end, but his flippant attitude about conversion to Christianity galled Jerome even more. Still brooding, at least a dozen years after the deaths of Praetextatus and Damasus, he writes from Bethlehem:

> That unhappy man Praetextatus, who died after he had been chosen consul, a profane person and an idolater, was wont in sport to say to blessed Pope Damasus, "Make me bishop of Rome, and I will at once be a Christian."

Given the role Praetextatus played in elevating Damasus to bishop of Rome and the fortune Damasus achieved upon attainment of that office, Praetextatus' *bon mot* is quite understandable. To Jerome, however, it was unforgivable, for it betrayed a total lack of seriousness about the very thing Jerome cared for most.[32]

---

[30] Symmachus, *Epp.* i 47-51; ii 53. See Dill, *Society*, 152.

[31] *Ep.* 23: 2-3 Cf. *CIL* vi 1779 for Paulina's assertions. Symmachus generously eulogizes Praetextatus in his communications to the emperors regarding his death, *Rell.* x and xi. See Bloch, "Document," 216.

[32] Jerome's report is found in *Against John*, 8. On the elevation of Damasus to bishop see above at n. 17. For the problems in dating Jerome's letter see the introduction to it in *A Select Library of Nicene and Post-Nicene Fathers of the Christian Church*, Second Series, vol. vi (Michigan, rpnt. 1979), 424f.

Praetextatus' attitude may be profitably contrasted with the famous account of a conversion that took place two years after his death. In his *Confessions* (VIII 6 [14]ff.), Augustine reports that Ponticianus told him the story of Anthony, the Egyptian monk, and how reading his *Life* had led to conversion. Augustine then reports his own profound reaction to the story, describes his physical discomfort and spiritual anguish. Then, as with Anthony:

> I heard the voice of a boy or girl coming from the Church (lit. Divine house) which repeatedly uttered in a sing-song manner: take up and read, take up and read ... I went hurriedly back to the place where ... I had placed there the copy of the Apostle ... snatching it up, I opened it and read in silence the first passage on which my eyes fell, "Not in revelry and drunkenness ... but put on the Lord Jesus Christ ..." (Rom 13: 13f.). No further did I desire to read, nor was there need.

Now here was a conversion to be reckoned with! A *kledon* leads Augustine to yet a second divination – the appropriate passage from Paul.[33] Augustine, who had grown up in Christian surroundings only to convert to Manichaeism and Philosophy, had finally come home.[34] Accordingly, his attitude toward conversion to Christianity differed radically from that of his pagan contemporaries.

These two remarkably different stories about conversion which I've just recalled are made all the more remarkable by the combination of their motifs in a roughly contemporary rabbinic legend on the same topic. As part of a series of *chreiai* about the early first century sage, Hillel, we read:[35]

> A story about a gentile who was passing behind a school house (synagogue) and heard the voice of a child reading,[36] "These are the garments ... a breastplate,

---

[33] *Conf.* viii 12 [29]. For the text and translation I am following the readings adopted in Lieberman, *Hellenism*, 197f. See the entire section there (194-99) on the nature of these forms of divination. Note also B. Hag. 15a and parallels (cited by Lieberman, n. 20) where a child's voice, reading from Scripture, is divined as a sign to apostasize!

[34] There is a voluminous literature on Augustine and his conversions. For bibliography see Brown, *Augustine*; Dudden, *Ambrose*; and Nock, *Conversion*.

[35] B. Shab. 31a with parallels in ARN A 15 (p. 61); ARN B 29 (p. 61); *Midrash Haggadol* Exodus 28: 4; Yal. Sh. 1 #379; and *Sefer Hamma*ᶜ*asiot* #13 (ed. Gaster, Hebrew p. 23). The version in the Babylonian Talmud is the earliest, upon which the others depend. They have, however, access to variant readings of that tradition. I date it late fourth to early fifth century because it is reported anonymously and clearly redacted into the cycle of Hillel legends collected on that folio. The Hebrew is late and, obviously, the motifs of the legend are also appropriate to the late dating. For more on the Hillel *chreia* see H. Fischel, "Story and History: Observations on Greco-Roman Rhetoric and Pharisaism," *A.O.S. Midwest Branch Semi-Centennial Volume* (1969), 59-88 and *idem.*, "Studies in Cynicism and the Ancient Near East: The Transformation of a *Chria*," *E.R. Goodenough Memorial Volume* Suppl. *Numen* 14 (1968), 372-411.

[36] Following the reading in ARN A, *Midrash Haggadol* and *Sefer Hamma*ᶜ*asiot.*

and an ephod, and a robe, and a tunic of checque work, and a mitre ..." (Ex. 28:4). He asked, Whom are these [clothes] for? They told him, For the High Priest. That gentile said to himself, I'll go convert so they can make me High Priest ... He came to Hillel who converted him and said, One cannot be made a king unless one knows the appointments of a king; go learn the appointments of kingship. He went and studied. When he came to the verse, "The stranger who draws near shall die" (Num. 1:51), he asked, To whom does this verse refer? [Hillel] replied to him, Even to David, king of Israel. The convert reasoned to himself *a fortiori*: If of Israelites ... it says, "The stranger who draws near shall die," a simple convert who has converted with his staff and wallet, how much the more so ... It is not appropriate for me to be High Priest ... He came to Hillel and said to him, Humble Hillel, may blessings rest upon your head for you have drawn me close, beneath the wings of the Divine Presence.

I think the parallels are obvious. Like Augustine, the voice of a child reveals a verse of Scripture that leads the hearer to conversion. Like Praetextatus, the listener is willing to convert on the condition that he become High Priest (= bishop of Rome). The rabbinic tale has combined these motifs to provide the background of a *chreia* about Hillel. The story differs from its Christian and pagan counterparts in that the convert comes to understand the inappropriateness of his motives for conversion through his study of Torah. Thus prepared, he converts for the sake of Torah itself.

These three stories of conversion must be seen in the light of imperial religious legislation in the late fourth century.[37] Paganism had become increasingly proscribed. The empire no longer supported the cult; it persecuted it. By 392 it was illegal to venerate an image in the privacy of one's own household.[38] The Jews, who were trained in such logic, could reason *a fortiori* about what to expect for themselves. And the Christians, for all that they harried one another and worried about the barbarians camped along their borders, were quick to assume the reins of power and crack the whip previously employed against them.

Hieronymus, cantankerous as ever, whinnies with delight at the triumph. He tramples his enemies under the beating hooves of his rampant rhetoric and assigns them to Tartarus. Praetextatus and his pagan followers, though they hear the death knell sounding, retain their liberal outlook and wry inability to take seriously Christian pretensions to exclusivism. And the rabbis, who could not hope to legislate their own exclusivism, turn to wistful legends of Hillel to voice the one hope they could have, and from which they drew their solace – that the truth of their Torah would accomplish what an empire could not.

---

[37] See n. 4 above for anti-pagan legislation. The anti-Jewish laws are conveniently summarized in J. Parkes, *The Conflict of the Church and the Synagogue* (New York, rpnt. 1969).

[38] *C. Th.* xvi 10, 4.

Bibliography

Albeck, H., "Midrash Vayikra Rabba," *Louis Ginzberg Jubilee Volume*, S. Lieberman, et al., edd. (New York, 1946)

Alföldi, A., "A Festival of Isis in Rome Under the Christian Emperors of the Fourth Century," *Diss. Pannon* ser. 2 vii (1937)

Bacher, W., *Die exegetische Terminologie der jüdischen Traditionsliteratur* (Leipzig, 1899)

Baer, Y., "Israel, the Christian Church and the Roman Empire from the Time of Septimus Severus to the Edict of Toleration of 313," *Scripta Hierosolymitana* 7 (1961) 79-149

Bagatti, B., *The Church from the Circumcision* (Jerusalem, 1971)

—, *The Church from the Gentiles in Palestine* (Jerusalem, 1971)

Baldwin, Barry, "Rereading Christian Literature," *Patristic and Byzantine Review* 9 (1990) 135-148

Bardy, Gustave, "Les Traditions Juives dans l'Oeuvre d'Origine," *Revue Biblique* 34 (1925) 217-252

Barnard, L. W., *Studies on the Apostolic Fathers and their Background* (New York, 1966)

Barnes, T. D., *Tertullian* (Oxford, 1971)

Baskin, Judith R., *Pharoah's Counselors: Job, Jethro, and Balaam in Rabbinic and Patristic Tradition* (Brown Judaic Studies, 47, 1983)

—, "Rabbinic-Patristic Exegetical Contacts in Late Antiquity: A Bibliographical Reappraisal," *Approaches to Ancient Judaism vol. 5: Studies in Judaism and Its Greco- Roman Context*, William S. Green, ed. (Atlanta, 1985) 53-80

Bauer, W., *Rechtgläubigkeit und Ketzerei im Ältesten Christentum* (Tübingen, 1964) [Eng. trans.: *Orthodoxy and Heresy in Earliest Christianity* (Philadelphia, 1971)]

Benin, S. T., "Commandments, Covenants and the Jews in Aphrahat, Ephrem and Jacob of Serugh," *Approaches to Judaism in Medieval Times*, David Blumenthal, ed. (Chico, 1984) 135-56

Benko, Stephen, "The Libertine Gnostic Sect of the Phibionites according to Epiphanus," *Vigilae Christianae* 21 (1967)

—, *Aufstieg und Niedergang der Römischen Welt* II 23.2 (1980) 1081-9

—, *Pagan Rome and the Early Christians* (London, 1985)

Bikerman, Elie, "La Chaine de la Tradition Pharisienne," *Revue Biblique* 59 (1952) 44-54

Billerbeck, Paul, and H. Strack, *Kommentar zum Neuen Testament aus Talmud und Midrasch* (München, 1922, 1926)

Bloch, H., "A New Document of the Last Pagan Revival in the West 393-394 A. D.," *Harvard Theological Review* 38 (1945) 216-17

–, "The Pagan Revival in the West at the End of the Fourth Century," *Paganism and Christianity in the Fourth Century*, A. Momigliano, ed. (Oxford, 1963)

Bobertz, Charles A., "For the Vineyard of the Lord of Hosts Was the House of Israel, Cyprian of Carthage and the Jews," *Jewish Quarterly Review* 82 (1991) 1–15

Bokser, B., "Justin Martyr and the Jews," *Jewish Quarterly Review* 64 (1974) 97–122, 204–211

–, *The Origins of the Seder* (Berkeley, 1984)

Bonner, S. F., *Education in Ancient Rome* (Berkeley, 1977)

Bonnet, M., *Acta Phillipi et Acta Thomae* (Darmstadt, 1959)

Borret, M., *Origene Homilies sur le Levitique II* (Sources Chretiennes 287, Paris, 1981)

Boucher, M., "Some Unexplored Parallels to 1 Cor. 11: 11–12 and Gal. 3: 28: The New Testament and the Role of Women," *Catholic Biblical Quarterly* 31 (1969) 50–8

Bowersock, G. W., ed., *Approaches to the Second Sophistic* (University Park, Pa., 1974)

Bowker, John, *The Targums and Rabbinic Literature* (Cambridge, 1972)

Braun, F. M., "La 'lettre de Barnabe' et l'Evangile de saint Jean. Simples reflexions," *New Testament Studies* 4 (1957/58) 119–124

Braverman, Jay, *Jerome's Commentary on Daniel: A Study of Comparative Jewish and Christian Interpretations of the Hebrew Bible*, (Catholic Biblical Quarterly Monograph 7: Washington, 1978)

Bregman, M., "Circular Proems," *Studies in Memory of J. Heinemann*, R. Sarason, et al, edd. (Jerusalem, 1981) 34–51 [Hebrew]

Brock, Sebastian, "Jewish Traditions in Syriac Sources," *Journal of Jewish Studies* 30 (1979) 212–232

–, "Sarah and the Akedah," *Le Muséon: Revue D'Études Orientales* 87 (1974) 66–77

–, "Some Syriac Accounts of the Jewish Sects," *A Tribute to Arthur Voöbus*, R. H. Fisher, ed. (Chicago, 1977)

–, "A Syriac Verse Homily on Elijah and the Widow of Sarepta," *Le Muséon: Revue D'Études Orientales* 102 (1989) 93–113

–, "Two Syriac Verse Homilies on the Binding of Isaac," *Le Muséon: Revue D'Études Orientales* 99 (1986) 61–129

Brown, Peter, *Augustine of Hippo* (Berkeley, 1967)

–, *The Body and Society: Men, Women and Sexual Renunciation in Early Christianity* (New York, 1988)

–, *The Cult of the Saints* (Chicago, 1981)

–, *Religion and Society in the Age of St. Augustine* (London, 1977)

Brown, Raymond E., *The Birth of the Messiah* (Garden City, 1979)

–, *The Gospel According to John XIII–XXI* (Garden City, N. Y., 1970)

–, "Not Jewish Christianity and Gentile Christianity But Types of Jewish/Gentile Christianity," *Catholic Biblical Quarterly* 45 (1983) 74–79

Brown, Raymond E., and J. Meier, *Antioch and Rome* (New York, 1983)

Büchler, A., *Studies in Sin and Atonement* (reprint: New York, 1967)

Burke, G., "Celsus and Justin: Carl Andresen Revisited," *Zeitschrift für die neutestamentliche Wissenschaft* 76: 1/2 (1985) 107–16

Burkitt, Francis Crawford, *Early Christianity Outside the Roman Empire* (Cambridge, 1899)

−, *Early Eastern Christianity* (London, 1904)

Cameron, A., "The Date and Identity of Marcobius," *Journal of Roman Studies* 56 (1966) 25−38

−, "The Theotokos in Sixth-Century Constantinople," *Journal of Theological Studies* 29 (1978) 79−108

Chadwick, H., "Christian Platonism in Origen and Augustine," *Origeniana Tertia*, R. Hanson and H. Crouzel, edd. (Rome, 1985) 215−30

−, ed., *Contra Celsum* (Cambridge, 1965)

Chandler, Karen, "The Rite of the Red Heifer in the Epistle of Barnabas and Mishnah Parah," *Approaches to Ancient Judaism* V, William Scott Green, ed. (Atlanta, 1985) 99−114

Chernick, M., "*Ribui Umiut*," *Proceedings of the American Academy for Jewish Research* 49 (1982), Hebrew Section, 105−22

Chiat, M., "Ancient Synagogues in Eretz Yisrael," *Conservative Judaism* 35 (1981) 4−18

−, *Handbook of Synagogue Architecture* (Chico, 1982)

Chilton, Bruce, D., *A Galilean Rabbi and His Bible. Jesus' use of the Interpreted Scripture of His Time: Good News Studies 8* (Wilmington, Del., 1984) [also published as *Jesus' Own Interpretation of Isaiah* (London, 1984)]

−, *The Isaiah Targum* (The Aramaic Bible, vol 11, Wilmington, Del., 1987)

Clark, E. *Jerome, Chrysostom and Friends*, Studies in Women and Religion 2 (Lewiston, NY, 1979)

Cohen, Jeremy, *"Be Fertile and Increase, Fill the Earth and Master It": The Ancient and Medieval Career of a Biblical Text* (Ithaca, 1989)

Cohen, N., "Leviticus Rabbah Par. 3," *Jewish Quarterly Review* 72 (1981) 18−31

−, "Structure and Editing in the Homiletic Midrashim," *AJS Review* 6 (1981) 1−20

Cohen, S. J. D., "Epigraphical Rabbis," *Jewish Quarterly Review* 72 (1981−82) 1−17

Cohon, Samuel, S., "Original Sin," *Hebrew Union College Annual* 21 (1948) 275−330

Connolly, R. H., trans., *Didascalia Apostolorum Syriacae* (Oxford, 1929)

Cumont, F., *Oriental Religions in Roman Paganism* (reprint: New York, 1956)

D'Ales, A., *L'edit de Calliste* (Paris, 1914)

−, *De paenitentia* (Paris, 1926)

−, *La theologie de Tertullien* (Paris, 1905)

D'Angelo, Mary Rose, "Theology in Mark and Q: *Abba* and 'Father' in Context," *Harvard Theological Review* 85 (1992) 149−74

Danielou, J., *Aspects du judeo-christianisme: Colloque de Strasbourg, 23−25 Avril, 1964* (Paris, 1965)

−, *Judeo-Christianisme: Recherches historique et theologique offertes en hommage au Cardinal Jean Danielou* = (*Recherches de science religieuse* 60, 1972)

−, *Origene* (Paris, 1948)

−, *The Theology of Jewish Christianity* (London, 1964)

Daube, David, "Public Retort and Private Explanation," *The New Testament and Rabbinic Judaism* (London, 1956) 141−50

−, "Rabbinic Methods of Interpretation and Hellenistic Rhetoric," *Hebrew Union College Annual* 22 (1949) 236−64

–, "Alexandrian Methods of Interpretation and the Rabbis," *Festschrift H. Lewald*, M. Gerwig, et al, edd. (Basel 1953) 27–44

DeLacy, P. H., and B. Einarson, trans., Plutarch, "On the Delays on Divine Vengeance," *Moralia* 7 (LCL, Cambridge, MA, 1959) 180–299

de Lagarde, Paulus, *Didascalia Apostolorum Syriacae* (Leipzig, 1854; Wiesbaden, 1967)

de Lange, N. R. M., *Origen and the Jews: Studies in Jewish Christian Relations in Third Century Palestine* (Cambridge, 1976)

Delling, G., *Paulus' Stellung zur Frau und Ehe* (Stuttgart, 1931)

Dill, Samuel, *Roman Society in the Last Century of the Western Empire* (New York, 1899; 2nd ed., rev., 1960)

Dimitrovsky, H. Z., ed., *Exploring the Talmud* I (New York, 1976)

–, *S'redei Bavli* (New York, 1979)

Downey, G., *A History of Antioch in Syria* (Princeton, 1961)

Drijvers, Han, "Jews and Christians at Edessa," *Journal of Jewish Studies* 36 (1985) 88–102

Dudden, F. Homes, *The Life and Times of St. Ambrose* (Oxford, 1935)

Dunn, J. D. G., ed., *Jews and Christians: The Parting of the Ways A. D. 70 to 135* (Tübingen, 1992)

Esser, G., *Die Buss-schriften Tertullians de paenitentia und das Indulgenzedikt des Papstes Kallistus* (Bonn, 1905)

Etheridge, John Wesley, *The Targums of Onkelos and Jonathan ben Uzziel on the Pentateuch* 2 vol. (London, 1862–65)

Feldman, Louis, "The Omnipresence of the God Fearers," *Biblical Archeology Review* 12 (May, 1986) 58–69

–, "Proselytism by Jews in Third, Fourth and Fifth Centuries," *Journal for the Study of Judaism* 24 (1993) 1–58

Ferguson, Everett, ed., *Studies in Early Christianity: A Collection of Scholarly Essays* (New York, 1993)

Fiensy, D., *Prayers Alleged to Be Jewish: An Examination of the Constitutiones Apostolorum* (Chico, 1985)

Fischel, Henry, "Story and History: Observations on Greco-Roman Rhetoric and Pharisaism," *AOS Midwest Branch Semi-Centennial Volume* (1969) 59–88

–, "Studies in Cynicism and the Ancient Near East: The Transformation of a Chria," *E. R. Goodenough Memorial Volume*, Suppl. *Numen* 14 (1968) 372–411

–, *Essays in Greco-Roman and Related Talmudic Literature* (New York, 1977)

Fox, H., "Circular Proem," *Proceedings of the American Academy for Jewish Research* 49 (1982) 1–31

Fox, Robin Lane, *Pagan and Christians* (New York, 1987)

Fraade, Steven, *Enosh and His Generation: Pre-Israelite Hero and History in Post-biblical Interpretation* (SBL monograph 30, 1984)

Frankel, Zacharias, *Über den Einfluß der palästinischen Exegese auf der alexandrische Hermeneutik* (Leipzig, 1851)

Frend, William H. C. "Jews and Christians in third century Carthage," *Paganisme, Judaisme, Christianisme: influences et affrontements dans Le mond antique: melanges offerts a Marcel Simon* (Paris, 1978) 185–94

–, "A Note on Jews and Christians in Third Century North Africa," *Journal of Theological Studies* 21 (1971) 92–96

– "A Note on Tertullian and the Jews," *Studia Patristica* X (*Texte und Untersuchungen* no. 107 [Berlin, 1970]) 291–96

Friedlander, Moritz, *Patristische und Talmudische Studien* (Wien, 1878)

Funk, F. X., ed., *Didascalia et constitutiones apostolorum* (Paderborn, 1905)

Gager, J., "Jews, Gentiles, and Synagogues in the Book of Acts," *Christians Among Jews and Gentiles*, G. W. E. Nickelsburg and G. W. MacRae, edd. (Philadelphia, 1986)

Gero, Stephen, "With Walter Bauer on the Tigris: Encratite Orthodoxy and Libertine Heresy in Syro-Mesopotamian Christianity," *Nag Hammadi, Gnosticism, and Early Christianity*, Charles Hedrick and Robert Hodgson, edd. (Peabody, Mass., 1986) 287–307

Gerson, D., "Die Kommentarien des Ephraem Syrus im Verhältnis zur jüdischen Exegese," *Monatsschrift für Geschichte und Wissenschaft des Judentums* 17 (1868)

Ginzberg, Louis, "Die Haggada bei den Kirchenvätern und in der apokryphischen Litteratur," *Monatsschrift für Geschichte und Wissenschaft des Judentums* 42 (1898) and 43 (1899)

–, *Legends of the Jews* 7 vols. (Philadelphia, 1909–1938)

Goldberg, A., "On the term *gufa* in Leviticus Rabbah," *Leshonenu* 38 (1974) 163–69 [Hebrew]

–, "On the Sources of Sections of Pesikta DRav Kahana," *Tarbiz* 38 (1969) 184–5 [Hebrew]

Goldenberg, Robert, "The Deposition of Rabban Gamaliel II: An Examination of the Sources," *Journal of Jewish Studies* 23 (1972) 167–190

Goldfahn, A. H., *Die Kirchenväter und die Agada* (Breslau, 1873)

Goldin, Judah, *Studies in Midrash and Related Literature*, Barry L. Eichler and Jeffrey H. Tigay, edd. (Philadelphia, 1988)

Goodenough, E. R., *Jewish Symbols in the Greco-Roman Period* vol. 3 (New York, 1953)

Graetz, H., "Haggadische Elemente bei den Kirchenvätern," *Monatsschrift für Geschichte und Wissenschaft des Judentums* 3 (1854)

Grant, Robert M., "Charges of Immorality Against Various Religious Groups in Antiquity," *Studies in Gnosticism and Hellenistic Religions*, R. Van der Broek and M. J. Vermaseren, edd. (Leiden: Brill, 1981) 161–170

–, "Jewish Christianity at Antioch in the Second Century," *Recherches de science religieuse* 60 (1972) 97–108

Green, William, ed., *Approaches to Ancient Judaism vol. 5: Studies in Judaism and Its Greco-Roman Context* (Atlanta, 1985)

Gregory, Timothy E., "The Remarkable Christmas Homily of Kyros Panopolites," *Greek, Roman, and Byzantine Studies* 16 (1975) 317–24

Grossfeld, Bernard, *A Bibliography of Targum Literature* (Cincinnati, 1972)

Gulick, C. B., trans., Athenaeus, *The Deipnosophists* 5 (LCL, Cambridge, Mass., 1963)

Harrington, Daniel J., and Anthony J. Saldarini, trans., *Targum Jonathan of the Former Prophets* (The Aramaic Bible, vol. 10, Wilmington, Del., 1987)

Harkin, P. W., *Saint John Chrysostom, Discourses against Judaizing Christians*, (The Fathers of the Church 68, Washington, 1979)

Hauptman, Judith, "Contemporary Talmud Research," *Association for Jewish Studies Newsletter* 43 (Spring, 1993)

Hayman, A. P., "The Image of the Jew in the Syrian Anti-Jewish Literature," *To See Ourselves as Others See Us: Christians, Jews "Others" in Late Antiquity*, J. Neusner and E. Frerichs, edd. (Chico, 1985) 423–41

Hayward, Robert, *The Targum of Jeremiah* (The Aramaic Bible, vol. 12, Wilmington, Del., 1987)

Heinemann, Isaac, *The Methods of Aggadah* [Hebrew] 3rd ed. (Jerusalem, 1970)

Heinemann, Joseph, "Chapters of Leviticus Rabbah with Dubious Sources," *Tarbiz* 37 (1968) 339–54 [Hebrew]

–, "Leviticus Rabbah," *Encyclopaedia Judaica* 11 (Jerusalem, 1972) 147– 50

–, "Proem," *Scripta Hierosolymitana* 22 (1971) 100–22

–, "Profile of a Midrash," *Journal of the American Academy of Religion* 39 (1971) 141–50

Heinrichs, A., L. Koenen, edd., "Der Kölner Mani Kodex," *Zeitschrift für Papyrologie und Epigraphik* 19, 32, 44, 48 (1975–82)

Hengel, Martin, *Judentum und Hellenismus, Studien zu ihrer Begegnung unter besonderer Berücksichtigung Palästinas bis zur Mitte des 2. Jh. vor Chr.* 2nd ed. (Tübingen, 1973)

Hennecke, Edgar, *New Testament Apocrypha*, W. Schneemelcher, ed. (Philadelphia, 1965)

Henrichs, A., *Kyriakon: Festschrift Johannes Quasten* (Munich, 1970)

Herford, R. Travers, *Christianity in Talmud and Midrash* (London, 1903)

Herr, M. D., "Midreshei Halakha," *Encyclopaedia Judaica* 11 (Jerusalem, 1971) 1522–23

Hirshman, M., "The Greek Fathers and the Aggada on Ecclesiastes: Formats of Exegesis in Late Antiquity," *Hebrew Union College Annual* 59 (1988) 155

–, "Midrash Qohelet Rabbah: Chapters 1–4; Commentary (Ch. 1) and Introduction," *Jewish Theological Seminary of America*, Ph. D. dissertation (1982)

–, *Mikra and Midrash: A Comparison of Rabbinics and Patristics* [Hebrew] (Hakibbutz Hameuchad, 1992)

Horbury, W., "Tertullian on the Jews in the Light of *De Spectaculis* xxx. 5–6," *Journal of Theological Studies* 23 (1972) 455–59

Jaffee, M., "The Midrashic Proem," *Approaches to Ancient Judaism* 4, W. S. Green, ed. (Chico, 1983) 95–112

Jaubert, Annie, "Le Voile des Femmes (I Cor. XI. 2–16)," *New Testament Studies* 18 (1971–2) 419–30

Jervell, J., *Imago Dei: Gen. 1.26f im Spätjudentum, in der Gnosis und in den paulinischen Briefen* (Göttingen, 1960)

Kadushin, Max, *The Rabbinic Mind*, 2nd ed. (New York, 1965)

Kafka, Franz, *The Great Wall of China: Stories and Reflections* (New York, 1970)

Kamesar, Adam, *Jerome, Greek Scholarship, and the Hebrew Bible* (Oxford, 1993)

Kelly, J. N. D., *Early Christian Doctrines* (London, 1958; 2nd ed., New York, 1960)

–, *Jerome* (New York, 1975)

Kennedy, George, *The Art of Rhetoric in the Roman World* (Princeton, 1972)

–, *Classical Rhetoric and its Christian and Secular Tradition from Ancient to Modern Times* (Chapel Hill, 1980)

–, *Greek Rhetoric Under Christian Emperors* (Princeton, 1983)

–, *New Testament Interpretation through Rhetorical Criticism* (Chapel Hill, 1984)

Kimelman, R., "*Birkat Ha-Minim* and the Lack of Evidence for an Anti-Christian Jewish Prayer in Late Antiquity," *Jewish and Christian Self-Definition*, vol. 2 (London, 1981) 226–44

–, "Rabbi Yohanan and Origen on the Song of Songs: A Third Century Disputation," *Harvard Theological Review* 73 (1980) 567–595

Kinzig, Wolfram, "'Non-Separation': Closeness and Cooperation Between Jews and Christians in the Fourth Century," *Vigiliae Christianae* 45 (1991) 27–41

Klein, Michael L., *Fragment Targum of the Pentateuch* (Rome, 1980)

–, *Geniza Manuscripts of Palestinian Targum to the Pentateuch* 2 vol. (Cincinnati, 1986)

Klijn, A. F. J., *The Acts of Thomas: Introduction – Text – Commentary* (Leiden, 1962)

–, "The Influence of Jewish Theology on the Odes of Solomon and the Acts of Thomas," *Aspects du judeo-christianisme: Colloque de Strasbourg, 23–25 Avril, 1964* (Paris, 1965)

–, "Jewish Christianity in Egypt," *The Roots of Egyptian Christianity*, Birger Pearson and James E. Goehring, edd. (Philadelphia, 1986) 161–175

–, "Review of Pritz, R.," *Vigilae Christianae* 43 (1989) 409–10

–, "The Study of Jewish Christianity," *New Testament Studies* 20 (1973– 74) 419–31

Klijn, A. F. J., and G. J. Reinink, *Patristic Evidence for Jewish Christian Sects* (Leiden, 1973)

Kraabel, A. T., "The Disappearance of the God Fearers," *Numen* 28 (1981) 113–26

Kraeling, C. H., "The Jewish Community at Antioch," *Journal of Biblical Literature* 51 (1932) 130–60

Kraft, Robert A., *The Apostolic Fathers: A New Translation and Commentary. Vol. 3, Barnabus and Didache* (Toronto, 1965)

–, "In Search of 'Jewish-Christianity' and Its 'Theology': Problems of Definition and Methodology," *Recherches de science religieuse* 60 (1972) 81–92

Krauss, S., "Antioch," *Jewish Encyclopedia* 1 (New York, 1904) 632

–, "Antioche," *Revue des etudes juives* 45 (1902) 27–49

–, "The Jews in the Works of the Church Fathers," *Jewish Quarterly Review* O. S. 5 (1893)

–, "Jesus of Nazareth," *Jewish Encyclopedia* VII (New York, 1904) 170–73

Kugel, James L., and Rowan A. Greer, *Early Biblical Interpretation* (Philadelphia, 1986)

Lachs, Samuel Tobias, *A Rabbinic Commentary on the New Testament: The Gospels of Matthew, Mark, and Luke* (Hoboken and New York, 1987)

Lake, Kirsopp, *The Apostolic Fathers* I (LCL, Cambridge, Mass., 1912) 383–85

Lamirande, Emilien, "Etude bibliographique sur les Peres de l'Eglise et l'Aggadah," *Vigilae Christianae* 21 (1967) 1–11

Lauterbach, J. Z., "Jesus in the Talmud," *Rabbinic Essays* (Cincinnati, 1951) 530–31

Lebreton, J., *Histoire du Dogme de la Trinite* (Paris, 1927)

Leibschuetz, J. H. W. G., *Antioch: City and Imperial Administration in the Later Roman Empire* (Oxford, 1972)

Leon, Harry, *The Jews of Ancient Rome* (Philadelphia, 1960)

LeSaint, W. P., trans., *Tertullian, Treatises on Penance* (ACW, 28, Maryland, 1959)

Levey, Samson H., *The Targum of Ezekiel* (The Aramaic Bible, vol. 13, Wilmington, Del., 1987)

Levine, Lee I., *Ancient Synagogues Revealed* (Jerusalem, 1981)

—, *The Rabbinic Class of Roman Palestine in Late Antiquity* (Jerusalem, 1989)

Lieberman, S., "The Discipline of the So-Called Dead Sea Manual of Discipline," *Texts and Studies* (New York, 1974) 200–07

—, *Greek in Jewish Palestine* (New York, 1942)

—, *Hellenism in Jewish Palestine* (New York, 1962)

—, "The Rabbinic Song of Songs," [Hebrew] *Gnosticism, Merkabah Mysticism and the Talmudic Tradition*, G. Scholem, ed. (New York, 1965)

—, *Tosefta ki-Fshutah Kippurim* (New York, 1962)

Lieu, Judith, John North and Tessa Rajak, edd., *Jews Among Christians and Pagans* (London, 1992)

Linder, Amnon, *Jews in Roman Imperial Legislation* (Jerusalem, 1987)

Loewe, R., "Apologetic Motifs in the Targum to the Song of Songs," *Biblical Motifs*, A. Altmann, ed. (Cambridge, Mass., 1966) 159–96

Lowe, M., ed., *The New Testament and Christian-Jewish Dialogue: Studies in Honor of David Flusser = Immanuel* 24/25 (1990)

Lüdemann, G., "The Successors of Pre-70 Jerusalem Christianity: A Critical Evaluation of the Pella-Tradition," *Jewish and Christian Self-Definition* 1, E. P. Sanders, ed. (Philadelphia, 1980) 161–73

MacLennan, Robert, "Four Christian writers on Jews and Judaism in the second century," *From ancient Israel to modern Judaism* vol. 1, J. Neusner, et al., edd. (1989) 187–202

MacMullen, Ramsay, *Changes in the Roman Empire: Essays in the Ordinary* (Princeton, 1990)

—, *Christianizing the Roman Empire* (New Haven, 1984)

—, *Corruption and the Decline of Rome* (New Haven, 1988)

—, *Paganism in the Roman Empire* (New Haven, 1981)

—, *Roman Social Relations* (New Haven, 1974)

Maier, J., *Jesus in den talmudischen Überlieferung* (Darmstadt, 1978)

—, *Jüdische Auseinandersetzung dem Christentum in der Antike* (Darmstadt, 1982)

Malina, B., "Jewish Christianity: A Select Bibliography," *Australian Journal of Biblical Archeology* 6 (1973) 60–65

—, "Jewish Christianity or Christian Judaism: Toward a Hypothetical Definition," *Journal of Jewish Studies* 7 (1956) 46–57

Margulies, M., ed., *Midrash Wayyikra Rabbah* (Jerusalem, 1972)

Maries, L., and Ch. Mercier, edd., *Hymnes de Saint Ephrem Conservees en Version Armenienne* (Patrologia Orientalis 30, Paris, 1967)

Marrou, H., *Histoire de l'Education dans l'Antiquite*, 7th ed. (Paris, 1977) [Eng. trans.: *A History of Education in Antiquity* (New York, 1956)]

McNamara, Martin, *The New Testament and the Palestinian Targum to the Pentateuech* (Rome, 1966)

—, *Targum and Testament* (Shannon, 1972)

Meeks, Wayne and Robert Wilken, *Jews and Christians in Antioch in the First Four Centuries of the Common Era* (Missoula, 1978)

Momigliano, A. ed., *Paganism and Christianity in the Fourth Century* (Oxford, 1963)

Mortimer, R. C., *The Origins of Private Penance in the Western Church* (Oxford, 1939)

Muffs, Y., "Abraham the Noble Warrior: Patriarchal Politics and Laws of War in Ancient Israel," *Journal of Jewish Studies (Essays in Honour of Yigael Yadin)* 33 (1982) 81–107

–, *Love and Joy: Law, Language and Religion in Ancient Israel* (New York, 1992)

Mulder, M. J., ed., *Mikra: Text, Translation, Reading and Interpretation of the Hebrew Bible in Ancient Judaism and Early Christianity* (Compendia Rerum Iudaicarum ad Novum Testamentum, Assen/Maastricht and Philadelphia, 1988)

Munck, J., "Primitive Jewish Christianity and Later Jewish Christianity: Continuation or Rupture?" *Aspects du judeo-christianisme: Colloque de Strasbourg, 23–25 Avril, 1964* (Paris, 1965)

Murmelstein, B., "Aggadische Methoden in den Pentateuchhomilien des Origenes," *Zum 40jährigen Bestehen der Israelitisch-theologischen Lehranstalt* (Wien, 1933) 13–122

Murray, R., "The Exhortation to Candidates for Ascetical Vows at Baptism in the Ancient Syriac Church," *New Testament Studies* 21 (1974) 59–80

–, *Symbols of Church and Kingdom: A Study in Early Syrian Tradition* (Cambridge, 1975)

Naveh, J., *On Stone and Mosaic* (Jerusalem, 1978) [Hebrew]

Neufeld, K. H., "Karl Rahner zu Büsse und Beichte," *Zeitschrift für katholische Theologie* 108 (1986) 55–61

Neusner, J., *Aphrahat and Judaism: The Christian-Jewish Argument in Fourth- Century Iran* (Leiden, 1971)

–, *Judaism and Scripture* (Chicago, 1986)

–, *A History of the Jews in Babylonia* vol. 1, The Parthian Period (Leiden, 1969)

–, "The Priority of Leviticus Rabbah over Pesikta Derab Kahana," *Proceedings of the American Academy of Jewish Research* 54 (1987) 141–68

–, *Religions in Antiquity* (Leiden, 1968)

–, *What is Midrash?* (Philadelphia, 1987)

Nickelsburg, G. W. E., and G. W. MacRae, edd. *Christians Among Jews and Gentiles* (Philadelphia, 1986)

Nistler, Johanna, "Vettius Agorius Praetextatus," *Klio* X (1910) 462–75

Nock, A. D., *Conversion* (Oxford, 1933)

O'Carroll, M., *Theotokos: A Theological Encyclopedia of the Blessed Virgin Mary* (Wilmington, Del., 1983)

Oppenheimer, A., *The Am Ha-Aretz* (Leiden, 1977)

Osborn, Eric Francis, *Justin Martyr* (Beiträge zur historischen Theologie 47, Tübingen, 1973)

Pagels, Elaine, *Adam, Eve and the Serpent* (New York, 1988)

Parisot, J., *Patrologia Syriaca, I: Aphraatis Sapientis Persae Demonstrationes* (Paris, 1894)

Parkes, J., *The Conflict of the Church and the Synagogue* (reprint: New York, 1969)

Pearson, Birger, "Christians and Jews in First Century Alexandria," *Christians among Jews and Gentiles: Essays in Honor of Krister Stendal*, G. Nickelsburg and G. MacRae, edd. (Philadelphia, 1986) 206–16

Perkins, Pheme, *Resurrection* (Garden City, 1984)

Poschmann, B., *Paenitentia secunda. Die kirchliche Busse im ältesten Christentum bis Cyprian und Origens* (Bonn, 1949)

–, *Penance and the Anointing of the Sick*, F. Courtney, trans. (London, 1964)

Prigent, Pierre and R. A. Kraft, *Epitre de Barnabe* (Sources Chretiennes 172, 1971)

Pritz, Ray, *Nazarene Jewish-Christianity* (Jerusalem, 1988)

Quasten, J., *Patrology* (reprint: Westminster, MD, 1968)

Rabbinovicz, R., ed., *Variae Lectiones in Mischnam et Talmud Babylonicum* (reprint: New York, 1976)

Rahner, K., *Theological Investigations XV: Penance in the Early Church*, L. Swain, trans. (London, 1983)

Ramsay, W., *Cities and Bishoprics of Phrygia* (Oxford, 1897)

–, *St. Paul the Traveller* (New York, 1896)

Richter, G., "Über die älteste Auseinandersetzung der syrischen Christen mit den Juden," *Zeitschrift für die neutestamentliche Wissenschaft* 35 (1936)

Riegel, S., "Jewish Christianity: Definitions and Terminology," *New Testament Studies* 24 (1972–78) 410–15

Ritter, Adolf Martin, "Chrysostomus und die Juden neu überlegt," *Kirche und Israel* 5 (1990) 109–22

Rivkin, Ellis, "Defining the Pharisees: The Tannaitic Sources," *Hebrew Union College Annual* (1969–70) 205–49

Roberts, C. H., *Manuscripts, Society, and Belief in Early Christian Egypt* (London, 1979)

Robinson, J. M., ed., *The Nag Hammadi Library in English* (New York, 1977)

Rokeah, David, *Jews, Pagans and Christians in Conflict* (Jerusalem and Leiden, 1982)

Sambursky, S., "On the Origin and Significance of the Term Gematria," *Journal of Jewish Studies* 29 (1978) 35–8

Sanders, E. P., *Paul and Palestinian Judaism: A Comparison of Patterns of Religion* (London, and Philadelphia, 1977)

Sanders, E. P., et al., edd., *Jewish and Christian Self Definition* 3 vols. (Philadelphia, 1980–83)

Sandmel, Samuel, "Parallelomania," *Journal of Biblical Literature* 81 (1962) 1–13

Sarason, R., "The Petihot in Leviticus Rabbah," *Journal of Jewish Studies* 33 (1982) 557–67

–, "Toward a New Agendum," *Studies ... in Memory of J. Heinemann* (Jerusalem, 1981) 55–73

Schäfer, P., "Die Petichta," *Kairos* 3 (1970) 216–19

Schechter, S., *Some Aspects of Rabbinic Theology* (London, 1909)

Schiffman, L., "At the Crossroads: Tannaitic Perspectives on the Jewish-Christian Schism," *Jewish and Christian Self-Definition* III (Philadelphia, 1981) 115–56

–, *Who was a Jew?* (Hoboken, 1985)

Schlatter, A., *Synagogue und Kirche bis zum Bar Kochba – Aufstand. Vier Studien zur Geschichte des Rabbinats und der jüdischen Christenheit in den ersten zwei Jahrhunderten* (Stuttgart, 1966) [written between 1897 and 1915]

Schoedel, W., *Ignatius of Antioch* (Philadelphia, 1985)

–, "Theological Norms and Social Perspectives in Ignatius of Antioch," *Jewish and Christian Self-Definition* vol. 1, E. P. Sanders, ed. (Philadelphia, 1980)

Scholem, G., *Gnosticism, Merkabah Mysticism and the Talmudic Tradition* (New York, 1965)

Scholer, D. M., "Tertullian on Jewish Persecutions of Christians," *Studia Patristica* 17.2 (1982) 821–28

Schürer, E., *The History of the Jewish People in the Age of Jesus Christ* (4 vol.) Rev. ed., G. Vermes, F. Millar, M. Black, M. Goodman (Edinburgh, 1973–1987)

Schwabe, M., "Letters of Libanius to the Patriarch of Palestine," [Hebrew] *Tarbiz* 1/2 (1930) 85–110

Schwartz, E., ed., "Proklos," *Acta Conciliorum Oecumenicorum* I (Berlin, 1927)

Schwartz, J., "Jerome and the Jews of Judea," *Zion* 47 (1982) 186–91 [Hebrew with English summary]

Schweizer, E., "Christianity of the Circumcised and Judaism of the Uncircumcised – the Background of Matthew and Colossians," *Jews, Greeks and Christians*, Robert Hamerton-Kelly and Robin Scroggs, edd. (Leiden, 1976) 245–260

Seeck, Otto, *Monumenta Germaniae Historica Auctorum Antiquissimorum* VI (1883)

Segal, Alan F., *Rebecca's Children: Judaism and Christianity in the Roman World* (Cambridge, 1986)

–, *Two Powers in Heaven* (Leiden, 1977)

Shanks, Hershel, ed., *Christianity and Rabbinic Judaism* (Washington, D. C., 1992)

–, *Judaism in Stone* (New York, 1979)

Shinan, Avigdor, "The Angelology of the Palestinian Targums on the Pentateuch," *Sefarad* 43 (1983) 181–98

–, "Live Translation: On the Nature of the Aramaic Targums to the Pentateuch," *Prooftexts* 3 (1983) 41–49

–, "On the Petihta," *Jerusalem Studies in Hebrew Literature* 1 (1981) 133– 43 [Hebrew]

–, "The 'Palestinian' Targums – Repetitions, Internal Unity, Contradictions," *Journal of Jewish Studies* 36 (1985) 72–87

Shukster, M. B., and P. Richardson, "Temple and Bet Ha-midrash in the Epistle of Barnabus," *Anti-Judaism in Early Christianity* vol. 2, S. Wilson, ed. (Waterloo, 1986) 17–31

Sigal, P. "An Inquiry into Aspects of Judaism in Justin's Dialogue with Trypho," *Abr-Nahrain* 18 (1978/79) 74–100

Sill, G. G., *A Handbook of Symbols in Christian Art* (New York, 1975)

Simon, Marcel, "La migration a Pella: legende ou realite?" *Recherches de science religieuse* 60 (1972) 37–54

–, "Problems du Judeo-Christianisme," *Aspects du judeo-christianisme: Colloque de Strasbourg, 23–25 Avril, 1964* (Paris, 1965) 1–17

–, "Reflexiones sur le Judeo-Christianisme," *Christianity, Judaism and other Greco-Roman Sects: Studies for Morton Smith at 60* (Leiden, 1975)

–, *Verus Israel: Etude sur les relations entre Chretiens et Juifs dans l'empire romain (135–425)* (Paris, 1948, 1964; Eng. trans., London, 1986)

Skarsaune, Oskar, *The Proof from Prophecy. A Study in Justin Martyr's Proof-Text Tradition: Text-Type, Provenance, Theological Profile*, Supplements to Novum Testamentum, Volume LVI, (Leiden, 1987)

Smelik, K. A. D., "John Chrysostom's homilies against the Jews," *Nederlands theologisch tijdschrift* 39 (1985) 194–200

Smith, Morton, "On the Shape of God," *Religions in Antiquity*, J. Neusner, ed. (Leiden, 1968) 315–326

–, *Tannaitic Parallels to the Gospels* (Philadelphia, 1951)

Smith, R. Payne, *Thesaurus Syriacus* (Oxford, 1903)

Spiegel, S., *The Last Trial* (New York, 1967)

Steinmetz, Devorah, "A Portrait of Miriam in Rabbinic Midrash," *Prooftexts* 8 (1988) 35–65

Stern, Menahem, *Greek and Latin Authors on Jews and Judaism* (Jerusalem, 1974–80)

Stern, David, "Midrash and the Language of Exegesis," *Midrash and Literature*, G. Hartman and S. Budick, edd. (New Haven, 1986) 105–24

–, *Parables in Midrash: Narrative and Exegesis in Rabbinic Literature* (Cambridge, Mass., 1991)

Strack, H., *Jesus, die Häretiker und die Christen* (Leipzig, 1910)

Strack, H., and G. Stemberger, *Introduction to the Talmud and the Midrash* (Minneapolis, 1992)

Strecker, G. *Die Juden-Christentum bei den Pseudo-Klementinen* (Berlin, 1958)

Stylianopoulas, T., *Justin Martyr and the Mosaic Law*, (Society of Biblical Literature Dissertation Series, Missoula, 1975)

Taylor, Joan E., "The Phenomenon of Early Jewish-Christianity: Reality or Scholarly Invention?" *Vigiliae Christianae* 44 (1990) 313–34

–, *Christians and the Holy Places. The Myth of Jewish-Christian Origins* (Oxford, 1993)

Telfer, W., *The Forgiveness of Sins* (London, 1959)

Tennant, Frederick, R., *The Sources of the Doctrines of the Fall and Original Sin* (New York, 1903, reprint, 1968)

Turlington, D. D., "Views of the Spirit of God in Mark and 'Q:' A Tradition-Historical Study," *Columbia University*, Ph. D. dissertation (1987)

University of Oxford, *Oxford Classical Dictionary* (Oxford, 1970)

Urbach, E. E., *HaZaL: Pirqei Emunot VeDe'ot* (Jerusalem, 1969, 1975) [Hebrew] [Eng. trans.: *The Sages*, vol. 1, 1. Abrahams, trans. (Jerusalem, 1975)]

–, "Homiletical Interpretations of the Sages and the Expositions of Origen on Canticles, and the Jewish-Christian Disputation," *Scripta Hierosolymitana* 22, (1971) 248–275 = *Tarbiz* 30 (1961) [Hebrew]

Veyne, Paul, ed. *A History of Private Life: From Pagan Rome to Byzantium* (Cambridge, Mass., 1987)

Visotzky, Burton L., "Most Tender and Fairest of Women: A Study in the Transmission of Aggada," *Harvard Theological Review* 76 (1983) 403–418

–, "Rabbinic Randglossen to the Cologne Mani Codex," *Zeitschrift für Papyrologie und Epigraphik* 52 (1983) 295–300

–, "Review of David Stern, *Parables in Midrash: Narrative and Exegesis in Rabbinic Literature*," *Catholic Biblical Quarterly* 55 (1993) 183–84

–, "Six Studies in Midrash and Methods," *Shofar* 10 (1992) 86–96

von Harnack, A., *Der Kirchengeschichtliche Ertraf der exegetischen Arbeiten des Orignes (= Texte und Untersuchungen* 42)

Vööbus, A., *Celibacy a Requirement for Admission to Baptism in the Early Syriac Church* (Stockholm, 1951)

–, ed., Didascalia Apostolorum Syriacae, *Corpus scriptorum christianorum orientalium* 407 (Louvain, 1979)

–, trans., Didascalia Apostolorum Syriacae, *Corpus scriptorum christianorum orientalium* 408 (Louvain, 1979)

Wallach, Luitpold, "The Textual History of an Aramaic Proverb," *Journal of Biblical Literature* 60 (1941) 403–15

Weis, P. R., "Some Samaritanisms of Justin Martyr," *Journal of Theological Studies* 45 (1944) 199–205

Weisen, David S., *St. Jerome as a Satirist. A Study in Christian Latin Thought and Letters* (Ithaca, 1964)

White, L. Michael, "Finding the Ties that Bind: Issues from Social Description," *Semeia* 56 (1991) 3–22

Wilken, Robert, "Byzantine Palestine: A Christian Holy Land," *Biblical Archeologist* 51 (1988) 214–27, 233–37

–, *The Christians as the Romans Saw Them* (New Haven, 1984)

–, *John Chrysostom and the Jews: Rhetoric and Reality in the Late Fourth Century* (Berkeley, 1983)

–, *Judaism and the Early Christian Mind* (New Haven, 1971)

–, *The Land Called Holy: Palestine in Christian History and Thought* (New Haven, 1992)

Wilson, R. McL., "The Early History of the Exegesis of Gen. 1: 26," *Studia Patristica* 1 (1957) 420–37

Wolfson, H. A., *The Philosophy of the Church Fathers* (Cambridge, Mass., 1956)

Woollcombe, K. J., "The Biblical Origins and Patristic Development of Typology," *Essays on Typology* (Naperville, 1957)

Wright, W., *Apocryphal Acts of the Apostles*; Vol. I: *The Syriac Texts*, Vol. II: *The English Translation* (London, 1871)

–, *The Homilies of Aphraates the Persian Sage* (London, 1869)

Wytzes, J., *Der Streit um den Altar der Viktoria* (Amsterdam, 1936)

Yassif, Eli, "Traces of Folk Traditions of the Second Temple Period in Rabbinic Literature," *Journal of Jewish Studies* 39 (1988) 228–9

List of First Publications

Fathers of the World: An Introduction
First Published in this volume.

Jots and Tittles
First published in *Prooftexts* 8 (1988) 257–69. Reprinted here by permission of
the editors.

Mortal Sins
First published in *Union Seminary Quarterly Review* 44 (1990) 31– 53. Reprinted
here with permission of the editors.

Trinitarian Testimonies
First published in *Union Seminary Quarterly Review* 42 (1988) 73– 85. Reprinted
here with permission of the editors.

Overturning the Lamp
First published in *Journal of Jewish Studies* 38 (1987) 72–80. Reprinted here with
permission of the editor.

Mary Maudlin Among the Rabbis
First published in this volume.

Anti-Christian Polemic in Leviticus Rabbah
First Published in the *Proceedings of the American Academy for Jewish Research*
56 (1990) 83–100. Reprinted here with permission of the publishers.

Text, Translation, Targum
First Published in *Prooftexts* 9 (1989) 93–98. Reprinted here with the permission
of the editors.

Lachs' Rabbinic Commentary
First Published in *Jewish Quarterly Review* 78 (1988) 340–43. Reprinted here with
permission of the publishers.

Segal's Rebecca's Children
First published in *Union Seminary Quarterly Review* 42 (1988) 64– 67. Reprinted
here with permission of the editors.

Two Types of Midrash Study

First published in *Conservative Judaism* 41 (1989) 65–71. Reprinted here with permission of the publishers.

Prolegomenon to the Study of Jewish-Christianities

First Published in *Association for Jewish Studies Review* 14 (1989) 47–70. Reprinted here with permission of the editors.

Three Syriac Cruxes

First Published in *Journal of Jewish Studies* 52 (1991) 167–75. Reprinted here with permission of the editor.

Hillel, Hieronymus and Praetextatus

First published in *Journal of the Ancient Near Eastern Society* 16–17 (1984–85) Ancient Studies in Memory of Elias Bickerman 217–224. Reprinted here with permission of the pubishers.

Index of Hebrew and Aramaic Sources

Bible

Index of Greek, Latin and Syriac Sources

New Testament

Patristic Literature

Index of Modern Authors

Subject Index

Wissenschaftliche Untersuchungen zum Neuen Testament

Alphabetical Index
of the first and second series

Wissenschaftliche Untersuchungen zum Neuen Testament

Heiligenthal, Roman: Werke als Zeichen. 1983. *Volume II/9.*
Hemer, Colin J.: The Book of Acts in the Setting of Hellenistic History. 1989. *Volume 49.*
Hengel, Martin: Judentum und Hellenismus. 1969, [3]1988. *Volume 10.*
– Die johanneische Frage. 1993. *Volume 67.*
Hengel, Martin and *Ulrich Heckel* (Ed.): Paulus und das antike Judentum. 1991. *Volume 58.*
Hengel, Martin and *Hermut Löhr* (Ed.): Schriftauslegung. 1994. *Volume 73.*
Hengel, Martin and *Anna Maria Schwemer* (Ed.): Königsherrschaft Gottes und himmlischer Kult.
  1991. *Volume 55.*
– Die Septuaginta. 1994. *Volume 72.*
Herrenbrück, Fritz: Jesus und die Zöllner. 1990. *Volume II/41.*
Hofius, Otfried: Katapausis. 1970. *Volume 11.*
– Der Vorhang vor dem Thron Gottes. 1972. *Volume 14.*
– Der Christushymnus Philipper 2,6 – 11. 1976, [2]1991. *Volume 17.*
– Paulusstudien. 1989, [2]1994. *Volume 51.*
Holtz, Traugott: Geschichte und Theologie des Urchristentums. Ed. by Eckart Reinmuth
  and Christian Wolff. 1991. *Volume 57.*
Hommel, Hildebrecht: Sebasmata. Volume 1. 1983. *Volume 31.* – Volume 2. 1984. *Volume 32.*
Kähler, Christoph: Jesu Gleichnisse als Poesie und Therapie. 1995. *Volume 78.*
Kamlah, Ehrhard: Die Form der katalogischen Paränese im Neuen Testament. 1964. *Volume 7.*
Kim, Seyoon: The Origin of Paul's Gospel. 1981, [2]1984. *Volume II/4.*
– »The ›Son of Man‹« as the Son of God. 1983. *Volume 30.*
Kleinknecht, Karl Th.: Der leidende Gerechtfertigte. 1984, [2]1988. *Volume II/13.*
Klinghardt, Matthias: Gesetz und Volk Gottes. 1988. *Volume II/32.*
Köhler, Wolf-Dietrich: Rezeption des Matthäusevangeliums in der Zeit vor Irenäus. 1987.
  Volume II/24.
Korn, Manfred: Die Geschichte Jesu in veränderter Zeit. 1993. *Volume II/51.*
Koskenniemi, Erkki: Apollonios von Tyana in der neutestamentlichen Exegese. 1994. *Volume II/61.*
Kuhn, Karl G.: Achtzehngebet und Vaterunser und der Reim. 1950. *Volume 1.*
Lampe, Peter: Die stadtrömischen Christen in den ersten beiden Jahrhunderten. 1987, [2]1989.
  Volume II/18.
Lieu, Samuel N. C.: Manichaeism in the Later Roman Empire and Medieval China. 1992. *Volume 63.*
Löhr, Hermut: see *Hengel.*
Maier, Gerhard: Mensch und freier Wille. 1971. *Volume 12.*
– Die Johannesoffenbarung und die Kirche. 1981. *Volume 25.*
Markschies, Christoph: Valentinus Gnosticus? 1992. *Volume 65.*
Marshall, Peter: Enmity in Corinth: Social Conventions in Paul's Relations with the Corinthians. 1987.
  Volume II/23.
Meade, David G.: Pseudonymity and Canon. 1986. *Volume 39.*
Mell, Ulrich: Die »anderen« Winzer. 1994. *Volume 77.*
Mengel, Berthold: Studien zum Philipperbrief. 1982. *Volume II/8.*
Merkel, Helmut: Die Widersprüche zwischen den Evangelien. 1971. *Volume 13.*
Merklein, Helmut: Studien zu Jesus und Paulus. 1987. *Volume 43.*
Metzler, Karin: Der griechische Begriff des Verzeihens. 1991. *Volume II/44.*
Niebuhr, Karl-Wilhelm: Gesetz und Paränese. 1987. *Volume II/28.*
– Heidenapostel aus Israel. 1992. *Volume 63.*
Nissen, Andreas: Gott und der Nächste im antiken Judentum. 1974. *Volume 15.*
Noormann, Rolf: Irenäus als Paulusinterpret. 1994. *Volume II/66.*
Okure, Teresa: The Johannine Approach to Mission. 1988. *Volume II/31.*
Philonenko, Marc (Ed.): Le Trône de Dieu. 1993. *Volume 69.*
Pilhofer, Peter: Presbyteron Kreitton. 1990. *Volume II/39.*
Pöhlmann, Wolfgang: Der Verlorene Sohn und das Haus. 1993. *Volume 68.*
Probst, Hermann: Paulus und der Brief. 1991. *Volume II/45.*
Räisänen, Heikki: Paul and the Law. 1983, [2]1987. *Volume 29.*
Rehkopf, Friedrich: Die lukanische Sonderquelle. 1959. *Volume 5.*
Reinmuth, Eckart: Pseudo-Philo und Lukas. 1994. *Volume 74.*
– see *Holtz.*
Reiser, Marius: Syntax und Stil des Markusevangeliums. 1984. *Volume II/11.*
Richards, E. Randolph: The Secretary in the Letters of Paul. 1991. *Volume II/42.*

Riesner, Rainer: Jesus als Lehrer. 1981, [3]1988. *Volume II/7.*
– Die Frühzeit des Apostels Paulus. 1994. *Volume 71.*
Rissi, Mathias: Die Theologie des Hebräerbriefs. 1987. *Volume 41.*
Röhser, Günter: Metaphorik und Personifikation der Sünde. 1987. *Volume II/25.*
Rose, Christian: Die Wolke der Zeugen. 1994. *Volume II/60.*
Rüger, Hans Peter: Die Weisheitsschrift aus der Kairoer Geniza. 1991. *Volume 53.*
Salzmann, Jorg Christian: Lehren und Ermahnen. 1994. *Volume II/59.*
Sänger, Dieter: Antikes Judentum und die Mysterien. 1980. *Volume II/5.*
– Die Verkündigung des Gekreuzigten und Israel. 1994. *Volume 75.*
Sandnes, Karl Olav: Paul – One of the Prophets? 1991. *Volume II/43.*
Sato, Migaku: Q und Prophetie. 1988. *Volume II/29.*
Schimanowski, Gottfried: Weisheit und Messias. 1985. *Volume II/17.*
Schlichting, Günter: Ein jüdisches Leben Jesu. 1982. *Volume 24.*
Schnabel, Eckhard J.: Law and Wisdom from Ben Sira to Paul. 1985. *Volume II/16.*
Schutter, William L.: Hermeneutic and Composition in I Peter. 1989. *Volume II/30.*
Schwartz, Daniel R.: Studies in the Jewish Background of Christianity. 1992. *Volume 60.*
Schwemer, A. M.: see *Hengel.*
Scott, James M.: Adoption as Sons of God. 1992. *Volume II/48.*
Siegert, Folker: Drei hellenistisch-jüdische Predigten. Part 1. 1980. *Volume 20.* – Part 2. 1992. *Volume 61.*
– Nag-Hammadi-Register. 1982. *Volume 26.*
– Argumentation bei Paulus. 1985. *Volume 34.*
– Philon von Alexandrien. 1988. *Volume 46.*
Simon, Marcel: Le christianisme antique et son contexte religieux I/II. 1981. *Volume 23.*
Snodgrass, Klyne: The Parable of the Wicked Tenants. 1983. *Volume 27.*
Sommer, Urs: Die Passionsgeschichte des Markusevangeliums. 1993. *Volume II/58.*
Spangenberg, Volker: Herrlichkeit des Neuen Bundes. 1993. *Volume II/55.*
Speyer, Wolfgang: Frühes Christentum im antiken Strahlungsfeld. 1989. *Volume 50.*
Stadelmann, Helge: Ben Sira als Schriftgelehrter. 1980. *Volume II/6.*
Strobel, August: Die Stunde der Wahrheit. 1980. *Volume 21.*
Stuckenbruck, Loren: Angel Veneration and Christology. 1995. *Volume II/70.*
Stuhlmacher, Peter (Ed.): Das Evangelium und die Evangelien. 1983. *Volume 28.*
Sung, Chong-Hyon: Vergebung der Sünden. 1993. *Volume II/57.*
Tajra, Harry W.: The Trial of St. Paul. 1989. *Volume II/35.*
– The Martyrdom of St. Paul. 1994. *Volume II/67.*
Theissen, Gerd: Studien zur Soziologie des Urchristentums. 1979, [3]1989. *Volume 19.*
Thornton, Claus-Jürgen: Der Zeuge des Zeugen. 1991. *Volume 56.*
Twelftree, Graham: Jesus the Exorcist. 1993. *Volume II/54.*
Visotzky, Burton L.: Fathers of the World. 1995. *Volume 80.*
Wagener, Ulrike: Die Ordnung des ›Hauses Gottes‹. 1994. *Volume II/65.*
Wedderburn, A. J. M.: Baptism and Resurrection. 1987. *Volume 44.*
Wegner, Uwe: Der Hauptmann von Kafarnaum. 1985. *Volume II/14.*
Welck, Christian: Erzählte ›Zeichen‹. 1994. *Volume II/69.*
Wilson, Walter T.: Love without Pretense. 1991. *Volume II/46.*
Wolff, Christian: see *Holtz.*
Zimmermann, Alfred E.: Die urchristlichen Lehrer. 1984, [2]1988. *Volume II/12.*

For a complete catalogue please write to the publisher
J. C. B. Mohr (Paul Siebeck), P. O. Box 2040, D-72010 Tübingen.